THE LOST SOUL
OF EAMONN MAGEE

An Authorised Biography

PAUL D. GIBSON

MERCIER PRESS

FOR EAMONN JR AND
TERRENCE 'DOC' MAGEE

MERCIER PRESS

Cork

www.mercierpress.ie

© Paul D. Gibson, 2018

ISBN: 978 1 78117 573 6

10 9 8 7 6 5 4

A CIP record for this title is available from the British Library

Printed and bound in the EU.

CONTENTS

ACRONYMS

BBBofC: British Boxing Board of Control

BUI: Boxing Union of Ireland

GAA: Gaelic Athletic Association

IABA: Irish Amateur Boxing Association

IBF: International Boxing Federation

INLA: Irish National Liberation Army

IPLO: Irish People's Liberation Organisation

IRA: Irish Republican Army

NICRA: Northern Ireland Civil Rights Association

OC: Officer Commanding

PIRA: Provisional Irish Republican Army

PPS: Public Prosecution Service

PSNI: Police Service of Northern Ireland

RUC: Royal Ulster Constabulary

UDA: Ulster Defence Association

UDR: Ulster Defence Regiment

UFF: Ulster Freedom Fighters

UVF: Ulster Volunteer Force

WBA: World Boxing Association

WBC: World Boxing Council

WBO: World Boxing Organisation

WBU: World Boxing Union

THE END

14 March 2017

'He pleaded guilty this morning.'

'At last.'

'Aye. Yesterday he was still pushing for manslaughter but he came in this morning and pleaded guilty to the murder charge.'

'Was he sentenced?'

'He's getting life but we've to go back to hear the minimum tariff. And I'll make sure he serves every second of it here and not in Turkey.'

'Did he look you in the eye?'

'No. No, he was smirking away yesterday, but he kept his head down today.'

'It's over then.'

'Not 'til I hear for how many years the bastard will rot away in an Irish cell.'

10 June 2017

'Eamonn.'

'Paul. Listen, it's about time I loosened my tongue a bit here.'

'Okay, mate. Go on.'

'I'm sitting here with tears streaming down my face and I swear to God I don't know ...' [heavy sobs]

'Take it easy, mate. Take it easy. What's happening?'

'Fourteen years? Fourteen fucking years? For a premeditated murder in cold blood? He was a hitman. He went tooled up. He knew how to use a knife because he'd learnt it in his military service in Turkey. He lay in wait for my son. For his prey. He stabbed his prey in the thigh and the buttock to drop it and then ended his life with two strikes through the lungs. Then he stabbed him some more ...' [more sobs]

'I'm sorry, Eamonn. Fourteen years is an insult.'

'Correct. A fucking insult. Someone has done a deal somewhere. But why would anyone help that bastard? He's wasted two years of everyone's time and public money. Two years prolonging our agony. Six separate counsels he's been through. All telling him the same: you're a murderer – stop with this manslaughter nonsense. He sacked them all. We had a jury sworn in and all at one point 'til he dismissed his counsel and set us back to square one. And now the fucking system helps him out …'

'It's a disgrace, mate. Who knows how–'

'I'm disgusted with them all. I'm disgusted with the PPS who have treated me like dirt from day one. Liaison officers supposed to be helping us and they never answered their phones. I'm disgusted with Judge Treacy. I was delighted when we got him for the trial. I'd have picked him out of a hundred judges cos he's a tough bastard. And then he hands down fourteen years. That day he got up and walked out of his own courtroom with his head down without even asking for the court to stand. I've never seen a judge leave his own courtroom like that. It showed me a deal had been done and he was ashamed of the sentence he'd just handed down. Fuck sake, he gave someone sixteen years the following week for attempted murder.'

'Seriously?'

'I'm fucking serious. Sure, I know people have done longer for armed robbery. Judge Stephens, too, in the appeal. They should all be ashamed. My own barrister and counsel couldn't have done more for me. Working 'til two or three in the morning every night so they were. But I'm disgusted with the whole justice system in this country. They've let me down. They've let my son down. What fucking justice?'

'I know, mate.'

[through heavy sobs] 'What fucking justice?'

PROLOGUE

'A book?' the passive-aggressive voice on the other end of the phone answers me incredulously. 'Listen, I've been beaten with baseball bats, I've had my throat slashed, I've been kidnapped and I've been exiled out of the country. My family's been held captive in our home as well. I've been shot twice, I've been in prison and my son's just been stabbed to death. Amongst all that, I was the welterweight champion of the world while drinking the bar dry and doing enough coke to kill a small horse every night. My life's not a book. It's a fucking movie script.'

These were the first words Eamonn Sean Terrence Magee ever spoke to me. I was sitting in a Madrid car park while he stood in John Breen's gym on the outskirts of Belfast. I still recall the pressure I felt, the fear that I'd lose him before I ever had him, the creeping sense of panic that I'd caught him on one of his supposedly many off days.

Magee is an alcoholic. More than that, I'd been warned he can be a truculent, temperamental, dangerous, depressive, paranoid alcoholic. I believed I had to time my call wisely. Weekends were likely to be a write-off, for example. Too early or too late on any day of the week may lead to an unfavourable response from the ex-boxer. I reasoned that after a mid-week gym session was probably my best bet. There was every chance he would have turned up for it reeking of the previous night's excesses, but hopefully he'd sweat and beat enough of it out of his system to be open to my suggestions. Having earlier spoken to Breen, his closest confidant in boxing, I knew that on this day Eamonn was scheduled to work with Marco McCullough ahead of the local featherweight's November outing in Belfast's Waterfront Hall. A text message from Breen was my cue that it was now or never.

'I don't want to talk about all this on the phone,' Magee decides after a couple of minutes listening to my rambling pitch. 'Come over here and we'll sit down face to face and see what happens.'

This is as good as I could have expected. He hasn't swung the door wide open, but neither has he slammed it shut in my face. The crafty southpaw has left it cautiously ajar so he can get a peek at me before making any definitive decision. I am heading home in a couple of weeks to watch the boxing bill McCullough is on anyway, so we choose the pre-fight weigh-in in the Waterfront Hall for our first physical encounter.

***

I see McCullough first, his soft features pale and drawn from the effects of days of rigorous abstinence to coerce his body down to the nine stone limit. Magee then comes into focus, lurking in the background, partially disguised by a flat cap pulled low and a scarf around his neck behind which he can tuck his chin. Magee's posture is striking to observe. All the damage, the attacks by blade and bullet and tooth and bat, has been inflicted onto his left side and, perhaps as a result, he now tends to subconsciously tilt his head and lean to the right. But, as always, his visible facial features are the dead giveaways: the flattened and fattened misshapen nose that dominates his countenance, underlined by thin, terse lips that remain pursed through habit to hide his once-missing front teeth. I can instantly pick his weathered and scarred, old-before-its-time face out of a cast of millions. He is an unmistakeable figure in Northern Irish life.

We shake hands, nod a greeting to one another and agree to find a quiet spot after the weigh-in formalities to sit down and discuss my vision for his story.

It would be disingenuous to say Eamonn Magee was ever a hero of mine, but certainly he is someone who has always fascinated me. There is nothing a boxing fan loves more than a hometown hero to support, and I am no different. I am a handful of years too young to remember Barry McGuigan in his prime, but I was there riding the mid-90s Celtic wave across the

Irish Sea with the rest of them as Steve Collins gate-crashed the golden era of British super middleweight boxing to dethrone Nigel Benn and Chris Eubank. Collins is from Dublin, of course, but Ireland is a small island and we get behind our own regardless of exact place of birth.

By the time the Celtic Warrior had hung up his gloves, Belfast's Wayne McCullough was a world champion, but his decision to relocate to the US left him out of sight and somewhat out of mind. As the new millennium arrived, the likes of Damaen Kelly and Brian Magee were quality professionals performing admirably, but they fell short in truly capturing my imagination. I needed something deeper than decent ring performances to grab onto.

As an extremely individual pursuit, boxing cannot rely upon the rabid tribal allegiances of team sports for its lifeblood. For that reason, solo sports tend to be more dramatic by nature and, like all good theatre, the success of the storyline is dependent upon the audience connecting with the portrayal of a character and his foe. It is largely irrelevant what emotion forges this connection – love, empathy, loathing, awe, whatever. All that matters is that enough people feel enough of *something* to want to watch an athlete in the boxing ring, or on the tennis court, or on the golf course and so on, over and over again. Magee achieved that, although to this day it is difficult to put my finger on exactly how he managed it. He has that aura particular to geniuses and cult figures that demands you pay attention to even the most insignificant moments of their existence. The sense of unpredictability that surrounds those who live their lives on a knife edge, coupled with Magee's constant underlying dark and volatile character, combines to convert the routine or mundane into a potential spectacle. He holds a magnetism that appears to attract trouble and tragedy in equal measure, with fleeting flashes of glory occasionally interspersing the two. Gifted and flawed: two characteristics guaranteed to produce a compelling subject.

***

I had expected the meeting place of which we earlier spoke to be somewhere either within the confines of the Waterfront Hall itself or alongside it in one of the neighbouring cafés or, much more likely, bars. As it turns out, Magee slipped out of range as soon as it was confirmed his fighter and their opponent had made weight, and decanted to a bar on the other side of the city centre.

'I'm in Madden's,' he says when I call looking for him. 'C'mon over here, it's a quiet spot.'

Madden's Bar is tucked away on the corner of Marquis Street and Berry Street where the black taxis lie waiting to ferry cargo out of the centre heading north or west. These black immigrants from the boroughs of London were introduced in the late 1960s for their ability to rumble over the remains of smouldering barricades and turn on a sixpence to dart down a side street and avoid the epicentre of a riot or disturbance. With the bus service regularly beaten into submission by the violence of those desolate decades, a black cab was often the only means of escaping the city centre as night fell. As with everything in the province at that time, the service was segregated, with separate associations for Catholic and Protestant drivers and passengers. It was felt to be safer that way but, of course, it also made it easier to identify what community a particular taxi was from or where it was headed, so it wasn't long before the dark vehicles became prey to terrorist assassination gangs.

Today the old hackney carriages enjoy a much safer existence on the streets of Belfast. One of the many fruits borne by the peace process has been the emergence of curious tourists to the Northern Irish capital and who better to lead them on a tour of the city, focusing on sectarian flashpoints and the gable-wall murals that tell a version of the story, than a wizened old taxi driver and his trusty black cab?

Madden's Bar has enjoyed a similar renaissance. It has always been a nationalist establishment but only since the turn of the century has it felt totally comfortable nailing its colours to the mast. A large mural depicting an old Irish fiddler playing at a table covered with pints of Guinness and prints of Irish language publications now proudly adorns the outside wall. *Fáilte Isteach*, or welcome inside, underscores the artwork and on either side of the front door *An ceol traidisiúnta* (and *an pionta*) *is fearr sa chathair* lets Gaelic speakers know the best traditional music and pint in the city can be located within. The Irish proverb *Is fearr Gaeilge bhriste ná Béarla cliste* (broken Irish is better than clever English) is another prominent and unambiguous sign that there is more green, white and orange than red, white and blue in this old watering hole's DNA.

Outsiders who visit today for a pint of Harp, a bowl of Irish stew and a traditional Irish music session may wonder why there would ever have been any fuss about such a public preponderance of Celtic lettering, but those who lived through the 1970s, 1980s and 1990s know differently. Scores have been murdered in sectarian attacks on the streets in and around Madden's over the years. The Ulster Volunteer Force (UVF) killed Roman Catholics on Marquis Street itself, as well as on neighbouring Millfield, North Queen Street and in Smithfield Market. The Irish Republican Army (IRA), meanwhile, shot and killed British soldiers on Berry Street and Chapel Lane, and murdered a Protestant civilian on Millfield. But the attack which resonates deepest with Madden's and its customers took place on 5 June 1976.

That evening, five members of the UVF's Shankill Battalion pulled up outside the Chlorane Bar on Gresham Street, four minutes' walk from Madden's, in a hijacked black taxi. One of them was Robert 'Basher' Bates, a leading member of Lenny Murphy's notorious Shankill Butchers gang, whose policy of abducting, torturing and murdering randomly chosen Catholics terrorised the nationalist community for almost a decade. The driver waited outside with the engine running as the four masked and armed passengers alighted and entered the bar. Once inside they told the stunned drinkers to divide into groups according to religion. Unusually for a bar in central Belfast in the 1970s, both Catholics and Protestants frequented the Chlorane and so the terrified customers were at this stage unsure as to the particular ecclesiastical persuasion of these killers. In the confusion a couple tried to make a run for it and all hell broke loose. When the gunfire died down and the murderers made their escape along North Street and back into the loyalist Shankill, five bodies lay lifeless on the bloodied barroom floor. Three were Catholic and two were Protestant. Ten days later any trace of the bar was forever destroyed in a bomb attack. The Chlorane was probably chosen for the ease with which the attackers were able to escape but it could just as easily have been Madden's.

Now, seventeen years on from the signing of the Good Friday Agreement that, theoretically at least, decommissioned the paramilitaries and brought an uneasy peace to the province, such a threat to innocent patrons in a bar like Madden's is basically zero. The Northern Irish are famed for their long memories but just in case the punters have one too many and lose sight of how far the city has come, a telling remnant from the past greets all who approach Madden's threshold. A buzzer on the door still alerts bar staff to someone waiting outside and allows them to check their identities and intentions via a CCTV camera and inside screen. It is one of the few city-centre bars that continues with this security measure.

As I wait for my Guinness to settle and then be topped off, an American couple standing at the bar, visibly emboldened by the effects of an afternoon supping a selection of Irish nectar, finally musters up the courage to enquire as to why such caution is still deemed necessary. The barman gives a masterful response that finds the perfect balance between granting the tipsy visitors sufficient reassurance that they have nothing to worry about and insinuating enough about the area's dangerous past to send them home with a famous story to tell about their day in a real, hard Belfast drinking den.

Magee is at the other end of the bar when I enter, still wrapped up in his coat, scarf and flat-cap ensemble, finishing off a pint of Harp. He pays for my pint, orders himself another, and we move to the corner for a bit of privacy.

Madden's is a dimly lit, claustrophobic, wooden box of a place, a comfortable coffin serving beer and whiskey. Photographs of revellers both young and old, local and international, now plaster the walls alongside posters promoting Irish folk festivals and vintage advertisements for products as varied as St Bruno tobacco, Diamond dyes and Bass ale. The cluttered bar is compact but stuffed with all the spirits and stout required for a decent night out. The foreign banknotes pinned to the wall above the platoons of liquor bottles are testament to the range of nationalities that have sampled the liquid delights within.

Wooden benches line the wooden panelled walls, with wooden chairs around wooden tables peppering the floor space. The only thing that isn't wooden is the craic guaranteed when the pints are flowing and the live music sparks up and grows outwardly and organically from a designated corner. *Please make these seats available to musicians after 9 p.m.* is written on the backrest of a bench. There's a hierarchy in these traditional pubs and a talented vocalist, fiddler or bodhrán player will always hold more sway than most. There'll be regular performers, but anyone with the ability to keep up is welcome to sit down with their instrument and play along. Some nights a session will begin with just a voice and a tin whistle and end with five or six times that number united as one within the controlled chaos that is live traditional Irish music in a heaving, bouncing, beer-soaked bar.

We are too early for a shindig on this afternoon, however. When we sit down at a table upon which *You don't miss the water until the well runs dry* is inscribed in Gaelic, there are no more than a handful of souls in the pub as a CD of Irish rebel songs plays softly in the background.

I quickly begin my pre-prepared spiel. I'm from the other side of town but essentially the same community. I'm nine years younger but also lived through the Troubles. I'm a boxing fan, I understand the sport. I'm a good writer, a good storyteller. I've the connections to get us a deal and do this properly. I'm passionate about this, willing to drop everything to focus on the project until it is complete. Basically, I'm the man for the job of telling your life story, Eamonn.

He listens intently and then begins with a warning. His is not what anyone would describe as a normal life, he says. He's going to tell me everything, the truth and nothing but the truth: that is how he puts it with more than a gentle nod towards his long and chequered relationship with the judicial system. I'm going to hear things that will shock and offend me. I'm going to hear things that could put me, him and the subjects of the anecdotes at risk from the police and, more worryingly, other forces that still patrol and control the streets of Belfast. He asks me if I take anything and from the look in his eye I know he's not referring to half a sugar in my morning coffee. A few lines of cocaine with his mates will be the only way to get all the best stories out of them, he continues. It's clear he wants to get a few things out in the open immediately so there are no surprises further down the line.

In truth, I am treating this as nothing more than a brief meet and greet, so I'm reluctant to start talking about any of the peaks and troughs of Magee's life and career. I want to go in prepared for those, armed and ready to delve as deep as I can and learn as much as possible from Eamonn in the process. But he's not really a man for small talk and his life rarely dabbles in the mundane that the rest of us recognise as daily existence, so we inevitably end up skimming over some of the more gruesome or glorious moments from the past forty-four years.

His narrow eyes dampen noticeably when I ask how he got through the recent memorial for his murdered son, Eamonn Junior.

'It's not easy,' is his understated response, 'and it's never going to be.'

It's a feeling he wouldn't wish on his worst enemy, he says, and he has a few of those. He tells me about a poem someone composed for Eamonn Jr that would break my heart. His son was an angel, he says; nothing like his old man.

We talk a little about his boxing, how his slick style contrasted so starkly with the thuggish image he has always carried as a violent street fighter.

He describes himself as a natural, clever fighter and his eyes sparkle briefly as he talks about spying a flaw in Jon Thaxton's footwork early in their 2002 bout. Magee noticed how, when he circled and manoeuvred the Englishman around the ring, Thaxton was prone to crossing his legs for a split second when forced into a particular position.

'I only had to wait,' Magee tells me with a sly grin, 'and then *bang* in the sixth round. Boxing is a game of chess, you see.'

The Thaxton victory led to the biggest moment of his career, fighting against Ricky Hatton. I still can't watch the fight without feeling frustrated that he couldn't finish the Mancunian in the second stanza when, having already been knocked down in the first, Hatton was buzzed again and in serious trouble. Magee famously left the arena to smoke a cigarette barely an hour before his ring-walk that night and I feel compelled to ask whether he has any regrets about how he lived his life between fights – a lifestyle that, it's fair to say, may have adversely affected his career.

'I don't regret anything and I wouldn't change a thing,' comes the immediate smiling reply.

I don't believe him, but I say nothing.

'My life has been great craic,' he concludes with another grin, but this one is unmistakably tinged with sadness.

My remark was an obvious reference to the booze and women and drugs and fags. He laughs when admitting that his old manager, the late Mike Callahan, would traverse the city depositing notes behind bars warning publicans not to serve Eamonn in the lead-up to a fight. But his reluctance to travel within the postcode of the straight and narrow had much more serious consequences than an inability to finish off a struggling foe in the ring.

He brings up the punishment shooting by the IRA himself. The Night of the Long Knives is how it was known in north Belfast: a famous occasion in 1992 when the republican paramilitary group handed down their own unique brand of justice to known drug dealers in the area. Thirteen were targeted that night and twenty-year-old Magee was one of them. Only the intervention of his father, who pleaded with the local IRA commander that his son was fighting for the Irish title in a couple of months, saved Eamonn from a bullet through his kneecap. That injury would almost certainly have ended any hopes of a boxing career. Instead he received a flesh wound to his calf for his troubles. He won that Irish title, by the way, fighting with a bandaged leg and wearing white socks that gradually reddened with his own seeping blood as the night went on.

The IRA attack is just one of the many contradictions that swirl around the ill-informed myth of Eamonn Magee. In general, sport in Northern Ireland is just another means by which segregation is maintained by those with a vested interest in keeping society divided and conquered. Yet, despite its roots in the working-class districts most embittered and affected by the Troubles, boxing has only ever united the two communities in the province. From Barry McGuigan and his dove-of-peace shorts, to Wayne McCullough carrying the Irish tricolour at the 1992 Olympic Games, any sectarian leanings have always been left at the gym door.

It has often been said that Eamonn Magee never got that memo. There is a belief that he carried his political baggage with him everywhere he went and, in exacerbating any underlying nationalistic tensions that existed, proved more divisive than unifying throughout his career. Those who hold this belief point to his father's republican past and Magee's own youthful dalliance with political violence. They point to run-ins with the law, allegedly laced with distinct sectarian undertones. They point to his in-your-face Irish nationalism at a time when a more restrained approach was urged.

I knew all this, but I had always sensed that the truth, as is its wont, was a more complex affair. If Magee was indeed a dyed-in-the-wool militant republican, why had the IRA shot and later exiled him? If he really was a dangerous bigot, how did his lifelong friendships with Protestants like McCullough or proud Englishmen like Hatton develop? If green, white and orange boxing attire truly defined him, what did it mean when he fought with the red hand of Ulster on his chest as an amateur representing his province?

The other topic Magee raises is the financial upside of spilling his heart onto the pages of my book. It soon becomes clear that the ex-fighter is still in possession of a rapier-sharp business mind. He has his own ideas for a title, release date, newspaper serialisation, a sequel and even a movie.

'Did you see that *Fighter* film?' he asks me. 'They made a movie about Micky Ward and the fella isn't fit to lace my boots.'

His eyes sparkle in such moments. As they do when he talks about beating 'the ex-British soldier and Plastic Paddy, Shea Neary', taking the piss out of a visiting *Guardian* newspaper journalist, or telling the promoter Barney Eastwood to shove his offer of 500 quid for ten victories up his hole. But the moments are fleeting and Magee's default mood appears to be a mixture of pensive sadness with an undercurrent of bitterness. He is always said to have a chip on his shoulder, too, but no one has ever identified who axed it into place. I haven't even begun to figure him out, have barely scratched the surface, but I'm hooked.

As night falls we rise to leave. The alcohol has taken its effect and dulled my senses somewhat, but it looks like we have a deal, sealed with a handshake and a silent acknowledgement that our word will be our bond going forward.

'So where do we start then?' he asks me as I put on my coat – he never took his off.

I had anticipated this question and have my response ready. While reading between the lines of an old *Irish Independent* piece on Magee, I thought I discovered the key to exploring this flawed and complicated man when the article touched very briefly on Eamonn's formative years and 'the scourge of internment'. This, I believed, was where his story must begin.

'Internment,' I say. 'I'd like to begin with Operation Demetrius and internment.'

'You'll need to speak to my mother then.'

1

ARDOYNE ON FIRE

In the little streets of Belfast
In the dark of early morn
British soldiers came a-running
Wrecking little homes with scorn
Hear the sobs of crying children
Dragging fathers from their bed
Watch the scene as helpless mothers
Watch the blood fall from their heads

'Men behind the Wire', written by Long Kesh internee Paddy McGuigan

I'm too polite to ask but some swift mental arithmetic places Isobel Magee at around seventy years of age. For a woman who has been through the trials and travails she has, who has survived the stresses and strains of mothering Eamonn Magee for forty-four long years, she looks remarkably fit and well. Eamonn is her baby boy, the youngest of four brothers, and, as they stand side by side in the kitchen of her house on the same street in which she has lived for over four decades, there is a definite resemblance in the facial features, particularly when the eyes narrow in preparation for a sly or coy grin. Such an expression soon appears when Isobel confesses that if this was her book it would be entitled *The Thorn in My Side*. A warm maternal laugh quickly follows as she grabs hold of Eamonn's arm, turns my way and, making direct eye contact for the first time, assures me that she loves her last-born with a passion. She holds my gaze as if to emphasise the point, to ensure I have taken it in. I sense that the explicit avowal of unconditional love for her son is a vital caveat Isobel wishes to declare before she opens up on some of the darker aspects of her family's life. It feels almost like a warning to brace myself.

Eamonn is here this morning simply to make an introduction and then leave the two of us alone. It is an approach we will repeat for virtually every person I meet and speak with to learn his story. A lot of what I need to hear is difficult for the interviewee to say and might be even tougher for Eamonn to listen to. Everyone is just more comfortable this way. He embraces his mother and departs with a final, solemn instruction. 'Tell him everything,' he says. 'Don't hold anything back.'

Now that it is just the two of us, I suddenly become very conscious that, having just met this great-grandmother, I now need to ask her to dredge up a very private, sensitive and painful past; that I'm going to pry and probe and ask questions that will force her to recollect events that in an ideal world she would never, ever have to think about again. More than that, I'm going to record every word she says and later put it in a book for the whole world to read. I feel quite tense, unsure of exactly where or how to begin, wishing I had more time to simply get to know Eamonn, his family and friends before I march into their homes and shine a naked, unforgiving light on their shared histories.

But the nerves I feel prove to be mere butterflies flittering harmlessly about the pit of my stomach and the warmth of a mouthful of freshly brewed tea soon calms their wings. In contrast, as I settle into a chair and fiddle with my dictaphone, I note that Isobel is clasping her hands together as if in prayer in a futile attempt to mask their tremoring. The anxiety coursing through her veins at the thought of the conversation ahead is clear. The hands soon part to jolt a Lambert & Butler from its silver box. She smokes two in quick succession during the next ten minutes. Isobel later describes herself as a nervous but strong woman and I can't improve upon that incredibly self-aware summation of her character.

The initial rapid nicotine intake turns out to be nothing more than a nerve-settler and the remainder of the pack is left untouched for over an hour as we become more comfortable in each other's presence. Contrary to Eamonn's instructions, Isobel does hold back at the outset. But by the time she is calmly enjoying a third smoke, we are returning to explore and embellish answers to questions originally judged too delicate for full disclosure. I cannot blame her for the former response and I am eternally grateful for the latter.

Isobel is my most accurate lens through which to view Eamonn's formative years on earth. She is key to setting the scene and beginning the journey to understanding this dangerously flawed man. I need her memory if I am going to get a true sense of what life was like for her kid growing up in north Belfast in the early 1970s.

I was another mother's kid growing up in east Belfast in the early 1980s, but the trip across town and, more importantly, the change in decade ensured I was raised in a totally different world. By Troubles standards, I had it easy. I still remember a British Army checkpoint at the end of my street, demanding some form of identification from my father upon arrival and departure, one squaddie brandishing a torch in my face in the back of the car while his companion quizzed my dad on his business that particular evening. They were generally polite but rarely friendly. I remember a few years later throwing apples at the same checkpoint before running giddily for cover on nearby waste ground. I remember army helicopters hovering for hours on end through the night, blazing their spotlights onto the streets and keeping me from sleep. I remember sleepovers with friends when we'd hear a bomb explode in the darkness, then bet each other the size in pounds of Semtex used and the exact location of the blast. I remember queueing in the rain outside shops in the city centre alongside my mother or grandmother for what seemed like an eternity because the handbag of every single woman was checked for incendiary devices before they could enter. Many must have slipped through the net for I also remember my mother dashing out the door to pick up a bargain in a shop advertising a bomb- or smoke-damage sale. I remember meeting my father when he finished work and the security gates were closing around the city centre, leaving it an empty and haunted ghost town by 6 p.m. I remember walking home in my Catholic school uniform and a motorbike cruising along beside me while from behind a darkened visor I was warned to take a different route home or the UVF would burn my school to the ground with all us wee Fenian bastards locked inside. I remember death. I remember a primary-school classmate being absent for a few weeks because her father opened the family's front door one night and was shot in the face by a member of the Ulster Freedom Fighters (UFF). I remember a friend being called out of class and sent home because the bookmakers at the end of his street, which his family members frequented, had been sprayed with Ulster Defence Association (UDA) bullets, leaving five dead and nine wounded. I remember seeing another girl from the year above me in school pictured on the front of the *Irish News*, crying uncontrollably at the graveside of her father, who was being buried as the latest victim of mindless, sectarian violence. Despite these memories, like I say, I know I had little to complain about by Northern Ireland Troubles standards.

By any standards, anywhere in the world, Eamonn Magee did not have it so easy. In truth, not many elite prizefighters do. It is just too tough a profession to enter voluntarily and excel at if your upbringing ensures alternative career options are on the table. If you have not become accustomed early on to life being a struggle, it is unlikely your soul will have been blessed, or cursed, with the resolve to do what it takes in the gym and ring to succeed at the very top of professional boxing. But everything in life is relative and, even in the company of his fighting peers, the narrative of Eamonn's childhood stands out as a particularly extreme version of the oft-told, ghetto-kid-against-the-odds, pugilistic chronicle. The boxes of poverty, adversity, substance abuse, an incarcerated father and problems with authority are all ticked with a bold, inedible marker pen, but what sets Magee apart is the ethno-political conflict that raged around the young fighter and consumed the community in which he grew up.

Magee was born and raised within the epicentre of Belfast's sectarian violence in the Ardoyne, a small republican enclave of barely 5,000 people, surrounded on all sides by the loyalist strongholds of the Crumlin Road, Glenbryn and the Torrens estate. It is what is known in Belfast as an interface area: a drop of green in a perilous lake of red, white and blue, separated from geographical neighbours by so-called peace walls, the barbed-wire-topped barriers that scar the city. The isolation naturally fosters a siege mentality, a belief that it is them against the world and they must fight to survive. The frequently dark reality of life within the north Belfast district during the Troubles proved that belief to be well placed more often than not.

By fluke of birth he arrived jabbing and hooking on 13 July 1971. The date gives rise to the family joke that his mother deliberately held him in her womb for longer than nature wished to ensure he was not born on the 'Glorious Twelfth', the most celebrated date on the Orange Order's calendar. On this day the Protestant fraternity remembers King William III's 1690 Battle of the Boyne victory over the Catholic King James II, which ushered in a Protestant Ascendancy on the island. Orange Order marches through the streets of Northern Ireland continue to heighten tensions and test cross-community relations every summer, no more so than in the Ardoyne, where a contentious parade along the Crumlin Road meets with annual resistance from local Catholic residents who find the music, banners and garb of the Orangemen sectarian, supremacist and unnecessarily triumphalist. The row of shops where the protestors gather and prepare to exchange insults and missiles with the passing marchers lies a stone's throw from the Magee family home.

In 2015, when I began this book, parade-inspired trouble in the area was regarded as being relatively tame. An Orange Lodge spokesman was charged with two counts of attempted murder after ploughing his car into a crowd of Ardoyne locals in broad daylight, seriously injuring a sixteen-year-old girl. A police officer lost most of his ear after being struck with a piece of flying masonry and twenty-three of his colleagues in the Police Service of Northern Ireland (PSNI) also required hospital treatment. Meanwhile, residents on both sides of the Crumlin Road boarded up their windows and hunkered down as youthful, alcohol-fuelled riots raged through the night. It is quite shocking that this is what passes as tame in north Belfast, but three or four decades ago, when Eamonn would have been the teenage rioter with a petrol bomb in one hand and a bottle of cider in the other, the situation on the ground was a damn sight worse. Back then the Ardoyne was a community at best under siege and at worst engaged in all-out guerrilla warfare. How it found itself in such trauma and turmoil will forever be disputed by the two sides, but for the locals who bore the brunt of it, it was simply the inevitable outcome of fifty years of Protestant, unionist misrule.

***

The state of Northern Ireland was only born when the Emerald Isle was partitioned by the 1920 Government of Ireland Act. The vast bulk of the Catholic-dominated country's Protestant community was embedded in the northeast of the island and, after some nimble gerrymandering, the six counties of Antrim, Down, Armagh, Derry, Tyrone and Fermanagh were cordoned off to form a critical mass for the desired demographic. Nobody was under any illusions as to the raison d'être of the fledgling nation and its new government, but James Craig, the Ulster Unionist Party leader and first prime minister of Northern Ireland, hammered home the fact just in case: 'All I boast of is that we are a Protestant Parliament and a Protestant State,' he declared in the Northern Ireland House of Commons, based in Stormont, before later describing the objective as being 'a Protestant government for a Protestant people'. This most certainly was not a *céad míle fáilte* to the significant minority of the newly formed country.

The problem from the outset was that the size of the Protestant majority never really matched the vehemence of the government's rhetoric. A census in 1926 revealed that the various Protestant denominations made up only sixty-two per cent of the population and by 1971 that figure had decreased to just fifty-three per cent. Despite those statistics, in 1921 unionists managed to secure sixty-seven per cent of the popular vote and seventy-seven per cent of the parliamentary seats on offer. Fifty years later, their share of the vote had dropped to forty-eight per cent, yet they still maintained sixty-nine per cent of the elected representatives. That absolute and seemingly unshakeable unionist majority at Stormont facilitated the creation of a framework that – through institutionalised discrimination against the Catholic community in areas such as electoral systems, employment, housing, policing and education – helped maintain a Protestant dominance of life in Northern Ireland for well over half a century.

The inevitable Catholic or nationalist discontent at the reality they faced never abated, but for the first four or five decades it was, by and large, kept simmering just below the surface. The 1922 Special Powers Act was crucial here, providing the authorities with a range of draconian powers with which they could swiftly quell any hint of dissent towards the established status quo. Then, in the mid-1960s, the built-up sense of oppression finally broke for air and manifested as a civil rights movement, modelled along the lines of counterparts in the USA, who had been battling racial segregation and discrimination for over a decade. The Northern Ireland Civil Rights Association (NICRA) emerged in 1967 and set about campaigning for electoral reform, fair allocation of government jobs and council housing, the repeal of the Special Powers Act and the disbandment of the hated and feared Ulster Special Constabulary, otherwise known as the B-Specials. It was a protest organisation whose modus operandi focused on marches, pickets, sit-ins and non-violent civil-disobedience measures in an effort to raise global awareness of the situation in Northern Ireland and pressure the Stormont administration into reforms. As it turned out, their wait for international headlines was not a long one.

By 1968 the country was an open tinderbox beneath a shower of sparks as paranoia on both sides of the political and religious divide grew daily; it was only a matter of time before the whole place went up in flames. When a civil rights march on 5 October 1968 in Derry was violently broken up by baton-wielding Royal Ulster Constabulary (RUC) officers, the jarring footage was beamed into television sets around the world. The forty-eight-year-old state stood on the edge of a dangerous precipice: unfortunately, it blindly jumped.

The unionist prime minister of the day, Terence O'Neill, promised limited reforms that only served to enrage his own electorate and exasperate the majority of nationalists who expected so much more than what was on offer. A civil rights march from Belfast to Derry in January 1969, organised by the student-run People's Democracy, met a wall of resistance at Burntollet Bridge and sparked days of serious rioting in the nationalist Bogside of Derry. In March and April loyalist paramilitaries attacked electricity and water infrastructure installations and blamed their republican rivals in the hope that it would cause O'Neill to halt his paltry reforms. That these two groups effectively marched and bombed to display their disgust at the exact same appeasing measures shows just how far apart the two sides sat in the polarising conflict. Disillusioned, O'Neill resigned in April and the cycle of violence between Catholic, Protestant and state forces accelerated.

Some say the Troubles began that aforementioned autumnal 1968 day in Derry. Others predate it a couple of years to May 1966 and the re-emergence of the UVF on the streets of Belfast. For many, the so-called 'Battle of the Bogside' in August 1969 – when Derry saw three days of intense rioting between nationalists, unionists and the RUC following a Protestant Apprentice Boys parade along the city's walls – was the definitive spark. Regardless, when the British Army began patrolling Belfast and Derry in the immediate aftermath of the Bogside unrest – a move named Operation Banner – it was clear that Northern Ireland was stumbling into uncharted and dangerous territory.

The Brits, as they were known, seemed to believe they would be in and, as soon as law and order had been restored, back out and home again. We now know it was the longest continual deployment in British military history, lasting thirty-eight long years. More than 300,000 army personnel were posted to the province before Operation Banner was finally wound down in July 2007. At one point in the mid-1970s there were over 27,000 soldiers stationed in the province. To put that figure in some context, the number of pairs of boots on the ground during the Afghanistan and Balkan conflicts never surpassed 10,000.

Ironically, given how history was to unfold, the majority of the Catholic community in Northern Ireland actually welcomed the British soldiers, famously serving tea and toast to the squaddies manning nationalist street corners in the north and west of the city. Fear of attack from loyalists was then the dominating emotion and so a belief that the army would protect innocents from the escalating mob violence that erupted when the sun went down was initially prevalent. For the people of Eamonn Magee's Ardoyne district, that belief proved wholly unfounded.

For three nights in the middle of August 1969, Belfast saw the very worst of the sectarian rioting to date. On Wednesday 13 August, NICRA demonstrations against the heavy-handed police actions in Derry were infiltrated by the IRA and turned violent. RUC stations on Hastings Street and the Springfield Road were attacked with stones and petrol bombs and when the police responded by sending Shorland and Humber armoured cars onto the streets, the vehicles came under fire from rifle shots and hand grenades. All over Belfast residents began hastily erecting barricades to demarcate an already segregated city along stark, sectarian lines, while local priests promised to ring chapel bells as an alert that their parish was under attack.

The following night the violence intensified and flooded into the Ardoyne. Loyalist mobs rioted outside Holy Cross Catholic Church before crossing the Crumlin Road to attack the nationalist homes of Brookfield, Herbert, Butler and Hooker Streets in what is known as Old Ardoyne. As RUC armoured trucks smashed through the makeshift barriers the locals had hoped would keep them safe, petrol bombs were lobbed over the police officers' heads and onto Catholic roofs and gardens. There was no huge IRA presence in the Ardoyne at that time, and what existed was conspicuous by its absence as the flames spread, so local men rallied together in an attempt to defend the neighbourhood. Ex-servicemen among their number dusted off old shotguns and fired towards the invaders: the response was RUC Sterling submachine-gun fire rattling down the narrow streets, killing two and wounding ten more.

Sammy McLarnon had just returned to his home on Herbert Street after helping his neighbours extinguish one of the many fires that were gutting houses in the area. As he and his pregnant wife debated whether to risk running up the road to leave their two children, aged two and one, with his mother, three RUC bullets came through the window. One entered Sammy's skull and, while his eldest son looked on, the blood and life drained out of him onto the living-room floor. The twenty-seven-year-old bus conductor was the Ardoyne's first official victim of the Troubles.

Barely an hour later, a second Ardoyne life was claimed. As spiralling petrol bombs lit up the night sky and scorched the earth where they shattered, Michael Lynch and a friend sheltered in a doorway on Butler Street, fearing for their lives. They were playing no role in the riots and their only wish was to make it home to Strathroy Park, about four streets away. Finally they made their move and ran, ducking across the road in the direction of Elmfield Street. A high-velocity bullet, fired from close range, pierced Michael's chest and he was dead before his body came to rest on the cold footpath.

It was a similar story on Friday night, with the British Army still nowhere to be seen in the Ardoyne. In a variation of the old cowboy, circling-the-wagons trick, locals hijacked fifty buses, parked them at the various entry points to the district and set them ablaze. Twenty people were injured by shotgun blasts that night and the official government investigation into the riots, the Scarman Report, later noted that an RUC armoured vehicle sat idly by and watched as a loyalist mob set Brookfield Street alight, house by house. In response, republican gunmen shot dead David Linton, an innocent man walking along the Crumlin Road and the first Protestant civilian to lose his life in the Troubles.

To celebrate their successes, loyalist lyricists quickly penned a vindictive song that they sang to the tune of Johnny Cash's 1961 ode to Ireland, 'Forty Shades of Green'. They named it 'The Night We Burned Ardoyne' and it soon became a favourite of the Orange Lodge flute bands based in north Belfast:

I have often thought and wondered, what the outcome might have been
If the army hadn't come in, to protect those men in green
Well they shouted all their insults, they threw their petrol bombs and shots
But on the 16th night of August we should have shot the lot

Do you remember Derry, Aughrim, Enniskillen and the Boyne?
But still fresh in my memory was the night we burned Ardoyne

We chased those Fenian gunmen, down Hooker Street they tore
And the song we sang and loved so well was 'The Sash my Father Wore'
So remember all you Fenians, you rebels to the core
The next time you start trouble, Ardoyne will be no more

On Saturday 16 August the British Army was finally deployed on the Crumlin Road to bring a degree of calm to communities that now considered themselves at war with one another. Scarman described it as the 'quiet of exhaustion' rather than any meaningful, peaceful cessation of violence and that is exactly what it was. The people paused for breath and emerged from what remained of their charred homes to look around at the devastation that had been wrought and take stock of the losses suffered. Seven were dead and over 750 injured. At least seventy-two Catholics and sixty-one Protestants had suffered gunshot wounds; 275 buildings were destroyed, of which eighty-four per cent were occupied by Catholics. Many decided to flee; 1,505 Catholic and 315 Protestant families were forced from their homes by flames or intimidation. Those who stayed, through necessity or defiance, hardened their stance and began preparing defences against future attacks. Almost overnight, an entire community had been politicised and radicalised, the events of August 1969 seared into their collective consciousness and destined to define much of what would happen in the Ardoyne for the next thirty or forty years.

Decades of perceived oppression and two summer nights of mayhem had combined to forge an atmosphere in which an armed and rebellious organisation could flourish. The riots, along with the old-guard IRA's apparent inability to protect their own community, also accelerated a split in the militant republican movement, which gave birth to the Provisional Irish Republican Army (PIRA) or Provos. Those who stayed put, the men and women who adhered to an ideology of revolutionary socialism rather than the romantic physical force nationalism of the Provos, became known as the Official IRA, or the Stickies, and gradually lost influence over the path the republican struggle was to follow.

Eamonn's father, Terrence, was one of the many young Ardoyne men who felt compelled to do something more to defend his people. As Isobel puts it, her husband simply 'got more involved'. Such euphemistic terminology is common in Northern Ireland when speaking of the Troubles. It derives from both a necessary reluctance and a genuine inability to make declarations as if absolute truths. Terrence would never have sat his wife and family down and explained that he was now a high-ranking member of the PIRA. He would never have told them about operations or where he'd be, who he'd be with and what he'd be doing. For their own safety, the less they knew the better.

For the next two years the sectarian violence established itself as another facet of everyday life in Belfast. The crude barricades that had sprung up around the city at interfaces between nationalist and unionist areas were soon reinforced with British Army barbed wire and later replaced by the ironically named 'peace walls' that continue to divide society to this day.

No-go areas for the Brits and other state security forces were declared in various parts of the Northern Irish capital. Full-scale riots erupted on a weekly basis and a tit-for-tat series of shootings and bombings was carried out by the rival paramilitary factions that were quickly gaining a stranglehold in working-class districts. The army and police patrolled the narrow streets in vehicles mounted with weaponry more suited to an open battlefield than the urban warrens that were now their daily beat. One blast of destruction from a .30 Browning machine gun mounted on top of a Shorland armoured personnel carrier was enough to scatter bricks and mortar the length and breadth of a street. Indeed, one high-ranking British officer commented that when he first arrived in Belfast and toured the devastation, he felt like he had stepped into a Second World War battle-scene photograph. He wasn't far wrong. CS gas and rubber bullets were now being used for the first time on the UK population and Ian Freeland, the British Army's overall commander in Northern Ireland, announced a shoot-to-kill policy towards the youthful petrol-bombers who peppered his men and vehicles at every opportunity. At one point in July 1970, 3,000 homes in the nationalist Falls area of west Belfast were placed under a thirty-six-hour curfew in which anyone found on the street was liable to be arrested or worse.

Death made an unwelcome return to the close-knit Ardoyne community as well during this period. In February 1971 Barney Watt emerged from the Ardoyne Working Men's Club on Chatham Street and a British Army bullet ended his life. The twenty-eight-year-old from Hooker Street had no connections with the IRA; he was just another innocent civilian making his way home to see his wife, six months pregnant with their first child. The following night the IRA shot dead Royal Artillery Gunner Robert Curtis in the neighbouring New Lodge district in revenge. The twenty-year-old, whose wife was also pregnant with their first child, was the first British soldier to be killed in the Troubles.

Through it all, Isobel fought to keep her family as safe as possible.

On the day she went into labour with Eamonn and entered the Royal Victoria Hospital, a British soldier was cut down by an IRA sniper in Andersonstown. On the day she was discharged with her bundle of joy wrapped tightly in her arms, the Provos repeated the trick on the Falls Road that runs past the hospital. This was the society waiting to greet Eamonn with open, poisoned, bloody arms. His three brothers provided him with a warmer welcome into their already cramped terraced house on Ballycastle Street, but within a fortnight the entire family was fleeing for their lives across the Oldpark Road and into the Ardoyne as their neighbourhood was ethnically cleansed. This time, the short fuse of sectarian violence was lit by Operation Demetrius and the introduction of internment.

***

Operation Demetrius, the British and Unionist governments' ham-fisted response to a security situation that had long since spiralled out of control, began at 4.30 a.m. on Monday 9 August 1971. Armed with a hopelessly outdated and inaccurate list of 450 Catholic males drawn up by the notoriously bigoted RUC Special Branch, the British Army swept through the Belfast ghettoes, their rifle butts smashing windows and skulls as they went. In total, 342 men were dragged from their beds under a barrage of baton blows and sectarian insults and taken to makeshift detention centres in various secret locations throughout the province that morning. The number would eventually rise to almost 2,000 and each was beaten, abused and interrogated. To exacerbate the tragic course of events, the British soldiers on the ground were not particularly diligent in their work. It later emerged that sons were taken in the absence of a wanted father, as well as *anyone with a beard* in such and such a house. It was standard procedure. The fact that the vast majority of those initially interned had no connection to militant republicanism whatsoever made the savage experiment all the more reprehensible. The so-called 'Fourteen Hooded Men' were singled out for particularly harsh treatment that included five techniques later ruled to be 'inhuman and degrading' by the European Court of Human Rights: starvation, forced stress positions, sleep deprivation, sensory deprivation and subjection to noise. Torture by any other name.

In response, Belfast violently imploded in an upsurge of sectarian shootings and bombings. Seventeen civilians were killed by the British Army in the following days, including eleven by the 1st Battalion Parachute Regiment in an infamous incident that would become known as the Ballymurphy Massacre. Among the dead was Father Hugh McMullan, the first Catholic priest to lose his life in the Troubles, shot by an army sniper as he went to the aid of a wounded man.

The second major flashpoint was the Ardoyne. There, the army shot three dead in the opening hours of Demetrius and most of the densely populated area was soon up in flames once again. Where before Catholic and Protestant families on the fringes of the district had lived side by side in an uneasy truce, they now retreated behind the dividing line of the ironically named Alliance Avenue. Such was the rabid hatred in the air, Protestant families opened the gas valves and burned almost 200 of their own properties on Velsheda Park, Farringdon Gardens and Cranbrook Gardens as they abandoned them, lest they fall into Catholic hands. In the process, fifty-year-old mother of nine Sarah Worthington was shot dead by the British Army as she prepared to exit her home through the kitchen door. An estimated 7,000 Catholics across the entire city were left homeless by the blazes that raged through the night, internally displaced in their own land. 2,500 of that number fled over the border to the south of Ireland and never returned. They were perhaps the lucky ones.

Isobel gathered up her four young boys and the family's meagre belongings and sought refuge in her father-in-law's house in the heart of Old Ardoyne. While she scrambled to secure a long-term roof over their head, the two middle brothers, Patrick and Noel, were sent to temporarily live with a family in the Irish Republic as part of a relocation programme for children in real danger from the sectarian strife. The Magees were entitled

in the late 1960s and early 1970s, Terrence's decision was more practical and emotional than political. He was an Irish republican in that, given a straight choice, he would have opted for a reunited and independent thirty-two-county Ireland, but were it not for the attacks on his district and the injustices he saw around him, he would never have taken up arms. The people of the Ardoyne viewed the IRA at that time as a legitimate military force and the only group with half a chance of protecting their vulnerable existence. IRA volunteers were freedom fighters, not terrorists. They were a disciplined army, focused on defensive attacks against members of the British state's security personnel. Whatever the IRA went on to represent in the years before it laid down its arms forever in 2005, this was the perception of the organisation in the Ardoyne when Terrence started fighting.

For the remainder of 1971 and throughout 1972, the Ardoyne continued to lose a disproportionally high number of its people in the violence of the Troubles. And as the district was the whole world back then to locals, who rarely, if ever, left its confines, the majority were murdered within sight of their own homes. A mile and a half north of Belfast city centre, the area is just a speck on the map, its perimeter little more than a one-mile walk all the way around. The so-called Old Ardoyne is a miniature maze of streets, entries and alleyways surrounding the Holy Cross Boys' Primary School, over which loomed the sniper-manned watchtowers of the Flax Street Army Barracks. Adjoined to the north is New Ardoyne, a grid of residential streets, six deep, bordered by the Ardoyne Road to the west, Alliance Avenue to the north, Etna Drive to the east, and Brompton Park to the south. Ardoyne Avenue leads east towards the Oldpark Road and through the Bone district, an even smaller Catholic neighbourhood with strong links to the Ardoyne. Removed from its urban setting and transposed onto a rural scene far from the city lights, the Ardoyne would be a village too tiny to warrant recognition in any guide book. With a population akin to a couple of twenty-storey residential tower blocks, everyone knew everyone in the tight-knit community. That meant that everyone knew each victim as well. Nothing was abstract about the deaths in the Ardoyne. They were not something that could be ignored or quickly forgotten by switching off the television and radio or flicking the page of a newspaper over after spotting another depressing headline. The conflict was very personal in the Ardoyne and the people soon became accustomed to living amongst violence and death.

On 28 October 1971 Michael McLarnon was standing in his doorway on Etna Drive when a bullet from a British Army patrol struck the twenty-two-year-old civilian and sent him stumbling into his house, crying out to his sister that he'd been shot. Five hours later, he died in the Mater Hospital. On 4 December 1972 Bernard Fox, a sixteen-year-old member of the IRA's youth wing, Na Fianna Éireann, was walking along Brompton Park when a British sniper positioned in the fortified observation post beside Holy Cross Church on the Crumlin Road ended his life. Eighteen other Ardoyne natives were killed on the district's streets in the time between McLarnon's and Fox's murders, the blood spreading from Etna Drive, along Eskdale Gardens and Strathroy Park, down Brompton into Butler and Flax Streets, staining everyone and everything it touched.

As the level of unrest on the street intensified, so the Magee family saw less and less of their father and husband. In another classic Belfast euphemism, Isobel describes Terrence as being 'out and about' a lot in those years. There were secret safe houses dotted all over the Catholic ghettoes to which men defending their patch could retire when tiredness conquered them. One of the fundamental reasons for such an arrangement was to protect their own families at home, a doomed effort to keep loved ones out of the war. It proved futile because the Brits continued to storm into houses at ungodly hours, regardless of whether they had intelligence to say their target was in situ or not. And the Magee household was a particularly popular hunting ground for young squaddies, who would kick in the door and barge their way into the front room and up the stairs in a volatile state of nerves mixed with adrenaline, fear and power.

THE LOST SOUL OF EAMONN MAGEE

Despite, or perhaps because of, his tender years, Eamonn remembers the ordeals vividly. He recalls the front and back doors being booted through by army patrols so many times that clocks could have been set by the unwelcome arrivals. Once inside the home, the destruction became almost routine as well. The fireplace was ripped out, floorboards torn up and pneumatic jackhammers jolted violently across the kitchen floor, drilling out chunks of concrete in a frantic but forlorn search for guns and bombs and bullets. Upstairs, clothes were strewn across bedroom floors as wooden drawers splintered and shattered against the walls. The damage was terrible and often irrecoverable but it is a much more intrusive memory that still lingers.

Eamonn shared a bedroom with his three brothers, a spartan affair with space for two single beds and little else. There they slept, two to a bed, head to toe, in perfect harmony. I find it hard to believe, but all four have sworn to me independently that there was never any discord within the bounds of those close quarters. At least not when the four Magee boys were left alone and in peace.

'Wake up!' barked a harsh English accent, as a rifle butt nudged Eamonn's leg and roused him from a deep slumber. He rubbed his eyes against the sleep and struggled to make sense of the scene in his bedroom. Looming over him was a tall British soldier, armed and ready for war.

'Downstairs! All of you! Now!'

Following his elder siblings' lead, he silently rose and traipsed down the stairs at the end of a single file, the pre-dawn cold biting at his bare feet and quickly penetrating the skin beneath his cheap, thin pyjamas.

'Stand there! In a line!' continued the military orders, always an unnecessary shout, when the boys had reached the living room. Another soldier then went along the line, taking a photograph of each of the four startled children as the rest of the patrol continued ransacking the house.

It must have been a frightening and surreal experience for four young brothers and their mother, and the thought of that unwanted photographer still causes Isobel to tilt her head and stare at me with a kind of sad bemusement when we discuss it. The memory almost appears to daze her as she half-rhetorically looks to me for answers.

'What were they doing?' she whispers. 'Why did foreign soldiers feel it necessary to wake my children in the middle of the night, march them downstairs, line them up and take their photographs? Why did they do it over and over again?' Finally she breaks into a melancholy smile and, almost wistfully, wonders where all those photographs are now.

The recollections of British Army harassment flow thick and fast from the mouths of all who lived in the Ardoyne at this time. Listening to the stories, it seems that, in addition to the deep-seated bitterness that was sown, the familiarity of the raids and searches bred an indifference to the constant invasions into private homes. It is also true that many have the gift, common amongst the Northern Irish of that generation, of finding humour – albeit forty years later – in scenarios that at the time were anything but funny. As much for my benefit as her own, Isobel uses that talent to manage the general tone of our conversation and intersperse or festoon a series of dark and depressing tales with lighter anecdotes that serve to brighten the mood somewhat.

One such example involved taking advantage of a particularly green squaddie, most likely fresh off the boat and without the faintest under-standing of the political realities on the ground. It was during one of the regular British Army raids on her home when Mrs Magee was left alone in the living room with the youthful private as his comrades aggressively scoured the upstairs bedrooms in another fruitless search for anything incriminating. A young IRA member had recently been killed while on active service and Terrence had left a plastic bag containing the volunteer's gloves, beret and Irish flag sitting on the sideboard in preparation for the funeral. The soldier, no more than a teenager himself, poked the end of his rifle into the bag to take a look and, clearly none the wiser, asked Isobel for an explanation. As usual her strength somehow overcame her nerves and she told her English visitor that it was just an Irish tricolour like every-one uses for Easter celebrations. Despite it being mid-October and the fact that black gloves and a beret were clearly not a traditional part of the Easter narrative anywhere in the world, her explanation was accepted and the squadron departed empty-handed.

The threat of a more frightening interaction with the British forces took place in the early hours of 31 July 1972. All through the previous night, Ardoyne residents had peered out their windows with a mixture of awe and fear as the lights of military vehicles on the surrounding hills appeared and grew in number until it felt like the entire might of the British Army was preparing to descend into the district. It was Operation Motorman, the state's attempt to reassume control of the IRA-dominated no-go areas that had emerged in the north and west of the Northern Irish capital. It was, by any standards, a massive operation – the biggest since the Suez Canal crisis in 1956 – and something never seen before or since on UK soil. According to the national archives, 30,000 troops were involved, including thirty-eight regular battalion-sized formations, twenty-seven of which were infantry battalions and two of which were armoured regiments. 5,500 members of the Ulster Defence Regiment (UDR), a ninety-seven per cent Protestant infantry regiment established in 1970 in a laughable effort to represent the entire community, also took part. The amphibious assault ship HMS *Fearless* docked in Belfast Harbour and unloaded a fleet of Centurion demolition vehicles, which were modified Centurion tanks fitted with bulldozer blades, to assist the armoured assault vehicles already in place. The paramilitaries, who had been forewarned and left their areas for the night, were not expected to offer any resistance, so the huge scale of the ground incursion was both a shock and a worry for local people hiding in their homes. Isobel remembers with an embarrassed smile that her main concern was the discovery of the illicit means by which she and every other family in the area received their gas and electricity supply at that time. With hindsight it is clear that the security forces had much bigger and more deadly concerns on their minds, but for the mothers of Ardoyne there was a mild panic that they would be led away in shackles for tampering with the electric metre and using the same single coin over and over again to keep the gas flowing into homes.

But it wasn't just the forces of the crown that would burst unexpectedly into the Magee home in those days. Around Christmas 1973 a group of young local men with guns strolled in through the unlocked front door and started up the stairs. Isobel recognised most of them and in a panic threatened to tell on them as if she was back in the schoolyard and an unruly classmate was stealing her pencil case or pulling her hair. It was an entirely empty threat but the intruders plied her with cigarettes in an effort to shut her up nevertheless. Isobel acquiesced and soon the gang was gone. She later learned they had intended to use the skylight in her attic for a sniper attack on a British military patrol as it passed the end of the road, but the vantage point turned out to be inadequate for their murderous requirements.

As she sat on her sofa, nursing Eamonn on her lap, distractedly gazing at the sparsely decorated Christmas tree and vigorously sucking on a cigarette to calm her nerves, her brother Tommy came into the house and immediately froze on the spot. His eye was fixed on a rifle left propped against the wall behind an armchair. As Isobel's pulse rocketed once again, the two siblings quickly concocted a plan to dispose of the weapon. Pushing the dog out the front door, Tommy followed it as if in pursuit and surreptitiously stuffed the rifle into the neighbour's overgrown hedge before swiftly grabbing the bewildered mutt and retreating to the house. The next day the IRA came knocking again, sheepishly asking if anyone had seen a missing Lee-Enfield. This time Isobel didn't even let them back across the threshold and, after divulging what she had done with the weapon, slammed the door shut in their faces. To this day she has no idea whether the IRA recovered the gun or whether her neighbour found it first and got rid of it herself. But she does know that less than a week later the hedge had been hacked down to below waist height so that such a disappearing trick could never again be repeated.

Absent-mindedness may have led to that IRA weaponry ending up in Isobel's home, but armaments were often deliberately stored there against her will. With another chuckle she depicts her sofa rising higher and higher off the living-room floor as rifles raided from a Stickie dump were stashed there for safekeeping. Stickie dumps were remote, supposedly secret locations where the Official IRA had disposed of weapons used in campaigns gone by. Again Isobel played her bluff – she threatened to hand over names to the authorities – and a few days later the guns mysteriously disappeared in the night. She knew, of course, that her husband was orchestrating the movement and storage of those arms, but Isobel's main concern was her youngest crawling under the settee and gaining an early taste for the feel of gun metal in his hands.

On another occasion she opened her back door to find a trail of unused bullets leading out to the back entry that ran parallel to her street. Fully aware that her innocence and lack of knowledge as to their origin would cut no ice if a British patrol came across them, Isobel improvised as only working-class mothers in the Troubles knew how. Two-year-old Eamonn was loaded into his pram and taken for an impromptu walk around the district. There he sat in his nappy, nestled on the bullets like a broody goose warming her eggs, while every time the coast was clear, his mother would reach in, pluck a bullet from under him, and furtively dispose of the deadly cargo through the gratings of a kerbside drain.

Such stories are what pass as light-hearted in the general Troubles narrative. Listening to Isobel tell them one after the other, I am almost lulled into a sense that, as tough as it was, maybe it wasn't really so bad. That maybe these games of cat and mouse with the British Army, or back and forth banter with the IRA, were all just a bit of close-to-the-bone craic in a working-class area similar to any other in the UK. As if reading my mind, she then brings me hurtling back to the stark and deadly reality of 1970s life in the Ardoyne.

Arriving home one night with a female friend after a couple of drinks in the local social club, Isobel spotted the lower half of a body lying across a hedge a few houses down from her own. Praying that it was just a drunkard a little the worse for wear, but deep down sensing it was something more sinister, the two women approached with caution to find it was a neighbour with a bullet in his head and blood oozing down his face and seeping into his clothes. The two women dragged him into Isobel's home while she forced her thumb into the wound to stem the flow of blood. It was May 1974 and the entire city was in a locked-down paralysis on account of the Ulster Workers' Council strike, called in opposition to the recent Sunningdale Agreement, which envisioned a degree of power-sharing between unionists and nationalists in the Northern Ireland government. There were barricades everywhere and the gas and electricity had been cut, leaving people living in the dark ages, cooking over open fires in their living rooms and shivering themselves to sleep.

Terrence and a comrade soon arrived, as did the shot man's frantic mother, and a decision was made to call an ambulance. Such was the fear of interrogation as to what they were doing with a gunshot victim that neither Terrence nor the mother wanted anything more to do with the macabre situation, and it was left to Isobel and her friend to accompany the critically wounded party to the hospital. The short journey there was akin to a military manoeuvre across a mixture of no-man's lands and open war zones. The paramedics instructed all on board to lie flat on the ambulance floor as they negotiated fierce riots on Tennent Street, traversed the loyalist Shankill, and approached the relative sanctuary of the hospital gates. By the time they had completed the handing over of their bloodied deposit to medical staff it was the early hours of the morning and the two women found themselves facing the very real problem of how to get home.

The security situation on the street was so dire that no buses or taxis were in operation and the offer of a lift in the back of a military Saracen truck to the old Ewart's Mill on Flax Street, now being used as an army barracks, was immediately refused in no uncertain terms. Regardless of the paucity of alternatives, no resident of the Ardoyne would be seen dead hitching a lift home in the back of an enemy vehicle. Unsure what their best bet was, they jumped in the back of a milk float heading vaguely in the direction they wanted and hopped off when they saw the Mater Hospital at the bottom of the Crumlin Road. There, they decided they would loiter until the sun rose, as the treacherous journey north towards the Ardoyne would feel somewhat safer in the early light of day.

That was the theory, anyway. In practice, their trek up the Crumlin Road was soon interrupted by gunfire at the junction with the Oldpark Road and, finding themselves caught in the middle of a shootout between the Provos and Brits, they dived for cover down the steps of some public toilets. There, in the cold morning air with the stench of stale urine burning their nostrils, they lay and waited for the battle to cease. When all they could hear was silence, the pair rose tentatively and made their way to the first army checkpoint on the Oldpark Road. Afraid to provide truthful answers as to either where they had been or where they were going, Isobel mustered the courage to lie that they had been visiting her friend's sick child in the Mater and were now trying to get home to Alliance Avenue. The soldier on duty bought the story and radioed the two through the various military posts that managed the flow of traffic and people along the road. Upon reaching Ardoyne Avenue, half a mile before their supposed destination as the army knew it, they suddenly turned left and sprinted for home without looking back.

It was an adventure that, even now, causes this great-grandmother to gently shake her head in disbelief at how a quiet drink with a friend in a local social club could turn out in the 1970s. But while she replays it all in her mind, the mischievous sparkle reappears in her eye as she once again unearths some mirth from a shockingly violent episode. While the doctors were frantically assessing the injured man's condition, the poor soul regained consciousness and began ranting and raving and spewing all sorts of unintelligible nonsense. Isobel's shocked friend looked to one of the doctors aghast and asked whether there wasn't something wrong with the victim's mind. 'Yes,' deadpanned the physician, 'he's got a bullet lodged in it.'

That man actually survived and lived to fight another day, but he was one of the lucky ones. Well over 1,000 people had by that point lost their lives since the Troubles' victims began being registered in 1969. In 1973 and 1974 the Ardoyne buried another thirteen of its people, with Highbury, Cranbrook and Holmdene Gardens now among the streets to be soaked in local blood. Terrence's appearances at home grew sparser and more fleeting, but Isobel understood the situation. Like practically every other young man in the area, he was obliged to do his bit to protect the district. What else could be done? Terrence and his comrades were like cornered cats clawing at a pack of rabid dogs that edged ever closer. Eventually one of the dogs would be sure to kill a cat, but the brave feline was determined to inflict some pain as it went. There was a certain hopelessness to that scenario that infected the entire community. It caused an anger that hung in the air like smoke. But at the same time the fighting was all that kept the Ardoyne's spirit alive. It gave the men, and by extension their families, a purpose in a life that was being torn to shreds in front of their eyes. When the housewives banged their metallic bin lids to sound the alarm and the men fired their bullets in response, they at least felt like they were doing something.

The PIRA was by now running the district, with seven small companies on active duty. Each company had little more than a couple of Armalite rifles and a submachine gun if they were lucky, but members were expected to collect their weapons from a call house each morning and patrol the streets in pairs, engaging with any crown forces that strayed into their territory. It was a perilous business to be involved in, with ten

IRA volunteers from the Ardoyne killed on active service between 1971 and 1974. In addition, Terrence and his peers found themselves regularly and randomly picked up by the Brits, often dragged from a local bar or social club, bound with plastic ties and quick-marched into the Flax Street Barracks for interrogation. Eamonn's father was normally released within hours, or the following day at the latest, but others who were moved further afield to be questioned were not so fortunate. The notorious Palace Barracks in Holywood, on the eastern fringes of Belfast, became infamous for sustained beatings, simulated drownings and victims being thrown blindfolded and terrified from a helicopter hovering a few feet off the ground. Combined with petty harassment on the street and the constant raids on Ardoyne homes, the plan was to break the spirit and resistance of the PIRA and its supporters. Of course, it had the exact opposite effect, as locals became even more united behind the republican paramilitaries who were seen as the only line of defence for the community.

Then, from not being around too often, Terrence was suddenly never there at all. During a particularly bleak period in 1974, the British forces launched a push to round up as many IRA members or supposed sympathisers as they could. Terrence, who normally slept in a safe house during this time, happened to be in his own bed for once as a British Army patrol crashed through the front door and pounded up the stairs in a pre-dawn raid.

Eamonn can't recall the morning his father was taken, but his mother remembers it as if it were yesterday.

'There were no charges or trials,' she says. 'The soldiers just banged through the door one night, came up the stairs, dragged him out of bed, and that was that. He was interned in Long Kesh. Eamonn would have been about three years old. It left me with the four boys on my own, and bombings and shootings and riots every night outside the front door.' Isobel stares at me, as if lost in the painful memory. 'It was a really bad time,' she finally says, 'very hard on all of us.'

The adjectives *bad* and *hard* are such subjective concepts, but even when they are prefixed by the intensifiers *really* and *very*, I can't help feeling that Mrs Magee is underplaying both the gravity of the security situation on the streets of Belfast at that time and the enormity of the hardships she must have faced in raising four young boys alone. Words such as *bad* and *hard* initially appear too bland, too common, to accurately depict the milieu of an internee's wife and her four young sons in the Ardoyne as Northern Ireland's bloody, sectarian implosion continued accelerating and careering out of control. But on reflection, there is not a lexicon broad enough to do justice to that dark state of affairs and she has probably articulated the circumstances perfectly. The Troubles were indeed *really bad*. And life for those caught in their epicentre was, quite simply, *very hard*.

***

The first question I ever asked Eamonn on tape dealt with his earliest memories of his father.

'Now you've asked a very good, serious question there,' he began as he continued rolling a cigarette and took another beer from his kitchen fridge. 'My first memories of seeing my father, and I mean this over my son's death bed, God rest him he's just dead, was going up ...'

At this point he turned his right shoulder up and away from me and lowered his chin, much as he did in the ring to deflect an opponent's left hook hurtling towards his jaw, and exhaled deeply. It took me a few seconds to realise he had broken down. His shoulders shuddered as he cried violently. I sat in silence, listening to him struggling to regain control of his breathing, before I apologised for starting the process on such a sensitive topic.

'Don't be silly,' he spat with renewed focus, wiping the tears away, and starting again. 'My first memory was going up to the Crumlin Road to get a bus that was run by volunteers because people couldn't afford to take the bus to go all the way up to the Kesh. And that was my first experience of meeting my fath–' He gets halfway through the word before breaking down again. 'That's what always sticks in my mind,' he finally manages to mumble after another torturous, prolonged pause.

***

The free mini-bus, run by the local Citizen Defence Committee, left from the back of the old Foreign Picture House where the Crumlin Star Club now sits. It was always crowded. Each family was designated two days per week for half-hour visits, one for wives only and the other for children as well. The site of Long Kesh is fifteen miles southwest of Belfast, about a half-hour drive, but to those who made the twice-weekly trip, it seemed so much further. Three-year-old Eamonn was already forging a reputation as a hellraiser and other women in the district would sometimes enquire as to whether he was booked on that week because, if so, they wouldn't be setting foot in the bus. He'd be in and out of handbags, clambering over everyone, pushing and pulling at whoever got in his way, and kids twice his age were already wary of his small, swinging fists. As much as they wanted to see their interned loved one, a one-hour round trip with wee Eamonn Magee was apparently just not worth the hassle.

It is another funny aside, but the truth is that visits to Long Kesh were genuinely harrowing experiences for the relatives of internees. Visitor permits would be checked in the car park before a wait that could often last longer than an hour in a freezing wooden hut with only a cup of tea provided by the Quakers to stop the blood running totally cold. One by one, names were eventually called and families boarded another bus for the short drive inside the camp. There a thorough search of each visitor was conducted by prison officers before another wait in another crowded, stinking hut. Finally, they were allowed through the wire and into one of the sixteen visiting booths where internees waited eagerly on one side of a desk. Throughout the thirty minutes of strained conversation, prison guards patrolled up and down between the desks.

Eamonn remembers the excitement of smuggling contraband in to his father on each visit: little pieces of fruit concealed about his person, or tiny letters, meticulously written in miniscule hand on both sides of a cigarette paper, folded up, encased in clingfilm and hidden under his tongue.

'We were always smuggling something in,' he says, 'even just for the craic. I'd have done it just for the buzz.'

But it is evident that he still finds it difficult to talk about this time and what are basically his first memories of life. There is a bitterness inside Eamonn that his increasingly curt responses to my gentle probing do little to mask. When I ask if he knows the exact reason for his father's arrest on the occasion he was interned, he replies that his old man was simply perceived as a threat to the British state and that was all the justification they needed. A perception.

'The British Army picked up anyone in those days,' he explains. 'Those were their orders from their prime minister and they're still doing it to this day.'

When I try to ascertain how long Terrence spent inside Long Kesh, Eamonn's response is short and not so sweet.

'A long time,' he almost whispers. 'When you're interned, you're interned until the Queen allows you out.'

✳✳✳

The negative impact an incarcerated parent has on a child has been well documented for decades and is often compared with suffering a bereavement. The symptoms that emerge are also eerily similar to those found in victims of post-traumatic stress disorder, with the psychological health of the child normally worst affected. Various studies have evidenced higher rates of attention deficit disorders and behavioural problems that manifest as aggression towards others. Speech, language and other developmental steps are often delayed. Linked to this, children with a parent in prison regularly achieve lower grades and have less chance of continuing to further or higher education. They are at higher risk of phobias and frequently feel stigmatised, which can in turn lead to low self-esteem, internalising personal problems and anger management issues. Rates of depression and anxiety are high and several studies have also reported a greater chance of physical problems such as obesity and asthma. Later in life, though not much later, kids who grew up with a jailed parent are more prone to substance abuse and more likely to be arrested and imprisoned themselves. On top of all this there is also the financial impact to consider, as poverty gaps already well established are almost always exacerbated for families with an incarcerated father. Basically, it is no way for a child to start their life.

What made it even worse for Eamonn, however, was that his father wasn't incarcerated in the normal sense of the term. Rather, he was interned. There was no arrest, trial and sentencing. He was simply picked up one morning and locked away. He was not in one of Her Majesty's standard prisons. He was held in a disused Royal Air Force base that had recently been converted into a rudimentary detention centre, modelled on a prisoner-of-war camp. There was no right to appeal, nor even a release date to look forward to. His imprisonment was indisputable and indefinite. This was the lot of a 1970s internee in Long Kesh.

Terrence and the rest of the men were caged like animals in ten separate enclosures, each one seventy paces long by thirty paces wide. A four-metre fence, topped with forbidding swirls of barbed wire mesh, kept them trapped inside. Within each cage sat a washroom and four Nissen huts, the prefabricated, half-cylindrical, corrugated steel structures designed for the British Army in the First World War. One of the huts acted as a canteen serving inadequate sustenance, while the internees slept in the remaining three. The huts measured just forty metres by eight, and at least forty fully grown men were crammed into each, lying on bunk beds that covered every square inch of the concrete floor. The flimsy roofs did little to shelter the occupants from the worst of the elements and together they huddled, fully-clothed and shivering, under paltry bedclothes as the cold rain dripped and biting wind whistled all around them. One small electric heater, placed out of reach on the inside of the rear gable wall, proved more of a sick joke than a provider of warmth. One or two in its immediate vicinity may have partially bathed an arm in the comforting convection current but the sight of it merely taunted the vast majority who lay beyond its pitiful range. Rats soon appeared, as did an outbreak of scabies. Migraines and severe attacks of depression were also common. It was a squalid and grim existence, made all the worse by the mental anguish the men suffered being locked up indefinitely without due legal process. Inevitably, some broke and were carted off to Holywell Psychiatric Hospital in nearby Antrim, their minds unable to take the torture any longer.

Meanwhile, on the outside, the families left to fend without a patriarch struggled on as best they could, often requiring financial aid from the Catholic Church just to put some meagre food on their children's plates. The more impoverished they became, and the worse the reports they read on their husband or father or brother or son's conditions inside the Kesh, the more embittered they grew towards the British state. All the while the political killings continued with a vicious, relentless abandon: eight people from the Ardoyne were murdered in 1975 and another nine in 1976.

Eamonn started Holy Cross Primary School around this time and proved himself bright enough when he bothered to apply himself to classwork. Isobel then began waitressing in the bar of the local Crumlin Star Social Club and so, in the evenings, Eamonn would wander over to where they were still rebuilding the houses destroyed in the riots and sit chatting for hours with the night watchman, Terry Diamond. If he found it difficult to dedicate himself to schoolwork, he had no problem absorbing information on the construction trade and would later lecture his mother on exactly how many bricks it took to build a wall and how long the entire house required for completion. Terry also gave young Eamonn his first driving lesson, lurching about conspicuously on top of a JCB digger.

Like any mother, Isobel encouraged her children to reach their academic potential but her biggest concern was with keeping the four off the street and away from the barricades and rioting that erupted on a nightly basis. Terry, Noel and Patrick distanced themselves naturally from the worst of it, but their baby brother was different. Even from his earliest years it was clear he was inexplicably drawn to danger and violence. He was just wired a little differently. What the others found frightening and shocking, Eamonn believed to be fun and exhilarating. He longed to be a part of it. Isobel tried to entertain him indoors as much as possible but it proved an impossible and thankless task.

At this stage, Terry and Noel, who attended Sacred Heart Primary on the other side of the Oldpark Road, had been boxing in their school's amateur club for two or three years, and Patrick, aged eight at the time, was due to join them for the thrice-weekly evening training sessions. In desperation Isobel pushed five-year-old Eamonn out the door with them, though he was technically still a couple of years too young to be regularly attending a boxing club. It was simply a means of keeping him off the streets and out of trouble for a few hours. In that objective it was to fail miserably, but it did prove to be the beginning of a relationship between Eamonn Magee and the 'sweet science' that endures until this day.

2

SACRED HEART

Sacred Heart was always much more than just a boxing club to the four Magee brothers. It was their saviour, a sanctuary from the chaos of the outside world. As such, its location on the first floor of the Sacred Heart parochial hall on Gracehill Street was entirely fitting. Built in 1924 with Irish-American money raised by the Irish White Cross Society, the robust, red-brick building emerged from the ashes of the early 1920s Belfast pogroms to provide a safe haven within which local Catholics could congregate and shelter from the sectarian violence that prowled the streets. It soon became an important social hub in the community and people travelled from miles around to the dances, educational classes and other activities organised by the parish. In the 1960s boxing was added to the curriculum.

Rain, hail or snow, three evenings per week, Terry, Noel, Patrick and Eamonn would set off on the ten-minute trek from Holmdene Gardens, down Etna Drive, left onto Brompton Park, across Havana Way and along Ardoyne Avenue before cutting through Ardilea Drive to reach the club. The notoriously inclement Northern Irish weather was the absolute least of their worries, however. More common difficulties included finding their route blocked by burning barricades or being forced to seek temporary refuge from a sudden surge in flying petrol bombs and the volley of rubber bullets fired in response. Upon arrival in the gym, they regularly struggled to pay their weekly dues but, seeing the state of their third- or fourth-hand gear, carried everywhere in well-worn, plastic supermarket bags, the coaches invariably turned a blind eye and allowed the quartet to train.

As far as their mother was concerned, they simply had to go. In her opinion a good gym and ring education was as important as the more traditional pedagogical guidance received from school teachers. Her own father, Emanuel Quinn, had been a professional fighter, winning seven of his fifteen bouts in the 1930s and 1940s, and he had bought his grandchildren a punch ball that they all hit relentlessly from the moment they could stand. Perhaps seeing the man her father was, Isobel instinctively knew that boxing was bound to have a deeper, positive impact on her boys. She also suspected that pugilistic talent may well run in the family. Isobel was one of Emanuel's thirteen children, eleven of which survived infancy, yet none had shown any interest in the sweet science. As genetic traits often do, the desire to box had skipped a generation, and it was soon obvious that Eamonn and his brothers were all magnetically drawn to the sport.

Being the eldest, Terry was the first to excel and when he reached the junior championship at the age of eleven he travelled down to compete in the 1977 All-Ireland in Limerick. Long before the era of easy and instantaneous long-distance communication, his three siblings were left in Belfast, impatiently jabbing their punch ball and wondering how their big brother was getting on against the best young boxers in the country. When he returned a couple of days later, a decorated soldier upon the culmination of a glorious battle, the boys listened in awe as he talked them through his three fights. Perhaps more inspiring than any words he could bequeath, Terry bore a marvellous black eye with pride, a most visual and wonderful indication of the heroic ring deeds he had committed in the name of the Magees and the Ardoyne.

With less than seven years separating the four brothers, it was natural that each individual's achievements spurred the others on and Isobel was soon struggling to find room in her small home for the medals and trophies that accumulated at pace. Third son Patrick was one of the best juniors in Northern Ireland at lightweight and only a steady job, and an even steadier girlfriend, prevented him going on to emulate his brothers in the senior and professional ranks. After a distinguished amateur career, Terry fought on into his late twenties and recorded twenty-one victories as a pro, including claiming the Irish super welterweight crown and losing a fight for the European equivalent. Noel was even more successful. As an eighteen-year-old he twice beat the great Steve Collins at senior level, picking up the Irish light heavyweight title as he did so. As a professional he mixed it with two world champions in Fabrice Tiozzo and Dariusz Michalczewski, fought for the British and European titles, won a Commonwealth belt and, at his peak, was ranked as high as number seven in the world by the World Boxing Council (WBC). Yet despite everything that Patrick, Noel and Terry would go on to achieve, it was clear from very early on that their youngest brother was gifted in ways of which they could only dream. From the moment Eamonn first laced up a glove, it was apparent he had the ability to surpass them all.

His first and only amateur trainer, Patsy McKenna, saw the potential as soon as he clapped eyes on the boy. Patsy, an old friend of the boys' father, is a small-statured, feisty man in his seventies, still apparently fit and ready for any argument that may come his way. He stays physically tense through conversations and has a tendency to shout random words of his speech, an intonational trait that hints at a life lived never too far from confrontation. More than anything, he is fiercely proud of where he comes from and his chest swells visibly when discussing Eamonn and the steady stream of quality amateur boxers his small district has produced through the years. Patsy's club was once one of the most successful in the country, often sending six or seven fighters to the All-Ireland championships with each coming home with a medal, and the Magees were a huge part of that. Money problems unfortunately mean the Sacred Heart Club is not currently in operation, but McKenna is a boxing fiend and he doubts he'll ever fully quit the sport. Today he goes five nights a week to the nearby Holy Cross gym to train the latest batch of north Belfast youngsters dreaming of becoming world champions.

Patsy remembers the little, red-haired Magee following his big brothers into the gym as a wiry five-year-old and immediately displaying skills well beyond the norm. A perfect storm of nature and nurture had forged a kid with innate boxing ability coupled with a fire in his heart that left him totally bereft of fear. On top of that, wee Eamonn simply loved to fight. He and a pal, Hugo Wilkinson, would give each other free bare-knuckle digs to the stomach until someone quit, contests that would often end in a draw after an hour's worth of punishment to the mid-section. In the house he would beg Terry and Noel to drop to their knees and box him like they meant it, and by the time he was seven he could throw every combination in the book. The elder boys naturally held back a little but if Eamonn's unrestrained ardour ever did cause the phony wars to spill into a genuine argument, the youngest would always insist on having the final word or, more likely, delivering the concluding punch. His brothers were tough young lads themselves, but Eamonn was something else.

That unfettered passion for physical conflict served him well as he began learning his trade in the breathless, frenzied flurries of leather that a couple of pint-sized juveniles serve up as a round of boxing in the gym. He stood out from the other youngsters so much that the senior coach, Eamon Maguire, couldn't help but notice his performances each evening. After a couple of weeks, Maguire whispered to Patsy, 'That youngest Magee lad has something about him. He's going to be very special.'

Eamonn overheard and walked home that night a couple of inches taller.

He had his first organised bout in the Clonard Boxing Club in west Belfast at the age of seven and immediately felt he belonged in the ring. Despite his street-fighter's heart, when the opening bell rang he fought with a controlled aggression that ensured he thrived in the tumult. He hit extremely hard for all the size of him, but it was the early traces of the slick, counter-punching, southpaw style he would later perfect that most impressed onlookers. On the street Magee would just get fucked into you, but between the ropes he treated fighting like a game of chess in which he was determined to stay two moves ahead. At that tender age, boys turn up at the designated club on fight night, line up according to a rough-and-ready amalgamation of age, weight and experience, and, after a series of nods and grunts from the wizened old officials, get paired with an opponent and pushed into the ring. It is such a rudimentary and relatively arbitrary matchmaking process that, coupled with the limited duration of the one-minute rounds, it tends to produce fifty-fifty confrontations that go the distance. Given the circumstances, it is simply very tough to differentiate yourself from the rest. Nevertheless, Eamonn won his first ten fights, many by stoppage, and ensured he was already being talked about in clubs up and down Co. Antrim. He wasn't bigger or stronger or fitter than the other lads, he was just naturally a much better fighter.

He lost his eleventh contest, a debatable decision against a home fighter in Beechmount Leisure Centre, and still recalls the empty feeling of defeat. Outwardly he took it on the chin but inside he felt disgusted with the judges and with himself for allowing them to make that decision. He privately swore that it wouldn't happen again and, in those days of fights being available almost every week, it wasn't a long wait to put things right. He became a regular in the boxing halls of north and west Belfast but frequent trips were made outside the capital as well. The fortnightly venture north to the Protestant town of Ballyclare on a Tuesday evening is still a particularly fond memory. There the gym was located above a grocery store and the owner of the premises would put on soup and sandwiches for the boys and open his private bar for the trainers throughout the night. But in truth, every venue was welcoming in its own way and Eamonn was eager to box in them all. No records are kept until a boxer is eleven years old but Eamonn guesses he had between eighty and 100 fights in those four years and the defeats could be counted on one hand, with a few fingers to spare.

***

Outside of boxing, life in general continued to harden Eamonn. As the baby of the family he still stuck close to his mother, often to the point of accompanying her on the one night a week Isobel ventured out for a social drink with friends. Their local was a no-frills, ladies-only establishment in a house in Old Ardoyne known as The Hole in the Knickers bar. The party invariably moved to the Magees' when last orders were called and Eamonn and his brother Patrick would be coerced into providing some light entertainment for the high-spirited, tipsy women by dancing to the Teddy Boy revival tunes of Showaddywaddy. Carol Copeland, the mother of the future Provo Godfather, Eddie Copeland, was always there, as was Betty Power, whose son, Billy, would gain fame as one of the Birmingham Six who spent sixteen years behind bars for crimes they had nothing to do with. Eamonn went to bed late those nights but still not late enough to prevent being woken by the exultations of Nailer Clarke, the patriarch of a well-known republican family in the district. Clarke would frequently stumble home in the early hours, three sheets to the wind, hollering at the top of his voice, 'What are yous all doing? Are yous all asleep? Wake up and fight the Brits! Up the RA! Never surrender to the Brits!'

When Eamonn and his brothers weren't in the gym, they were quick to turn their hands to whatever other sport or athletic endeavour was available. Often they'd be found proudly representing Holmdene Gardens in the highly organised and competitive games of street football that ran all year round within the Ardoyne and the Bone. Only when the darkness became pitch did the players reluctantly accept full time and heed their mothers' increasingly threatening calls to come inside. Functioning street lights were a rarity in the 1970s, the lamp posts serving as goalposts more than anything else, so when nightfall draped a black, smothering blanket over the district, even the most contrary of the bunch had to admit that the game was up.

The darkness was metaphorical too. Just as quickly as the daylight would dissipate, a heavy air of discontent would emerge and fog the night sky. Instinctively, the boys all sensed it, the foreboding aura of a brief calm before an intense and violent storm. The vast majority, Terry, Noel and Patrick among them, turned their backs and walked away from the promise of trouble, but Eamonn never quite could resist the dangerous allure. He'd seek out the like-minded minority intent on getting as close to the action as possible. As the rumbling engines of the Saracens drew closer and the smell of petrol filling glass bottles spread through the district, his brothers or mother would have to physically trail him back home by the scruff of the neck.

***

It is difficult to know for sure why the youngest of the pack differed so fundamentally from the rest, but Patsy soon developed his own theory to explain the waywardness of his prize pupil.

'You see that woman over there,' Patsy said quietly to Eamonn, while motioning to Isobel with a jutted chin.

'Aye, my ma,' Eamonn fired back guardedly as he stuffed his gym gear into a plastic bag.

'That's not your mother.'

'What do you mean?' the boy demanded. 'That *is* my ma.'

'It's not. It can't be. You were adopted. You were a stray. She picked you up from the care home.'

'No she didn't!'

'She must have. Why else would her other three sons be going straight back to their house after training every night while you're out on the street in your gang, building your own wee barricades, running wild and looking for trouble?'

'Fuck off, Patsy,' Eamonn muttered under his breath as, for the first of many times, he walked away from someone trying to talk some sense into him.

***

At this stage, Eamonn was still too young to graduate to the bona fide barricades and find the sort of trouble that would draw the attention and wrath of the British military and put his life in genuine danger. Even so,

THE LOST SOUL OF EAMONN MAGEE

the youthful mischief he sought out and invariably found was still a level above the average hijinks of your run-of-the-mill schoolboy tearaway.

He joined a local gang around the age of six, just about negotiating his way through an initiation ceremony that included running past the crosshairs of homemade rubber ring guns which made a stinging impression on any bare skin that became their target. Soon he had an earlobe scarred by a back-street piercing involving a red-hot needle and, in similar circumstances, a few years later he inked the initials E and M onto his left forearm.

One of his favourite pastimes, particularly during the cold and frosty winter months when an icy grey sludge coated the local street surfaces, involved hunkering by the kerbside on a homemade sledge, waiting to grab the bumper of a passing car. When judged correctly, the result was a free and potentially lethal sleigh ride until grip was lost or an irate driver slowed and made to deliver a swift and summary punishment upon the unwanted freeloader. When Isobel found out, she marched her baby boy down Brompton Park, onto the Crumlin Road and into the Holy Cross Church so he could explain himself to the parish priest in an impromptu confession-cum-disciplinary hearing.

Eamonn had developed an early natural aversion to authority figures in whatever guise they took, but back then he was still young enough to remain a little wary of the mystic powers of the Irish Catholic clergy. As such, a slightly cowed version of the young terror stood before the local padre, his dirty clothes soaked through from a particularly energetic session of car hopping.

'What have you been doing, Eamonn?' began the old priest with a gentle, neutral tone.

'I was hopping cars, Father,' was the matter-of-fact response.

'Hopping cars?'

'Aye, you wait 'til one's going at the right speed, then you grab the back and slide along behind it down the street.'

'Why would you do that, son? Can you not see how dangerous that is?'

A shrug from the boy.

'And what about your mother, worried sick about you?'

Another shrug.

'And look at your lovely duffle coat, Eamonn, and your gloves as well, absolutely soaked and filthy.'

Eamonn glanced down at the incriminating evidence but still offered no verbal response to his mild-mannered interrogator. The priest misread the silence as the contrition and acquiescence he was subtly digging for and continued his monologue in the same vein, albeit with renewed vigour.

'Your poor mother, Eamonn. She just wants the best for you. She works so hard to look after you. She gives you a roof over your head. She buys you all these clothes to keep you warm. She makes you your dinner every evening–'

A mistake. A factual error and just the inch a kid like Eamonn needs to take a mile.

'I get my dinner in school,' he interrupted in defiance, convinced now that this holy old goat didn't know what he was talking about. Eamonn wasn't about to let this ignorant priest start bossing him around. Even back then, Eamonn adhered to a particularly zealous interpretation of the thou-shalt-suffer-no-fools ideology.

He was soon back out hopping cars and, just as quick, Isobel was frog-marching him home, administering her feared and abrasive knuckle-shuffle into her boy's scalp as they walked. Insolently unperturbed, Eamonn simply grinned up at his exasperated mother with a smile dripping with provocation. 'Are you not going to take me back to see that priest again?' he enquired with mock innocence.

***

The reason Isobel had resorted to a trip to the sacristy in an attempt to scare her boy straight was that her husband was once again absent from the family home. When the Queen said Terrence could finally leave Long Kesh in late 1975, he emerged an even more psychologically damaged individual. Physically, he appeared all right: he had lost some weight but remained a big, imposing figure who walked purposefully and carried himself proudly at all times. For years Terrence had been the life and soul of the district, a larger-than-life figure who lit up the room and kept spirits high in the darkest of times. 'Doc' they called him, after Doc Holliday, the old gunslinger who sported a black trench coat similar to that which Terrence wore. A builder by trade, he employed half the neighbourhood at one time or another, often hiring three men when one would have sufficed. His own family had very little but Terrence still tried to make sure other families in the district got some of it. He had a rich singing voice and was easily encouraged into a song to entertain family and friends at home or in the pub. He loved the lonesome twangs of country and western music, with the likes of John Denver, Patsy Cline and Glen Campbell amongst his favourites.

But he sang less after his release and the light that used to dance behind his eyes grew dimmer each day. He did his utmost to shield Eamonn and his brothers from becoming party to the damage internment had inflicted upon his mind, heart and soul, but it was an extremely difficult period. He was more fragile within himself as bouts of depression attacked him with increased frequency and more debilitating force. He hit the bottle harder than ever and added sleeping pills to his doomed course of self-medication. And, exacerbating everything, his enemy – the British Army – continued to patrol his streets and harass his family.

It was a Sunday afternoon in 1977. Terrence liked to dress smart on a Sunday. He polished his shoes, ironed a shirt and put on his suit and tie before meeting some friends for an afternoon drink in the Shamrock Social Club on Ardoyne Avenue. As he supped his pint, Isobel prepared a late lunch in the house while outside on the street his four boys and their teammates from Holmdene Gardens FC enjoyed a mass kick-about and warmed up for the next big Ardoyne derby. Suddenly, heard before seen, two Saracen armoured personnel carriers rounded the corner at Etna Drive and steamed towards the Magee house. The footballers moved to the side, pressing their backs against walls and hedges, as one of the six-wheeled beasts mounted the footpath while the other simply cut its engine in the middle of the road, the Browning .30 machine guns mounted on their turrets thrusting out ominously at the wary kids.

After a brief pause, the rear doors of one Saracen were flung open and the army patrol inside spilled out onto the tarmac and up the narrow path into Eamonn's home. Immediately, Noel, a fine long-distance runner, set off to fetch his dad. Eamonn stood on his spot against a neighbour's low wall, mulling the situation over. 'Fuck it!' he said to himself and sprinted towards the empty Saracen that had just delivered a batch of hostile foreign soldiers to his family's front door. In one fluid movement he bounced inside, stepped onto the low-lying side-bench and propelled himself up and through the turret opening towards the blue skies overhead. At six years of age he was too young to fight the Brits with his fists or shoot them with the IRA's guns, so this was his contribution to the war. At the sight of his red hair and pale, cheeky face emerging onto the roof of the enemy vehicle, the other kids erupted in defiant roars of laughter. As a soldier exited the front passenger door and made to grab the unwanted hitchhiker by the feet and drag him back to earth, the boys began joyously kicking their footballs with all their might against the side of the resting Saracens and into the belly of the beast that had left its doors open.

By the time Noel returned with his father, a breathless calm had briefly descended on the scene outside. Apart from their boxing gloves, the boys' football was their most prized possession and British soldiers now had in their possession the footballs of every family on Holmdene Gardens. Terrence, his blood boiling with rage and alcohol, didn't know the full story but neither did he care. Seeing a patrol of six young squaddies crammed into the back of their Saracen, passing his children's football to each other with provocative glee, was more than he could take.

'Give it back,' he demanded before, anticipating the negative response, he piled in himself, one fist clenched and swinging wildly at bodies and the other open wide and grabbing desperately at the ball. Again the kids roared in jubilation but as the blows of the soldiers quickly overpowered Mr Magee, their buoyancy soon sank. With his suit ripped and torn he was kicked from the vehicle and onto the road before being trailed into his own home for the beating to continue on his living-room floor in front of his wife.

Outside, the other children, unsure how to react to such broad-daylight brutality, slowly moved uneasily away. The four Magee boys were left standing on their own, looking towards their front door, the emotions of fear, hatred and despair fighting one another for prominence.

Not long after that incident, Terrence was once again removed from his family. This time the exile was further afield than the Kesh and his old friends in the IRA, rather than the forces of the crown, were to blame.

In addition to their role as defenders of the district against the invasion of foreign soldiers and loyalist paramilitaries, the Provos soon assumed responsibility for policing their own people. Almost a decade of the Troubles had undermined old value systems and caused law and order to gradually break down in many of the working-class ghettoes of the city. Added to the fact that the RUC were unable or unwilling to enter many Catholic areas, there was an undeniable policing vacuum in pockets of north and west Belfast. Seizing an opportunity to cement their authority within the nationalist community, the IRA decided to fill the hole and formed its Administrative Branch in 1977 to deal with crime, from the petty to the deadly, however they saw fit. It was the beginning of the era of the organised punishment beating.

Terrence's offence was bouncing a cheque he wrote for a couple of thousand pounds, a misdemeanour that would have struggled to raise an eyebrow within the traditional justice system. Yet despite the relative levity of his infraction, he was given a straight choice: a one-way ticket out of the country or a low-velocity bullet to the knee pit. Terrence wisely took the boat to England.

***

Two and a bit years later, Isobel was hanging some washing on an accommodating neighbour's line. With four rambunctious boys and herself to clothe, there just wasn't the space to get everything dry in her own small abode. As she sorted through the wet boxing gear, the neighbour came out to reveal that the IRA had been asking about her. It was nothing to worry about, apparently, they just wanted a word. The following week when she arrived again with a fresh load of clean but damp clothes the neighbour invited her inside for a cup of tea. There, sat at the kitchen table, a local, high-ranking IRA man was waiting for her.

'How are you doing, Mrs Magee?' he asked.

'Not bad,' Isobel tentatively replied. 'We're surviving.'

The Irish are known to be great talkers but militant republican operatives prefer to get straight to the point as far as business is concerned.

'Would you want to have Terrence back, Mrs Magee?'

Isobel's heart skipped a beat.

'I would, yes,' she blurted out. 'Of course I would. He's my husband and the father of my children. I'd like him back with his family. All he did was bounce a wee cheque, he never hurt anybody.'

'Okay, Mrs Magee, leave it with me.'

A few days later the same man appeared at the Magee's back door. Isobel's heart skipped two beats this time.

'The IRA has granted permission for Terrence to return to the Ardoyne, Mrs Magee,' he announced once inside the kitchen. 'You have my word that your husband will not be harmed by anyone from the organisation upon his return.'

Physically tremoring, Isobel barely managed a whispered thank you as the man exited. Gently, she closed the door behind him, leant with her back to it and slid down onto the floor in an exhausted collapse of relief.

From the shadows of the adjoining coal cove, Terrence emerged to join her.

✱✱✱

It turned out that nine months of English life, an Irish Sea away from his home and family, was all Terrence could take. One night, under the cover of darkness, he snuck back into Holmdene Gardens. For the next eighteen months, he did not leave that small, cramped, two-up, two-down terraced house. The attic, a draughty, hollow space with a pitched roof whose apex sat well below head height, became his entire world. Only his wife and sons knew the situation, a time that was perhaps the absolute lowest point the family reached. It was worse than Terrence's period of internment because this way it was as if they were all imprisoned. Ardoyne people are famous for their habit, even today, of leaving the front and rear doors of their homes unlocked for family and friends to enter with little more than a notifying rap as they cross the threshold. Neighbours came and went throughout the day, borrowing, lending or simply stopping by for a chat. In a community that tight-knit, there is an openness that only exists when everyone is in the same boat, when all are committed to the same cause.

But suddenly, the Magees' doors were locked. Suddenly, the curtains were always drawn. Suddenly, the boys' friends were no longer able to drop in unannounced. But for Isobel's mother, herself totally unaware of her son-in-law's presence a few feet above her head, there were soon barely any visitors at all. The boys dreaded the weekend when their dad would descend with a few more beers in him than usual. The alcohol drew out his belligerent side and the family were all terrified he would try to go outside, an action that would almost certainly cost him his life. It was a life that had taken a very heavy toll on Terrence Magee. The alcoholism and depression, being chased out of his home by murderous, sectarian mobs, internment and exile – they all chipped away at his psyche to ensure that, mentally and psychologically, he was not a well man when he entered that attic. But by the time he walked free from it, eighteen months later, it was as if he had finally been irrevocably broken.

***

In my first recorded conversation with Eamonn, late one Friday night in the winter cold of his unheated kitchen, he alluded to those attic years, but I hadn't fully understood. He'd been drinking heavily all day and as soberness departs from Eamonn, paranoia often arrives to take its place. An innocent mistake on my part earlier in the day probably hadn't helped the situation.

We'd arranged to meet at Madden's bar and when I arrived I sat down and joined him and two of his acquaintances sitting outside, seemingly content to suffer the bite in the air in order to enjoy a smoke with their pint. Conversation was limited but at one point they casually joked about the wrong twin brother being targeted in a punishment shooting the previous night.

Suddenly a noise emanated from my pocket and I realised that my dictaphone had been left unlocked and a movement had inadvertently started playing an old recording. My temperature steadily rising, I removed the offending device from inside my jacket as nonchalantly as I could and switched it off. A brief awkward silence ensued, followed by a sideways look from Magee.

'Were you recording all that?' he asked with a smile struggling to totally rid itself of suspicion. 'I'm beginning to wonder about you.'

He was joking – ninety percent joking anyway – but a dangerous seed had been planted and it was now set to break ground.

After Madden's, I enjoyed a couple of hours with his brother Noel in Newcastle, Co. Down, while Eamonn sat apart and alone, steadily dispatching half-litre tins of lager. This was my first time meeting face to face with members of his family and the reality of it apparently spooked him. He began questioning what we were doing and what he'd get out of it. Where's the contract? Where're the guarantees? Where's the money? I had spent most of the uncomfortable forty-five-minute drive back trying to calm the situation and reassure Magee that he could indeed trust me. But back in the Ardoyne, as he told me through sobs about visiting his father in Long Kesh, he was still only partially convinced. I then asked him how it felt when his dad was released and came back home.

'I can't tell this story, I can't tell this story, I can't tell this story,' he muttered under his breath as he paced up and down the small kitchen with yet another tin of Carling in his hand. Suddenly he plunged his free hand into a coat pocket and took out a fistful of Sean Graham betting slips. They were all covered with his own unruly scrawl and, pulling one of the tiny gambling pens from another pocket, he scribbled something down on one of the few blanks amongst the pile. 'A reminder,' he continued almost inaudibly without looking up. 'I'll need to ask my mother that question.'

The pacing and slurred muttering then resumed.

'Two years. Two fucking years. He spent two years. Was it two years? Or two months? No, two years. Could it be two years?'

His pacing stopped then, right in front of where I was perched on top of the kitchen's sole stool.

'Walking from here to there. There to here,' he suddenly shouted with flecks of saliva gathering at the corner of his mouth. He was pointing from the sofa of his adjoining living room to his kitchen's back door, a distance of no more than three metres. 'There to here and here to fucking there!' he roared.

The anger visibly rose and erupted from him and, for so many different reasons, it was intimidating. Sitting outside in the car ten minutes before, I'd thought twice when he told me to come into the house to finish the conversation. I was now starting to regret ignoring my gut feeling that this was neither the time nor the place to be engaging with Eamonn on his father.

'Hiding from the other boys,' he went on, back to a drunken mumble that I hoped signified his rage had peaked and was now subsiding with no collateral damage caused. He finished his beer, crunched the can in his hand, took another from the fridge and began rolling a joint.

'Oh aye. Fuck, ask my ma about it tomorrow. Oh aye, we had our own wee code to get in and out of the house and everything. Oh aye. Nobody fucking knew. Everyone on the street used to think my da was dead. In school the kids were slagging me, your da's dead, your da's dead. And he was in the house the whole time, the silly bastards. But I couldn't say that to any of them.'

The joint was ready now. He lit it, opened his beer and started to cry.

***

There is no universal or accepted response to witnessing your alcoholic and depressed father interned in a cage, physically assaulted by foreign soldiers while his house is ransacked by their cohorts, exiled by comrades he would recently have died for, or living like a secret hermit in the family attic, fearful for his life. Amongst young and impressionable minds in particular, it is impossible to predict the impact of such traumas. Certainly, there was no uniform reaction from Eamonn and his brothers, although three of the clan developed relatively similar personalities and character traits that contrasted sharply with the fourth. The three oldest boys made a conscious decision to avoid the life that may eventually lead to their father's fate. By his late teens Patrick had moved out of the Ardoyne, found a secure job, was married and had the first of his three children to care for. Terry moved even further afield and settled in Wales at the age of sixteen, a rare Irishman abroad who never again took a drink or smoked a cigarette. Noel knuckled down to working and training in Belfast, later Stoke-on-Trent in England, and finally found a comfortable suburban life with his wife and two children in the coastal town of Newcastle, thirty miles south of the violent capital. It was only Eamonn who found it difficult not to follow in his father's footsteps.

His mother thinks he was twelve when he first had a drink, but Eamonn admits he was just nine years old. In Isobel's version he came asking her for fifty pence to go to a tea party at his friend John O'Hare's grandmother's house. He admitted that the granny would not be there and Isobel, perhaps wrong-footed by this unusually open concession and the absurd image of Eamonn and his merry band sat around a table enjoying freshly brewed cups of Nambarrie, handed him the coin and watched him stroll away. Three hours later, she watched him totter back up the path and stumble into the house, filled with drink.

Old Mrs O'Hare's place had been taken over for the night by a rabble of young teens smoking dope and drinking cheap cider and beer. As the youthful intoxication intensified, so too did the noise exuding from within until O'Hare's dad was alerted and burst through the front door. Eamonn scampered up the stairs and exited through a bathroom window onto a yard wall and down into a back alley before Mr O'Hare could identify him. But there was nothing he could do to hide his drunken state from his mother when he arrived home.

To the best of her knowledge, that was Eamonn's first serious experimentation with booze. In reality, the poisonous tangle of the alcoholism that would later consume her son had taken root three years earlier, before he'd even reached double figures. His opening tipple was stolen too, a two-litre bottle of Blackthorn cider he spied tucked down the side of a delivery driver's seat. Instinctively, he snatched it and ran without looking back. He knew as well that there was only one place to drink it. Back to his empty house he headed and straight up through the trapdoor into the attic. There, as his father had for the previous two years, Eamonn sat alone and drank the cider, letting the alcohol numb him.

***

The 1980s arrived and Terry left. He was selected to represent Ulster at a boxing tournament in Wales and never came back. He was barely midway through his teenage years but something about the calmness of

Carmarthenshire and the charms of a particularly friendly landlady obviously appealed to him. He settled in Betws, a small village in the protective shadow of the Black Mountain with the sleepy River Amman drifting by, a million miles from north Belfast. Betws derives from the Anglo-Saxon word *bed-hus*, or house of prayer, and means chapel in Welsh. Perhaps the etymology influenced Terry as he even briefly considered joining the priesthood before dedicating himself to boxing. Later, he would become a fireman and well-known charity worker throughout southwest Wales.

It wasn't until his own mid-teens that Eamonn visited his eldest brother and it was perhaps even longer before he fully understood and forgave Terry's decision to leave. The way he saw it as a naïve youngster, the four boys should have stuck together no matter what and, with Terrence Senior's health and state of mind deteriorating badly, Terrence Junior had abandoned the family when they needed him most.

The dangers the nine-year-old Eamonn faced on the streets were very real. One night he was walking home from the youth club just after 9 p.m. with his friend, Neilly Shevlin. They had just emerged from Brompton Park Entry and started up Berwick Road towards home when a car slowed almost to a standstill alongside them and then accelerated away. The vehicle continued on up Berwick before slowing again beside another figure walking the pavement. This time the windows of the car lowered and the UDA murder squad inside fired bullets into twenty-six-year-old local man Paul Blake. He was a Catholic victim chosen totally at random, Eamonn and Neilly presumably passed over as a couple of years too young to be slaughtered that night.

Around this time a twenty-seven-year-old republican prisoner by the name of Bobby Sands was elected to Westminster and began refusing food in an effort to have the British government recognise him and his comrades as political prisoners. Sixty-six days later, Bobby died of starvation.

'Mr Sands was a convicted criminal. He chose to take his own life,' declared an unmoved Margaret Thatcher as sectarian violence on the streets of Northern Ireland surged back towards early-1970s levels. The 1981 hunger strikes, and Thatcher's cold-blooded handling of the tragic ordeal, boosted IRA recruitment and increased popular support for the paramilitaries in the nationalist community. So too did the continuing acts of state brutality, like the night young Danny Barrett lost his life.

The Barretts lived in Havana Court, just round the corner from the Magees. Danny was born within a few months of Eamonn's brother Noel and the two boys were close friends. He was a regular teenage kid and the night he was killed he'd been playing pool and watching *Top of the Pops* with his mates. Only the fact the Magees were all working up a sweat in the nearby Sacred Heart gym meant none of them were part of the group sitting on the Barretts' front wall, enjoying the summer warmth and waiting for the local disco to fill up.

The previous day Joe McDonnell had become the fifth hunger striker to perish and his sacrifice had sparked riots on Brompton Park the night before, which continued to flare up sporadically throughout the following day. Shots suddenly rang out and the boys all charged inside the Barrett home and waited until calm had returned. When it did they re-emerged into the pleasant dusk and Danny re-took his position facing his house, perched upon the two-foot wall that surrounded the front garden. Again, the hollow crack of gunshots splintered the evening air and everyone but Danny hunkered behind the wall. Danny waved away his friends' protestations that he should get off the wall and join them. Seconds later, Danny did drop from the wall.

Standing in the doorway, his father Jimmy believed his son had descended voluntarily in search of cover. It took a few more seconds before he processed the meaning of the pool of dark blood that grew around his son's head. Danny had been shot through the back of the neck by a Welsh Guard manning the observation post of the British Army barracks in neighbouring Flax Street. As Jimmy knelt, cradling his son and whispering the Rosary into his blood-stained ears, an ambulance arrived and a medical team in the nearby Mater Hospital was notified and stood ready to save Danny's life. At that precise moment there was still a chance, but by the time the ambulance had been stopped by a mobile RUC patrol and two army checkpoints, each demanding the names and details of all on board, the life had bled from the bullet hole in Danny's neck. At just fifteen years of age, he was pronounced dead a few metres short of the hospital gates.

Meanwhile, back at Havana Court, where family and friends were gathering in a state of shock and tears, the Brits raided the Barrett home and the houses of Danny's friends. They found nothing. At a later inquest, an unnamed soldier insisted Danny had been firing a rifle. This was an unfounded and false allegation that forensic tests soon dismissed out of hand. Danny's anonymous killer was never prosecuted.

Walking home from the gym that night, the three Magee brothers still residing in the Ardoyne learned what had happened. It was an explosive time to be a young Catholic male coming of age on the streets of the north Belfast ghettoes. A time when Eamonn needed more close authority figures or potential positive role models around him rather than less. But with his father slowly drifting away and his eldest brother establishing a new life overseas, he had never felt so alone and vulnerable.

***

In 1982 Eamonn turned eleven. For a boy moving from primary to secondary school, and a boxer progressing from the juveniles to junior championship level, this was a landmark year. Part of him was sad to leave the Holy Cross Primary School in which he'd spent seven good years, a time in which he'd become something of a Godfather figure behind those blue gates. Always one with a strong sense of what was fair, Eamonn had more or less eliminated bullying during his reign, with any incidents stamped out quickly and – for the bully at least – painfully.

His early boxing successes had afforded him a large degree of respect and he loved bringing his trophies and medals into class for pupils and teachers to take a look and beg for a blow-by-blow account of how he claimed the shiny pieces of metal. Now he had to leave those comforts behind and start again in St Gabriel's on the Crumlin Road. St Gabriel's closed its doors permanently in 2008 but not before it had cemented its reputation as one of the toughest schools in Belfast. The students were hard in St Gabe's, and the teachers even harder.

Like a convict on his first day in a notorious prison, Eamonn believed he had to assert his authority in his new environment as quickly as possible. He wouldn't go looking for trouble, but if it arrived he'd certainly deal with it. He got his chance on the third day during a game of pitch and toss with a boy four years his senior. When he finally flicked his penny closer to the wall to break a losing streak and win back his losses, the older kid seriously misjudged the situation and refused to hand over what was rightfully Magee's. Despite a severe age, height and weight disadvantage, Eamonn administered a savage beating that only relented when a passing teacher heard the commotion and dragged him off his bloodied foe. His brand-new uniform was in tatters and his mother was soon standing fuming beside him in the principal's office, but Eamonn didn't care: he had proven a point and guaranteed his fellow students would think twice before crossing him during the next five years.

The incident also ensured his card was marked as far as the teaching faculty was concerned. It was as if battle lines were immediately drawn and within a term Eamonn had made sworn enemies of half the staff room, with Vice-Principal McGartland his prime nemesis. A 'hateful cunt' is Magee's admittedly partisan assessment of the man as he recalls an icy revenge he took on the VP for keeping him and his classmates waiting outside the dinner hall in sub-zero temperatures for no apparent reason. While packing a snowball until it was more solid ice than snow, Eamonn instructed his two pals either side of him in the line, John Connolly and Joe Carmichael, to dry their hands and warm them in their pockets. He then launched the cold boulder towards the back of McGartland's head and was doing the same as soon as it had left his grasp. The hurtful ball found its target with a direct hit and a stunned McGartland turned and stormed straight up to Magee and his mates. Disappointed that an inspection of the three unveiled no incriminating signs of cold and damp palms, he ordered the trio to his office and told them to forget about their dinner that day.

On the way there, commanding officer Magee issued the instructions.

'He has no proof that it was one of us so don't be admitting anything and don't be taking no slaps from him.'

Inside the office, McGartland demanded once more to know who was responsible and was again met with three heads shaking their denials.

'Hand out, Carmichael!'

Much to Eamonn's dismay, Joe consented and received six stinging whips from a well-used cane.

'Hand out, Magee!'

No chance. The refusal further enraged an already seething McGartland, who began swiping at Eamonn's legs while the guilty snowballer danced out of range and deflected the worst of the blows with his schoolbag. Sweating and panting, McGartland gave up and moved on to Connolly, an interested spectator at the end of the cane queue.

'Hand out, Connolly!' he barked, at which point John turned on his heels and sprinted out the door, ignoring McGartland's bellowed threats chasing him down the corridor.

They weren't all like McGartland, however, and Principal McGleeson is one who is described as harsh but fair. Mr McGleeson won Magee over when he took the young pupil's side over a zealous form teacher midway through first year. Irish class, the one subject that Eamonn just couldn't get his head around, sparked that particular dispute. Tired of failing the monthly tests, Eamonn snuck into Mr Rice's *gaeilge* classroom and pinched a copy of the following day's exam. He was careful not to overplay his hand and instead filled in just enough correct answers to guarantee a pass in the low forties. The perfect crime, he thought, but Eamonn was never exactly

Mr Inconspicuous, despite his best intentions. Rice had calmly watched Eamonn's harmless cheating throughout the test and when a buoyant Magee deposited his paper on his teacher's desk as he swaggered towards the door, Rice thanked him for his efforts and wrote '0%' across the front page in a bold, red marker pen.

Eamonn took his six whacks from his Irish teacher's yardstick with little fuss, for he knew he deserved them and had been caught fair and square. But when his form teacher, Miss McNeill, tried to repeat the punishment, Eamonn refused to play ball. A brief verbal back and forth led to an agreement to take it to Principal McGleeson and let him arbitrate on the matter. But when Eamonn turned his back on McNeill to walk out the door, she lashed him viciously across the back with a leather strap. The pain was like a lightning strike and, instinctively, Magee turned and as he did so threw a punch that whistled past his form teacher's ear. Shocked and visibly shaken as she looked into young Eamonn's cold, blue, unblinking eyes, McNeill quietly ordered the boy to follow her to McGleeson's office. Once there, Eamonn sat outside listening to her relay her version of events to the principal. When Eamonn was called in, he didn't say a word. He merely removed his jumper and shirt and stood with his bare back to McGleeson, the raw welt almost glowing in its intensity.

'Okay, Eamonn, put your shirt and jumper back on and go on home now,' he said.

Eamonn put his shirt and jumper back on and left the room but he didn't go home. Not just yet. He stood outside with his ear to the door and listened with immense pleasure while McGleeson warned Miss McNeill never to strike a child like that again in his school. A few minutes later when a chastened, red-faced McNeill left the principal's office, Eamonn was there waiting for her. His eyes were still unblinking as they stared into her own but they were now underlined by a massive, goading grin. He needed her to know that he had won, even if it was weeks before the strap mark left his pale, white skin.

Eamonn had barely missed a day of primary school as during those years he was largely able to resist the lure of street mischief until the home bell rang. But secondary school was different and there were occasionally days when he just didn't fancy it. He was now thick with John Connolly and one day the pair decided that they deserved an unscheduled mid-term break. Skipping a class or two was no bother, and a random day could easily be skived here or there as well, but they had their hearts set on a slightly longer holiday. After batting various schemes back and forth amongst themselves, they arrived at the conclusion that an injury of some kind would do the job. Drawing inspiration from the recently released classic *Escape to Victory*, it was decided that a couple of quick arm breaks would serve their purposes. Connolly, displaying a level of bravery that quickly wandered into the realms of stupidity, went first and lay on the ground with his bare arm bridging the gap between a breezeblock and the roadside kerb. Magee jumped and came down two-footed on his best friend's limb. The sharp crack of the bone was still echoing down the street as Connolly's fervid, high-pitched squeals began, and Magee, the boxing star, began to have second thoughts.

After meeting a wall of silence and denial from Eamonn, Isobel soon got the truth out of his partner in crime who, in comparison with her son, broke relatively easily under interrogation. Years later she joked about it with Connolly and he revealed that after she had mentally abused the real story out of him, Eamonn was waiting outside the door with a dose of physical abuse to punish him for talking. On this occasion, Connolly got a couple of days off for his trouble as the plaster set and the pain subsided, but Eamonn was straight back to school. It was just another youthful example of him choosing the extreme and dangerous route when more level and sedate paths were easily accessible.

***

All the while, Eamonn's amateur boxing career continued going from strength to strength and he was now excelling in the organised championships that eleven-year-olds were eligible to enter. These are the first, necessary steps that every amateur fighter hopes will culminate in an appearance at the Olympic Games. He quickly became Antrim champion. Then Ulster champion. Then Irish champion. For years he didn't lose a fight and successfully defended those three titles right the way through to senior level. The first All-Ireland win in 1983 was the one that left those close to him in no doubt that Eamonn had the potential to go all the way to the top of the amateur game.

Patrick still talks about his younger brother's performances in an almost whispered awe. Stocky and robust in build, with an unmistakeable red-haired tinge despite his shaved head, I can see some physical resemblances between Eamonn and the brother he is closest to in age. But like his older siblings, Patrick shares precious few character traits with the youngest of the family. He's a measured and reserved father of three, who values a quiet life above all else. In our first meeting he sits straight-backed and slightly tense at his kitchen table and I have the impression his mind is in a constant whirl as it gauges how much to reveal to the stranger that has just entered his home. He only really relaxes and opens up when the topic is Eamonn in the ring.

If the first All-Ireland victory suggested greatness for the youngest Magee, an Ireland versus USA event the following year made it an indisputable truth in Patrick's mind. Sacred Heart Belfast and Sacred Heart Newry joined forces to compete against an American team in the border town. The Americans had sent over their best fighters, including a kid in Eamonn's weight class who hadn't lost in over thirty fights and was earmarked as the next big thing. Many thought it was a wasted trip for the young superstar as no Irish trainer would want to put their own boys in with him. Without hesitation, Patsy McKenna and Eamon Maguire made the fight. Magee will take him on, they said. Magee did, and comprehensively out-boxed the hot prospect to earn a deserved, unanimous decision.

He by now had a self-confidence about him; he almost knew he was unbeatable. Unlike the vast majority of junior amateurs, he was never a cover-up fighter, never one to simply tuck his chin behind a high guard and randomly trade leather. He had a gift that allowed him to see punches before his opponent threw them, a kind of pugilistic clairvoyance. He could judge distances instinctively and he used that talent to draw rivals in before catching them with sharp counters. In addition to his natural gifts, he was hungry to learn and quick to pick up and perfect new additions to his armoury.

By the age of fourteen he was already bounding into the gym excitedly to tell Patsy he'd been watching a certain professional fighter the night before and noted a particular punch or combination that he was determined to master. The pair would then work on it for weeks before unleashing it on an unsuspecting opponent.

One famous example was a lightening double left from the southpaw stance, and the Holy Family Club's Billy Boyle was the unfortunate guinea pig on that occasion. It was in a packed Dockers Boxing Club in Belfast city centre's Sailortown district and Eamonn, facing the large mirror that adorns the side wall, squared Billy up and then debuted his new combination. There was bedlam from ringside as Boyle lay motionless on the canvas floor. The two left hands were so quick, and thrown with such deceptive power, that most onlookers missed the punches and thought the Holy Family fighter was taking a dive!

It was during this time that Eamonn built a strong and lifelong friendship with Wayne McCullough, the future bronze-medal-winning Olympian and bantamweight champion of the world. Their paths would have crossed before in the juvenile club shows but it was only at the age of eleven that they properly met. Wayne, born and raised on the staunchly loyalist Shankill Road, was the first Protestant with whom Eamonn ever had a full conversation. Trained by Harry Robinson and fighting out of the Albert Foundry Club in west Belfast, McCullough was a dogged, relentless fighter with a granite chin. Harry and Patsy became firm friends as well and the two men would take turns sharing driving duties to transport their charges to championships all over Ireland. Upon arrival they'd share digs together, a hostel room, a church hall or, when in Dublin, the home of Tommy and Teresa Dowell, friends of Patsy who welcomed the northerners in year after year. The time together gave Eamonn and Wayne plenty of opportunity to talk and discover that, despite having almost nothing in common, they enjoyed one another's company. In addition to his upbringing in the polar opposite – politically, at least – of republican Ardoyne, Wayne was a naturally shy and quiet kid who from day one dedicated himself to learning the profession of boxing. He neither smoked, drank nor partied, and he was certainly never out rioting or making a name for himself among security force and paramilitary circles.

***

Eamonn bristles when I suggest that he and McCullough must have made for particularly strange bedfellows back then.

'Why?' he fires back aggressively before I've a chance to make my point. When I elaborate, highlighting his extra-curricular activities at the barricades, he is quick to cut me off.

'Listen, no one can help where they were born, right? I'm from the Ardoyne. I'm Irish and make no apologies for that. I was involved on the street as a kid, fighting the Brits. But, that was just the way it was. That was nothing exceptional. All the boys I hung about with did the same. We'd sit around at night under the sniper towers in Flax Street mill, listening to rebel tunes, brainwashing ourselves, really. Then when the riots started we'd join in. And yes, we called the Brits our enemy. But I don't hate any group of people and I certainly never hated Protestants in Northern Ireland. I didn't give a fuck that Wayne was a Protestant from the Shankill. He was, and is, a beautiful man, impossible not to like. It's as simple as that.'

***

There was calm for Eamonn within boxing, but right up until he climbed through the ropes, life on the streets of north Belfast continued to challenge and harden him. Just walking to and from the Sacred Heart gym proved to be an adventure. One day he set off and saw a collection of British Army and RUC vehicles and personnel at the end of his street. The police looked on while the army kicked through Fitzy Mulholland's front door in search of guns, bombs or ammunition.

As Eamonn paused to take in the scene, he saw Ma Brown walk through and away from the commotion sporting a long cream coat that almost reached her ankles. Mulholland's next-door neighbour was known to everyone as Ma Brown, an octogenarian fixture in the district for as long as anyone could remember. It was her strangely stilted gait that caught his attention on this occasion, however, and he followed the form of her unbending, limping leg down to her ankles where he saw the muzzle of an Armalite rifle peeping out. At twelve years of age he was already more adept at sniffing out armaments than seasoned soldiers paid to do the job.

He smiled at the old grandmother edging her way to safety through the array of military uniforms and turned his attention back to the raid where Mulholland's ginger dog was yapping incessantly at the troops ransacking his master's house. By now a small crowd had gathered to watch the show and the slight increase in pressure caused one young private to snap. Suddenly, the soldier spun round and put a plastic bullet in the dog's head from point-blank range. The death of the mutt sparked an intense riot that night but by the time the first petrol bomb soared – on this occasion, at least – Eamonn had entered the gym and was busy going through his drills with Patsy.

The barricade on Etna Drive was almost permanent at this stage and, as such, was a focal point for the worst of the rioting. Patsy started telling the Magee boys to walk to the gym with him by going out the back of his house on Etna, along the entry and across the waste ground to reach their destination. It circumnavigated the missiles and plastic bullets, but general harassment from the army was impossible to avoid altogether.

On one occasion three young Brits were patrolling the area when they spied Patsy, Patrick and Eamonn cutting across in the direction of Jamaica Street. A cry to halt rang out but the Irish trio initially chose to ignore it. They were more familiar with the landscape than their foreign visitors and were determined to first place themselves on the other side of an expansive, shallow-looking puddle. They knew that, due to a natural dip in the land at that point, the body of water was a lot deeper than it appeared and if the Brits were intent on tormenting them that evening, they were going to have a little fun of their own. Sure enough, when they stopped in their tracks at the second English-accented yell, the soldiers marched forward into the puddle and within a couple of steps had sunk up to their knees, the filthy water well over the top of their boots. Struggling to hide their amusement, the two young fighters and their coach then opened their bags to be searched by the probing ends of the privates' rifles.

'Boxers, eh?' one of the soldiers piped up. 'I used to do a bit of amateur boxing myself.'

Before his brother or Patsy had a chance to respond, Eamonn decided to nip the attempt at friendly discourse in the bud. 'You can't have been very good or you wouldn't be stood here now with a rifle in your hand.'

The reply belied an intensity within Eamonn, still not even a teenager. He had never known anything other than the foreign occupation of his streets and, just like all the other kids of his age, the message 'Brits out!' had been drummed into him for as long as he could remember. But while other youngsters paid little more than lip-service to these militant republican ideals, watching his father's struggles and absorbing into his bones the violence he witnessed daily on the street had caused Eamonn to think about the situation more deeply than most. *I belong here, you don't*, he thought as he looked up and stared down that squaddie and his gun. He was fearless. Five minutes later he was in the gym with his gloved fists thumping the padded ribs of a heavy bag that represented every British soldier who had ever raided his home or beat his father.

The antagonism from British forces followed Magee and the other Sacred Heart fighters to the very edge of Northern Ireland. Today, the journey from Belfast to Dublin is less than two hours in a straight line and you breeze over the border without even realising the dialling code has changed. But back in the early 1980s the journey was closer to three-and-a-half hours of winding roads and a long, often stressful, delay at a heavily fortified border. Eamonn, now eligible to fight in the All-Ireland championships and always flying through the qualifiers to comfortably earn his place, made the trip south at least once a year. It was as far from home as most Ardoyne kids could hope to travel in those days and he always enjoyed the liberating buzz of being out on strange roads.

Ten kids were piled into the dilapidated red minibus on the way from the 1984 All-Ireland finals on this occasion, with three adults sitting up front. Approaching the border from Dundalk, the young fighters were halfway through a raucous alphabet game that required the naming of as many animals as possible with each letter until you stuttered and lost one of your three lives. As the bus slowed to join the sullen queue of vehicles waiting to pass through the military checkpoint, Patsy called for some decorum until they were safely out the other side. Not that the men necessarily expected any trouble ahead: they had their papers and all the proof even the most fastidious soldier could desire that they really were just a group of young and innocent amateur boxers returning home from a national competition. But back then, nothing was ever certain.

'Everyone out!' yelled the squaddie, motioning from the bus to the side of the road with the tip of his loaded rifle.

Out into the evening darkness they traipsed, clothes soaking instantly in the steady rainfall.

'They're only kids, for fuck sake,' protested Patsy as he was roughly searched beside the drivers' door.

'Everyone, on your knees, hands behind your head!' was the barked response to reason.

Every personal bag on the bus was then rummaged through by soldiers while the remainder of the patrol stood guard over the kneeling line of a dozen wet, shivering eleven- to fifteen-year-old boys.

'Right, up and on your way,' they were then instructed after the Queen's forces satisfied themselves that the small red minibus was indeed transporting nothing more than sweaty sports gear and a team of tired, frightened and now further embittered and politicised young boys.

The incident changed Eamonn. He could see no justification whatsoever for the army's actions at the border. They had done that to him and his friends purely out of badness. Back on the Ardoyne streets, he decided that two could play at that game.

He still never missed training and continued to win all of the fights or tournaments that Patsy entered him into, but away from boxing he gravitated towards a harder crowd and stepped up his contributions to the war against the Brits. Gone were the days of building fake barricades with his pals and hurling little more than verbal abuse at passing soldiers and Saracens. He was now stealing up to the front line of the riots, alongside teenagers four or five years his senior, and it was stones and rocks and paint bombs he now hurled the soldiers' way.

Isobel did her best to limit his participation but she was always fighting a losing battle. Friends would knock on the door to warn her that Eamonn had been spotted wearing his rubber gloves in the thick of the trouble and she would go running into the heart of the riot in her slippers and grab him by the neck. As she physically pushed him home she'd hear onlookers describing her as a lunatic, while press photographers snapped pictures of the darkly comical scene.

Spinning her youngest son around to face the long lenses, she'd shout, 'Go ahead! Take his photo and put it on the front page so maybe they'll lock him up and keep him safe!'

***

The police authorities were not aware of Eamonn just yet, but the gang of teenage lads he was now associated with had been making a name for themselves in other circles. One day Eamonn was walking through the district on his way to the shop when he spied his pals waiting at the bus stop.

'What are yous doing?' he shouted across the road.

'We've been summoned to Connolly House,' came the reply. 'C'mon with us, sure.'

'All right then, I'll go for the craic.'

Connolly House was the Sinn Féin headquarters on the Andersonstown Road, five miles and two bus journeys to the west of the Ardoyne. It was the political home of the Provos and Eamonn's mates were due to attend an informal hearing to discuss reports of their increasingly antisocial behaviour. Upon arrival, the group of five stood, heads bowed, and listened to the charges against them and warnings on the direction their lives were headed. Suddenly, a tall, bearded man entered the room and went along the line issuing individual and personalised threats.

'Breakable. Shootable. Shootable. Breakable.'

At Magee he paused, perhaps a little taken aback by the youth of the thirteen-year-old apparently involved in the sort of shenanigans that tended to be the domain of the four sixteen-year-olds he had just decided could be either shot or have their bones broken if they continued with their antics.

'You be in bed every night by nine o'clock,' was Eamonn's sentence that day, a verdict that proved a great source of hilarity amongst his mates as they travelled back to the Ardoyne.

He was already well known to local republicans. He was Doc's son, the wild one. The older three were good boys but Eamonn liked to get involved in whatever was going on. One morning as he dressed for school, three men knocked on the door, walked him several streets away, and blindfolded and spun their captive to disorientate him, before depositing him in a supposedly unknown house. There he was laid on the floor of a back room, his arms spread wide as if in crucifixion, with heavy men kneeling into his back and forcing him to maintain the stress position until his muscles trembled in agony. They wanted names and information on neighbourhood vandals, drug peddlers and joyriders but Eamonn wouldn't open his mouth. He could hear the sound of the house-owner's own children readying themselves for school in the bedrooms above. When the house fell silent he was pushed out the door and sent on his way. Eamonn went to school that day and said nothing about what had happened, but he knew what house he had been in and who had done the interrogating.

Almost thirty years later, he saw the man in the Shamrock Club, in his late sixties now, a recently retired town councillor. Eamonn, filled with drink and anger, couldn't bite his tongue any longer.

'Do you remember what you did to me that morning?' he whispered menacingly into the man's ear as he sat at the bar. 'I was a kid getting ready for school. Just like your own kids were getting ready for school that morning. And you dragged me out of my mother's house and tortured me.'

The man, physically shaking, got up to leave as others tried to calm Eamonn.

'For what?' Eamonn shouted after him at the top of his hoarse voice. 'For what!'

***

The drunken mischief and misbehaviour for the sake of it was frowned upon, but there was no doubt that kids like Eamonn, when their natural exuberance was controlled and directed in a way that suited republican needs, were extremely useful to the movement during that period. He was monitored for another year and then they approached him with an invitation to join the IRA's youth wing, Na Fianna Éireann. Without hesitation he accepted. After all, he hated the Brits and he wanted them out of Ireland. Within days he was sworn in and out on active service.

His first job was siphoning petrol from the cars of unsuspecting owners to guarantee there was an ample supply for the petrol bombs that were hurled at the army whenever a riot erupted. Five gallon drums were secretly deposited in street drains and it was Eamonn's responsibility to ensure the hidden fuel sources in his area were kept topped up and ready to go.

Soon he progressed to securing the second vital element of a petrol bomb: a glass receptacle to hold the combustible liquid. This required trips to the Old Ardoyne streets in the early morning to hijack the local milk float and relieve the startled driver of every empty glass bottle in his vehicle. The orders when hijacking vehicles were clear and unambiguously followed to a tee. The most important of all was that drivers were always to be left unharmed and allowed time to gather all personal belongings and exit their vehicle. Both parties to the hijacking knew this and violence during the process was thus almost unheard of. The replica guns the young Provos carried and waved in drivers' faces also helped avoid heroic and potentially deadly responses from the hijackees.

Life in the Fianna was much like any other walk of life. As you progressed, you naturally learned your trade and received more responsibility. Around this time, various well-known establishments began burning to the ground in the dark of night. The Ardoyne bus depot was a six-man job. One ladder up the wall and another down the other side. One hundred buses were then silently soaked in petrol and only when the final vehicle was drenched in siphoned 4-star petrol and five of the squad were safely back over the wall did the remaining volunteer set the entire fleet alight. They were disciplined, military operations in which the success of the mission was the only focus. Each operative carried a walkie-talkie to benefit from the eyes of lookouts posted around the vicinity of the target. There was never any verbal communication but if radio silence was broken by the noise of static it was taken as a direct order to abort and exit immediately. The benefits of such discipline soon became apparent when the RUC interrupted an attack on a local Honda dealership and each member of the Fianna company on action that night was able to walk away undetected as flames engulfed every car in the showroom.

Despite their somewhat chaotic appearance to the untrained eye, the riots were often highly organised manoeuvres as well. They could be used as a measure of control or a distraction while the IRA got on with questioning someone, moving something or making something. The riots also sometimes coincided with putting the district on complete lockdown, a situation that could be secured within a couple of hours. Fianna volunteers took the lead in closing off the four entry points into the area: the junction of Alliance Avenue and the Deerpark Road; where Alliance Avenue meets Ardoyne Road; where Brompton Park joins the Crumlin Road; and where Ardoyne Avenue connects to the Oldpark Road. The easiest way to do this was to hijack a number of cars, vans or buses, drive them into position and set them on fire. A group of youths hurling petrol bombs from behind the burning barricades guaranteed that the district was virtually impregnable. Anyone with an arm and some fire in their belly could lob a projectile, but it was a mark of honour to be trusted with a hijacking.

Personal vehicles were always off limits but anything with a logo on the side was regarded as fair game. At times there were virtual open goals. A British Telecom worker tinkering with wires thirty feet up a telegraph pole was only too happy to drop his keys and say no more, for example. If the back of the van was then packed with the type of technical and heavy duty tools an IRA company in the Ardoyne could make good use of, they'd be offloaded at the egg factory on Jamaica Road before the empty vehicle formed an integral part of a burning barricade.

On other occasions, however, even the best-laid plans could go dangerously awry. Shortly after the aforementioned telecommunications transit was dropped off, a hijacked Interflora model was cruising down the Crumlin Road when an RUC officer from Flax Street pulled his revolver and gestured for the vehicle to stop at the checkpoint. Instead, the young driver put his foot down. Swerving in and out of the queueing cars, he sped away down the Crumlin Road and hung a left onto Hillview Road. Seconds later he was screeching around the corner onto the Oldpark

Road before another left took him onto Ardoyne Avenue. He dove right up Jamaica Street before making a final sharp left into the square where the BT van and other vehicles destined for the barricades were waiting patiently. Unfortunately, three or four RUC Land Rovers had also joined the party. With no time to react, the Interflora van was crashed into a fence and the driver bolted before it came to a complete stop. By the time the police on the scene could react, the young hijacker was in the front door of one sympathetic house, out the back, across the street, through the front door of another and into the coal bunker in the back yard. There he lay, as still and silent as the hard black rocks of carbonised plant matter that surrounded him, for two hours until he was sure the coast was clear.

It was an exhilarating game for a young teenager to play, but the stakes were extremely high. At least nineteen of these child soldiers, one a twelve-year-old girl, were killed during the Troubles and countless more fell into the hands of security forces and spent hours or days in godforsaken places like the Castlereagh Detention Centre in east Belfast. Within this rectangular box of a building the RUC would beat and torture confessions out of hundreds of people, many of them entirely innocent. Cigarettes were stubbed out on faces; lighters were held to testicles; legs were stamped on until bone fractured; severe beatings were administered; mock strangulations were carried out and even reports of waterboarding have emerged years after the events. It was a notorious hell-hole, not just amongst nationalists but throughout the world. As late as the early 1990s, Amnesty International were still issuing urgent action appeals on behalf of youths trapped within Castlereagh's walls, held without charge or legal representation, suffering unimaginable physical abuse at the hands of police officers paid to serve and protect.

Eamonn was picked up by the RUC and taken to Castlereagh in the mid-1980s. His next-door neighbour was also arrested and would eventually be charged with hijacking a city bus. Eamonn was only fifteen at the time and his father was allowed to accompany him in the back of the police Land Rover, through the doors of Castlereagh and then into a series of interrogations. The teaching back then was to say nothing at all, so Eamonn didn't open his mouth. Three different RUC detectives tried their luck but he wasn't for budging. Finally, after hours of unwanted monologue, the police appeared to give up and walked their prisoner back towards reception. On the way they paused by an open door. Inside the room, black blinds were pulled down over the windows and a young man was sat in a chair receiving a savage beating from two policemen. Eamonn was halted and forced to look as the blows, all headshots, rained down and the man's blood speckled the white walls. Eamonn's interrogator looked at him.

'Men are paid to make boys like you talk, you know,' he said in a matter-of-fact tone before leading Eamonn and Doc into one final interrogation room. Eamonn's lips remained sealed.

The intention was to embed a sense of fear inside Magee but, instead, it merely deepened the reservoir of defiance that had been steadily building over the years. He responded the only way he knew how, back on the street hijacking buses and lobbing petrol bombs. The men paid to beat confessions out of teenagers in Castlereagh never did catch up with Eamonn, but it wasn't long before one of their colleagues did.

He had just left the gym where he was fine-tuning things with Patsy ahead of the following week's 1987 Gaelic Games, a four-nation tournament involving Ireland, Scotland, Wales and Canada. It was to be the first time Eamonn would represent his country and he couldn't wait to slip on that green vest with the shamrocks on the shield. Sixteen now, his body was filling out and after weeks of intense sessions in the Sacred Heart, his muscles were hard and taut across his chest and down through his biceps. He'd never been in better shape and, looking back, that level of fitness probably saved his life.

Other international amateur boxing stars may have continued on up Etna Drive and into their houses when they saw the commotion on

Brompton Park, but not Eamonn. A full-scale riot was raging and he was drawn to it like a moth to a flame. Sprinting down the street, he stashed his gym bag behind a garden wall and found some Fianna comrades distributing petrol bombs from a side entry near the barricades. He slipped on a pair of rubber gloves, took a milk bottle filled with gasoline and emerged onto Brompton Park, where he bent over to light the soaked cloth wick that flowed out of the neck of the glass bottle.

At the same time, an RUC Humber Pig had turned the corner from Balholm Drive and was heading towards the flame-haired rioter, the noise of the chaos masking its approach. From the hatch on the roof of the armoured vehicle, an officer appeared and pointed his rifle towards his target. When no further than ten metres away, he pulled the trigger. As Eamonn was still hunched over and struggling with his lighter, the three-inch plastic bullet whizzed past the tip of his nose and struck him square on the right side of the chest. He reeled back, but he didn't fall. By the time the shock had subsided and the pain taken over, he found himself in a safe house being attended to by the local IRA nurse. The muscles of his upper torso had protected him from more serious harm but he was ruled out of the Gaelic Games and it was decades before the shadowy bruise totally disappeared from beneath his chest hair.

***

I heard that story in the homemade gym that Eamonn's brother Noel has set up and still uses twice a week in his garage.

'Louie the Lip, I've always called him,' Eamonn told me on the drive to meet his second oldest sibling. 'On account of that big lower lip of his. He's an absolute gentleman and a scholar. You'll meet him and you'll wonder how the fuck he's related to me.'

Pugilistic achievements aside, it is certainly difficult to discern many similarities between the two. Physically, Noel is a much taller man with softer features and a darker complexion. He moved to Newcastle in the early 1990s and believes he never knew what it was like to feel totally at ease until he settled in this tranquil slice of Co. Down. Politics or the war on the street never interested him and the first thing he did when he left Belfast was to enrol his kids in an integrated, non-denominational school to ensure they grew up without a sectarian bone in their body. In contrast to Eamonn, he comes across as an open, unguarded and more innocent human being.

'That's right,' Noel said, as Eamonn pulled up his top to show me exactly where the bullet had struck him. 'Wrong place, wrong time as usual. You were just coming home with a pint of milk or something, weren't you?'

Noel, like the rest of the family, had never heard the true story. There was a pause before Eamonn – somewhat sheepishly, it appeared to me – enlightened him.

The plastic bullet that thumped into Eamonn that day was just one of the estimated 125,000 that the RUC fired throughout the Troubles. It was not until a man threatened to kill his two young daughters in north Wales in 2002 that the first bullet of this kind was shot by police on the British mainland. Perhaps life was less valuable in the Catholic ghettoes of Northern Ireland. Indeed, plastic or rubber bullets have ended at least fourteen lives in the province over the years, and blinded or maimed many more. The British government was fully aware of their lethal nature shortly after their introduction in the 1970s, but preferred out-of-court settlements when someone raised an objection, rather than allow scientific reports recommending their removal from the conflict to see the light of day. Instead, it issued rules of engagement for utilising the deadly munitions that included not opening fire within less than twenty metres and always aiming for the lower part of a target's legs. The bullet that hit Eamonn was fired from within a range of ten metres and struck him a few inches below his neck.

'That bastard shot to kill that night,' Eamonn said as he looked from his brother to me and back again. 'He tried to murder me.'

3

THE AMATEUR

By the late 1980s Doc was struggling badly with the drink. He kept himself topped up throughout the day with what he and his friends mysteriously referred to as a *hurley gurley*. Local barmen knew to fill the largest glass to hand with the strongest fortified wine in the pub when this was the order. By nightfall he was drunk and belligerent and, at times, violent when he returned home to Eskdale Gardens, where the family was staying while Holmdene Gardens was renovated. In the end Isobel couldn't take it any more and when the Holmdene house was fixed up, she moved back and Terrence stayed in Eskdale. After more than twenty years of an eventful marriage, the pair separated for good.

Though he was loath to show it, or any other emotion that could be interpreted as weakness, his parents' break-up hurt Eamonn. The youngest child in the family is often the worst affected by marital splits and at this time he was the only boy still living at home. But he was also very close to his dad in that embarrassed-to-express-it manner so common in Irish father-son relationships. By now he was through with school, departing with a score of ninety-nine per cent in his final technical-drawing exam, and could often be found working alongside his old man in the construction business. Doc called his son 'Rocky Two', never explaining the necessity of the numeral addendum. Rocky lost to Apollo Creed first time around before winning the rematch, so perhaps that had something to do with it.

Together they rebuilt or repointed much of the brickwork in the Ardoyne and they later worked on the chimneys of the Unity Flats a mile down the road towards the city centre. Eamonn would carry the hod and then lay the brick while Terrence renewed the cement pointing between the masonry. They were a good team for, despite a shared weakness for the bottle, the two Magee men were blessed with a strong work ethic and enjoyed the tired sense of satisfaction that a day's physical graft brings. For years as a kid, Eamonn had earned decent money by scouring the district for empty gas canisters and returning them to a local supplier. When even younger, he worked the stalls of summer carnivals on the Holy Cross football pitch and the famous Mickey Marley hand-picked him to be his Ardoyne helper when the street entertainer and his faithful steed, Joey, trotted into the district with their hobby-horse roundabout. Eamonn had never been afraid of putting in a shift, but this now was real, tough work and not without its risks, both from the nature of the job and the special circumstances of Northern Ireland at that time.

Once, while they were repointing the brickwork of an old building on Belfast city centre's Lower Donegall Street, Terrence's ladder gave way and he landed teeth first on the pavement. He lost a couple of his prized pearly whites in a pool of his own blood that morning, but a few months later father and son were standing outside a Belfast courthouse determined to gain fair compensation. They had limbered up for the negotiations with a few dawn pints in the nearby Docker's Club and Eamonn was in the mood to play hardball by the time he had the lawyer in his sights.

'Six thousand,' the solicitor offered by way of an opening gambit.

'No,' was Eamonn's succinct and firm response.

'Eight.'

'No.'

'Ten?'

'No.'

When the beleaguered brief raised it to £12,000, sixteen-year-old Eamonn shook his hand and accompanied his smiling father on one almighty all-day session to celebrate.

On another occasion they instinctively ducked for cover when the rattle of machine-gun fire rang out from across the Lower Ormeau Road.

'Someone has just been murdered,' Eamonn remarked to his dad as he hoisted the long-handled brick hod back onto his shoulder. In actual fact, five had been killed and another nine were injured when two UDA men sprayed a betting shop with forty-four bullets from a semi-automatic rifle and a 9mm pistol. It was a violent reminder that the Troubles were pervasive across every square mile of the city.

Eamonn truly loved his mother, but there were certain things he would only ever tell Doc and Isobel knew it. Like where he went at night. But Isobel would still head out and look for her baby boy. In a riotous, balaclava-clad group of a hundred, she was still able to pick Eamonn out in a heartbeat. Some days she'd come home in the afternoon and find some militant republican paraphernalia – a pair of gloves, a whistle, a replica gun even – carelessly left lying around, and would swiftly toss it over her back wall into a derelict site behind the house. When she later challenged Eamonn on it he'd always brush her off.

'Fuck sake, Ma. I'm not in the RA, okay?' he'd snap back.

But Isobel was always aware that Terrence knew more than she did. When they were still together, she had heard him slip out of bed on many an occasion to ease open the bathroom window and allow Eamonn and his Fianna comrades to scale the drainpipe and squeeze into the house. She knew that behind the scenes Terrence was using what was left of his influence to take care of things for Eamonn when he ran into trouble too deep for a teenager to handle alone. More than her other three boys, Eamonn was clearly his father's son.

The day before St Patrick's Day in 1988, Terrence set off for Milltown Cemetery on the Falls Road. There, in the republican plot, the three IRA volunteers shot dead by the SAS in Gibraltar the week before were due to be buried in front of thousands of mourners. As the final coffin was being lowered into the ground, UDA member Michael Stone threw two hand grenades into the crowd and began shooting indiscriminately. As people panicked, scattered and dived for cover behind gravestones, dozens of youths and young men chased after the loyalist assassin as he ran towards the M1 motorway. Every ten or fifteen yards, Stone would turn to hurl another grenade or fire from the two guns he was brandishing. Finally he was caught and beaten unconscious before the RUC arrived just in time to spare him fatal mob justice. By the time the smoke and debris had settled and Gerry Adams had resumed his graveside oration, three were dead and sixty injured from the gunfire, grenade shrapnel and flying shards of splintered marble. Back in a friend's house in the Ardoyne, Eamonn watched the footage of the massacre on television and immediately threw himself wholeheartedly into the riots that were erupting in nationalist districts across the city.

Isobel was at home on her hands and knees scrubbing the kitchen floor when a neighbour burst in to warn her that Eamonn had just been arrested. She sprinted down to the barricades only to be told by onlookers that he'd been put in the back of an RUC jeep and driven away. A couple of hours later she was back in her house, staring out the front window in silent prayer, when she spied Eamonn walking up the path. Running out in near hysterics she grabbed her son and, shaking him violently, screamed at the top of her voice, 'Do you want to get shot! Is that what you want? Give me a gun and I'll shoot you right now if that's what you want!' The certainty of firing that bullet into her own child may have been easier to live with than the constant worrying and wondering where her baby was and what danger he was in.

But, in truth – despite his actions that day – Eamonn was gradually drifting away from that lifestyle. Now approaching his seventeenth birthday, he had a decision to make on how committed he was to the IRA's violent war against the British occupation. It would have been the easiest thing in the world to continue down the path he was on, but deep down he knew it wasn't for him. He had seen friends die on that path, and others play a leading role in atrocities that any man would struggle to live with until the end of his days.

***

The ease with which he, or any young, disenfranchised man born in the Ardoyne in the 1970s, could have chosen the Armalite over the ballot box still numbs Eamonn today. I ask him if there was one watershed moment, one defining incident so traumatising that it repelled him from the militant republican cause. But he just shakes his head and leaves a heavy, pregnant silence hanging in the air. After what seems like an age, in which I wonder whether he has forgotten my presence, I start to move on to boxing matters when he suddenly interrupts.

'See the likes of Bootsy Begley, the Shankill Road bomber,' he begins. 'We were the same age and knocked about with each other all our lives. We were in the Fianna together, we drank together and yet I had no idea he was in the RA. I hadn't a fucking clue. Neither him nor Sean Kelly, who I see every day working in the shop round the corner.'

He pauses again, as if still amazed by the fact, before continuing. 'That could very easily have been me, you know. Wee things like that, it's hard to stop thinking about them. And wee Bootsy was a total gentleman. I know what he done was totally wrong and absolutely disgusting, but he was always a gentleman.'

Another pause and this time I drift away too, back to that Saturday afternoon in 1993 when Begley and Kelly walked into Frizzell's fish shop on the Shankill Road with a bomb on an eleven-second fuse. They were to clear the civilians out and blow up a UDA meeting believed to be taking place upstairs, but the bomb exploded prematurely, killing nine Protestants and Begley himself. It was later revealed that the UDA meeting had ended early and the intended targets were long gone when the blast ripped through the building. In the bloody aftermath, loyalists murdered fourteen civilians inside a week, and eight in one sitting when a UDA gunman yelled 'trick or treat' before opening fire on a Halloween party in Greysteel with an AK-47.

Shaking his head, Eamonn finally murmured, more to himself than me, 'I wonder how Sean Kelly can live with that.'

***

Boxing instead began to take up more and more of Eamonn's time as, together, he and Patsy McKenna won title after title in the juniors. A mixture of pride and the knowledge that Eamonn would probably just lose it has caused Patsy to keep hold of Eamonn's old amateur record book to this day. Watching him thumb through the wad of thin, faded pages where the letter L for loss is a rarity, I can see that footage of the fights is flickering vividly in the old man's mind. He proudly points out the big medal-securing victories but other, seemingly less significant bouts, appear to stir more emotion.

He remembers Tommy McMenemy, a big strong fella from Twin Towns in Donegal. He was more powerful than Patsy's guy but Eamonn had the class and would cut him to shreds each time they fought. Another Donegal man, Anthony McFadden from Dunfanaghy, was even more ferocious. He had knocked McMenemy out inside sixty seconds and Patsy sent his charge out with a warning about his punching prowess.

'First round, bang, and Eamonn is all over the place,' Patsy recalls with a laugh. 'I honestly thought it was all over. But he stayed on his feet, and he held on for dear life, and then his head cleared and he totally out-boxed the kid to victory.'

Magee could bang too, however. Patsy's eyes widen when he describes how he left a lad from Enniskillen sprawled on the ring floor in the National Stadium in Dublin. As the young boxer lay prostrate on the canvas, his left leg suddenly began twitching horribly. As he stood in the neutral corner, the blood drained from Eamonn's face and he stared, transfixed by that spasming limb, and willed his beaten opponent to rise.

'I didn't mean to do it, Patsy,' he said quietly as his trainer led him away.

'You're all right, son. Don't worry, he'll be fine.'

The passing referee then made an ill-advised and insensitive remark about Eamonn being a vicious bastard and Patsy almost jumped him.

'What do you want him to do!' he yelled. 'It's a boxing contest, he's trying to win and so is the other guy.'

Half an hour later, boxer and coach were sat in one of the arena's back rows grabbing a bite to eat in between bouts. Patsy always brought a big cool box of sandwiches and salad and chicken legs so neither he nor his fighters would have to go looking for food as the tournament progressed.

'Patsy?' Eamonn whispered.

Patsy looked over and saw Eamonn nodding his head down the row of seats to where the young fella who had just been unconscious on the canvas was sat on his own.

'Go and offer him a sandwich and a drop of tea,' Patsy suggested.

Unsure what reception he'd receive, Eamonn approached somewhat timorously with a chicken sandwich in one hand a mug of hot tea in the other. Tentative and uneasy with each other at first, they were soon chatting side by side until Eamonn was called to get ready for the final. They didn't mention what had just happened in the ring but both boys understood that it was just an unfortunate occupational hazard of the sport they loved.

'Good luck in the final, mate,' Eamonn heard his new friend shout as he strode towards the ring.

Patsy liked to see that side of Magee, a confirmation that his kid had a good heart. For although Eamonn had earned a reputation as the best junior in the country, he was also gaining notoriety amongst the boxing authorities as the biggest troublemaker on each Irish squad he made. At times it was deserved – as when fire extinguishers were let off in a Cork hotel – but at other times it was not, like when he was accused of stealing beer in Scotland when the theft took place while he was battling it out in the ring. Either way, such spirited hijinks were little more than devilment to Patsy and he was generally happy to turn a blind eye so long as nobody got hurt or arrested. Only when alcohol was involved did he begin to worry. Particularly if he smelled it on a boxer's breath during the fight.

One such incident comes quickly to mind, for both Patsy and Eamonn. It was the morning of the 1987 Ulster finals and Eamonn woke early with a hangover from hell. He rolled out of bed, crawled to the bathroom to empty his stomach of toxins, and did his best to avoid the daylight that exacerbated the headache busy splitting his cranium in two. His friend, Budgie, looked on with a rueful countenance.

'There's only one thing for it, mate,' Budgie stated with self-assumed wisdom.

'What's that?' Eamonn croaked in response.

'Hair of the dog. Get up, let's go.'

Still nowhere near sober, the best young welterweight in the country struggled to the local Gaelic Athletic Association (GAA) clubhouse where he knew an early morning pint would be easy to find. With the previous night's excesses still coursing through his veins, his bloodstream only needed a gentle top up before Eamonn was again borderline blotto. Never one to do things by half, Magee downed six more lagers before sauntering into St George's Boxing Club in the Markets area of Belfast with his gear slung over his shoulder. He was up against his old friend, the hard-hitting Anthony McFadden, and Patsy looked on in bemusement as Eamonn waltzed around the Donegal man throughout the first round and then tottered back to his stool. Three steps from the corner, Patsy's jaw dropped.

'I can smell the fucking drink off you from here, for fuck sake!' he hissed, as Eamonn pursed his lips, breathed through his nose and proffered his denial with a sheepish shake of the head. He still won the Ulster title that day but, of course, that wasn't the point. Patsy tried to reason with him and even invited ex-Olympians and pros to the gym to help hammer home the point that there was only a very small window to forge a successful boxing career. That you can't live that life and expect to succeed in the ring. That it takes sacrifices beyond what the average man on the street is willing to make. It broke Patsy's heart that he wouldn't listen but the trainer knew enough about alcoholism to understand he just had to carry on and do for Eamonn the best he could.

The other major threat to his fledgling boxing career was street fighting.

As the most famous boxing family in north Belfast, the Magee boys received respect and provocation in the district in almost equal measure. As the brother marked out as the future superstar, Eamonn was presented with the lion's share of the challenges, at least one a week throughout his entire young adult life in his own estimation.

'I never went looking for it,' he still insists. 'Trouble just always found me.'

They came from outside the district to try their luck as well, particularly New Lodge. When the Ardoyne or Bone locals separated from the New Lodge crowd upon exiting the Glen Park Bar and the alcohol and testosterone-fuelled young men started squaring up to one another, Eamonn was invariably called out to deal with multiple threats in a single night. Finally, he decided to end the confrontations once and for all. He gathered a gang of his most trusted cohorts together one evening, and they sat drinking indoors, preparing for the decisive battle while the New Lodge lads enjoyed themselves in the bar. Just before closing time, Eamonn positioned his men in various alleyways and entries surrounding their target. It was raining heavily that night so they each tied a plastic bag over their head. It made for an intimidatingly comical look, but passers-by were much more concerned by the hurley sticks that each grasped in their hands as they waited for their quarry to exit the bar. The attack was swift, bloody and decisive. Around forty young men struggled back to the New Lodge that night and never again returned to the Ardoyne.

At other times, the three brothers still living in Northern Ireland joined forces, as they did when Patrick began receiving hassle from some thugs in neighbouring Ligoniel. They were a formidable trio to go up against but, in reality, Eamonn on his own could normally take care of any situation that arose. One night the three came out of the Shamrock and were saying their goodbyes. Noel and Patrick were now married and both wives were present, while Eamonn was on crutches having damaged his leg in a fall a few days earlier.

Suddenly there was a shout of 'Magee!' and the group of five turned to see an angry young man making a beeline for Eamonn. The attacker was a nasty piece of work, a known bully clearly desperate to take a shot at the boxing champ with a few drinks in him. He was across the road and on top of them before the women could scream or Noel and Patrick could get their fists up, but in one fluid movement Eamonn had let the crutches fall, put all his weight on his good foot and stretched the attacker out cold on the Ardoyne Avenue pavement with one short left cross. Neither his brothers nor their partners could believe the speed at which the shocking incident had transpired.

On another occasion, a vanquished foe did manage to make a clawing contact with Magee and a trip to the Mater Hospital was required for three stitches in a torn eyelid. Budgie accompanied him and after the doctor's needle and thread had patched Eamonn up, the pair walked on down the Crumlin Road to get some food in a Chinese takeaway at the Carlisle Circus roundabout. While they waited for their dinner, a pair of hard-looking characters entered, placed an order and immediately left. Budgie was half cut but Eamonn had his wits about him and could innately sense the threat of violence in the air. He pulled his friend outside with him and, sure enough, the same two guys rounded the corner with baseball bats.

'Run!' Eamonn yelled and took off up the Antrim Road. Budgie, drunk and not an athlete, was soon flagging and it wasn't long before the attackers caught up with him. Looking back, Eamonn saw him on the ground, writhing and kicking and attempting to dodge or deflect the worst of the blows. Magee didn't hesitate. He ran back, clotheslined the two baseball aficionados off his cowering friend and then raised his fists in anticipation of a battle.

At that precise moment a siren wailed in the near distance and the aggressors turned on their heels and fled. It turned out to be an ambulance rather than a police van and it picked up poor Budgie and brought him to casualty. By the time they were back in the Shamrock a few hours later,

Budgie had three of his own stitches to match Eamonn's. The only diffe-rence was that his were holding his lower lip together, and for the rest of the night there was great hilarity as half of each mouthful of Budgie's beer leaked through the wound and dribbled down his chin.

I once asked Patsy if he knew how often his most valuable asset was scrapping bare-knuckled on the street.

'Of course I did,' he barked at me in his own indomitable fashion. 'Everyone in the district knew what he was like. He missed a multi-nations tournament in Italy in 1988 with two broken knuckles after dealing with some guy behind the Shamrock.'

So was he not concerned when Eamonn came into the gym every week with cuts and bruises and a tournament just around the corner?

'That was a rarity,' he replied with a wry smile. 'Not many were ever able to land a meaningful punch on him.'

***

Around this time, another family tragedy hit Eamonn hard. He had been in the Shamrock drinking with Nipper, his mum's younger brother. Eamonn loved spending time with his young uncle and the pair of them had great craic that night, drinking and laughing until closing time when they said their goodbyes.

'See you tomorrow, Nipper.'

'Good man, Eamonn.'

The next morning Isobel shook her son awake.

'Eamonn, son, Nipper's dead.'

'Aye right, Ma,' Eamonn mumbled as he rolled over to go back to sleep. It was 1 April and, despite the hangover, you'd need to get up earlier than that to make a fool of him.

'No, really, son. He's dead,' Isobel continued tearfully but Eamonn was snoring again.

When he finally rose from his bed a couple of hours later, he learned that it was true. Nipper had gone to sleep in an armchair in a friend's living room and never woke up. He was only thirty-three years of age and his seventeen-year-old nephew was the last person to see him breathing.

***

1989 was the year Eamonn announced himself on the world stage. Despite still being technically a junior, he was so good that he began competing against the seniors – grown men who may have had ten years or more on him.

In May of that year he finally got to take part in the Gaelic Games in Canada, the tournament that an RUC bullet had previously prevented him from boxing in. It wasn't long ago that Eamonn believed the world ended at Ardoyne shops and now here he was, trotting around the globe with his boxing pals. His friendship with Wayne McCullough continued to strengthen but he also grew close to southerners like Paul Griffin from Dublin and the Cork trio of Michael Roche, Gordon Joyce and Paul Buttimer. Magee, Griffin and Roche became particularly thick and were invariably found at the centre of any mischievous goings-on. In Canada, midnight escapes through bedroom windows were made and the team coach was pulled over following police reports that those in the back seat were partial to baring their rear ends to shocked locals in every town they passed through.

On another night, Eamonn brought a young lady back to the hotel room he shared with three of the other boxers. She was a stunning older woman, like no one he had come across in the Ardoyne, and he wanted to make the most of this one night he would spend with her. After hours of waiting patiently outside, Griffin and the others began banging on the door, demanding to be allowed to their beds. The two lovebirds giddily ignored the pleas for so long that security was called and proceeded to open the door. Unperturbed, Magee continued with his conquest with the other three looking on, although the pressure eventually got to him and he was forced to conclude his business in the privacy of the en-suite bathroom.

It was largely harmless stuff but it was still behaviour in stark contrast to the likes of McCullough, who was early to rise, earlier to bed and breathed pure boxing throughout the day. Nevertheless, it was Magee – scratching his crotch furiously between rounds on account of a virile dose of crabs he had contracted before leaving Belfast – who flew home with a gold medal and the coveted boxer of the tournament award after a series of impressive victories.

In August the Irish Amateur Boxing Association (IABA) sent him to Puerto Rico to fight against the world's elite in the world junior championships. The opening ceremony took place exactly eighteen years to the day from the beginning of internment and the macabre anniversary seemed to inspire Magee, who fought magnificently to reach the final. He benefitted from a walkover in the preliminaries, when Costa Rica's Francisco Campos withdrew, before stopping a durable Bulgarian, Ivan Ivanov, inside a minute in the next round. In his quarter-final he had the gold-medal favourite from Cuba, Josef Sanchez, down in the first and third stanzas on his way to a comfortable 26–13 victory. He then faced a local star, Victor Perez, in the semi-final and had too much for his Puerto Rican foe, running out a 29–17 winner with a performance that endeared him to the Caribbean natives. Nerves got the better of him in front of 8,000 fans shouting his name in the final, however, and he lost out to the East German Enrico Berger. But a silver medal from a world championships is a prized possession for any boxer. Shane Mosley and Joel Casamayor were two other young hopefuls to medal that year.

Eamonn arrived home to praise being showered on him from all corners of the boxing fraternity. 'Eamonn High' read the headline in a *Belfast Telegraph* feature that described Magee as 'a rarity in the sport in that he can box or fight depending on what is required' and 'a clever boxer with a punch that comes naturally to him'. Irish head coach Frank Gervin endorsed that view: 'This boy has everything going for him. There is no doubt in my mind that one day he can become an Olympic champion.'

The undisputed Godfather of Irish professional boxing, Barney Eastwood, tried to tempt him into turning pro then and there but Magee was still focused on amateur glory and the 1990 Commonwealth Games in Auckland in particular. 'I always wanted to go to the Commonwealth Games,' he said, 'and I knew that if I came home from Puerto Rico with a medal I would be in line for a trial.'

A fortnight later that dream was dashed by a vote in the Ulster Boxing Council that vetoed the idea of Magee fighting a trial against Eddie Fisher to see who deserved the spot on the plane to New Zealand. The legendary Northern Irish sports writer Jack Magowan described the move as a 'surprise thumbs-down for Ireland's brightest young talent' and IABA president Felix Jones concurred. 'The selection of an Ulster team is not my business,' Jones began, 'but you can't ignore the fact that Eamonn not only stopped a Bulgarian in Puerto Rico, he had the Cuban favourite twice on the floor and then beat a very good Puerto Rican in front of 8,000 wildly partisan home fans. And standards there, in my view, were higher than in either the Ulster or Irish championships!'

The apparent lack of support from his own council was a major blow to Eamonn but much worse was to follow just a week later. Standing in the queue beside John Connolly in a pizza takeaway on the Antrim Road, he felt a tap on his shoulder.

'Have you a fag, mate?' asked the stranger.

'No I don't, buddy,' Eamonn replied honestly.

Minutes later he was walking down the narrow Phoenix Entry carrying his pizza box when he felt a strange warm sensation flowing down his back. Reaching to the side of his neck he was able to fit four fingers into a gaping wound up to his knuckles.

Turning around he saw the stranger who had just requested a cigarette with the remains of a broken bottle in one hand and an iron bar in the other. Blood was dripping from the jagged edge of the bottle. The man dropped it and swung with the metal pole but Eamonn managed to avoid the swipe and get his hand on the weapon. After a brief struggle he wrenched it free and went on the offensive himself. Despite the hurt he had inflicted when he slashed the sharp end of a fractured glass bottle across Magee's throat, the attacker knew better than to continue the fight now Eamonn was armed. He immediately spun and fled into the night.

Eamonn dropped the bar and stumbled forward onto the Antrim Road. Somehow, there was no pain, just an awful warm feeling over his skin as the crimson blood continued to pour freely from the three-inch gash on the side of his neck. By some miracle there was an ambulance waiting at the nearby traffic lights and it sped him to the Mater Hospital and straight into the operating theatre. Dozens of stitches were required, both inside and out of the wound, but surgeons assured him he was a lucky young man. Had the glass thrust into his flesh just a few millimetres to the side, his external jugular vein would have been severed and he'd be lying dead in Phoenix Entry.

His mother wept openly, and his father privately, when they saw their boy in the hospital bed, but Isobel confesses that her overriding concern was that Eamonn would go looking for revenge as soon as he was discharged. As it happened, it was taken care of within a week. It turned out that the attacker was from the New Lodge, possibly one of the many who suffered that beating with the hurley sticks outside the Glen Park, and he was soon tracked down and given a severe kicking that culminated in several layers of skin from the man's face being left on a pebble-dashed wall. A few days later the police lifted one of Eamonn's friends, brought him to the station and stood him in front of the victim.

'Is this the man who slashed Eamonn Magee?' an officer asked.

'No, that's not him,' was the reply.

The officer then turned to the young man with the freshly scarred face. 'Is this the man who attacked you?' he asked.

'No,' came the reply.

That was the end of that incident. Eamonn still sees the man who was within millimetres of murdering him walking about north Belfast on an almost monthly basis. They may even nod a silent greeting to one another as their paths cross, but they have never talked about the horrific violence that passed between them.

Incredibly, Eamonn was back in the ring within six weeks. At the end of November he won four fights to become the Irish intermediate champion, which was the final stage before competing for the senior title. In December he travelled to Rome to take part in a multi-nations event and returned, three dominant victories later, with another boxer of the tournament accolade and a papal blessing from the Pope when John Paul II spotted the Irish fighters from his balcony during mass in St Peter's Square.

The serrated scar on his neck was still in its raw, angry infancy and Eamonn took to wearing turtlenecks to cover it up when he left the house. It made for an interesting conversation starter with women in bars but at that moment in time he only had eyes for one.

Mary Grogan grew up in Balholm Drive, a couple of streets away from Holmdene Gardens, but she had never before met Eamonn Magee. Her father, himself a boxing fan, managed the Crumlin Star Social Club where Isobel waitressed, but while she had heard all about the Magee boys and what great fighters they were, Mary had never actually laid eyes on Eamonn. More than boxing, the Grogans were a Gaelic games family, heavily involved with the local Kickhams GAA Club. It was in the clubhouse bar one night just before Christmas that Eamonn approached and introduced himself.

'I've been chasing you for months and you haven't even noticed me,' he opened with a roguish smile.

He called her Mary Doll and they chatted all night. There were nine years between them but it didn't seem to matter. Now in her fifties, Mary is still a beautiful woman, but back then, as the 1980s drew to a close, with her big shoulder pads and even bigger blonde hair, she turned heads on the street.

In January 1990 they got together and the following month Eamonn helped her move furniture into a new house on Rosapenna Street, just outside the Ardoyne between the Oldpark and Cliftonville Roads. A mutual friend decorated the property to make it look like a home and Eamonn liked it so much he decided to stay. Soon Mary was pregnant. They were in love.

***

Now aged eighteen, Eamonn had his first full year as a senior in 1990. He made the final of both the Ulster and Irish championships and each time dropped a decision to fellow Belfast man Eddie Fisher. Indeed, Fisher got the better of Magee on the three occasions they met as seniors, although both Patsy and Eamonn are convinced that they deserved the nod in at least two of those contests.

There were other narrow defeats around this time as well, however. He won one and lost one on a tour of the US, before Robert McCracken, the future middleweight world-title challenger and head coach of the British Olympic boxing team, beat him by a point in the 1990 World Cup. Such was Magee's undeniable talent, Patsy wouldn't accept the losses as a case of the better man winning. He knew the difference was the lack of dedication on the part of his charge. He also knew that Eamonn's inability to live right between tournaments was forcing him to compete at least one weight class above where he should be operating. But Patsy had learned within weeks of meeting Magee as a precocious five-year-old that if there was one thing he did not like, it was being given a direct order. He would have to believe that the idea to drop a division came from himself and, when Fisher nicked another one from Eamonn in the 1991 Ulster final, Patsy began the process.

'You're the quickest welterweight I've seen, Eamonn,' the wily old trainer surmised as Magee shadow-boxed in the gym one night. 'As quick as any light welter in Ireland, that's for sure.'

As they walked home together a month later, he poured some water over the little seed now germinating in Eamonn's mind. 'Did you hear Billy Walsh is coming down from 71kg? He's campaigning as a welter now. And Joe Lowe has just switched in the opposite direction. Last year Fisher moved from light welter to 67kg. Just shows you, guys are moving up and down all the time.'

And then he fertilised the soil while holding the heavy bag as Eamonn whaled away during training. 'You're hitting it hard, son. Imagine if you could bring that power down to 63.5kg.'

A few weeks later, Patsy's flower sprang forth.

'Patsy, I'm thinking of trying to get down to light welter,' Eamonn said one night. 'What do you reckon?'

'That sounds like a fine idea, Eamonn,' Patsy beamed.

The weight came off relatively easily. Eamonn always worked fiercely when he was training but, perhaps lulled into a false sense of invincibility by his natural gifts, he had often undone a lot of that good work in Ardoyne watering holes as soon as he left the gym. For a couple of months after his decision to switch class, he drank less beer, ate less pizza and ran a few extra miles per week and by late 1991 he was comfortable operating in the 63.5kg light welterweight class.

His first outing in the new division came at the 1992 Ulster senior finals in Belfast, held in November and December 1991 with an eye on affording the country's top boxers the best preparation possible for the upcoming Barcelona Olympics. Any lingering doubts over whether it was the right weight for Magee were dismissed in explosive fashion as he powered his way to stoppage victories and his first senior Ulster title. In the final he knocked out the accomplished Billy Cowan barely a minute into the contest, as if to underline his intent to dominate the domestic light welterweight scene.

The change in division did nothing to ease the journey to a national title, however. In addition to the likes of Cowan and his nemesis Eddie Fisher, quality, seasoned campaigners such as Neil Gough and Billy Walsh were also fighting as light welterweights during this period. Gough, from the St Paul's Club in Waterford, appeared in eleven consecutive senior finals, won eight of them and also fought a record seventy-five internationals for Ireland, while Walsh, from St Colman's in Cork, appeared in three consecutive finals, winning one. Magee knew he would probably have to face one or both every time he travelled south to fight for a national title. But before that he began 1992 with a bout against a man who would go on to become a bona fide legend of world boxing.

Sugar Shane Mosley was born just a couple of months after Eamonn in California, USA, and while Magee was sweating his way to a silver medal in the world junior championships in Puerto Rico in 1989, Mosley was doing the exact same thing two divisions below the Irishman. By 1992 the American had filled out and when he arrived in Ireland in January of that year, he was already widely regarded as one of the best amateur light welterweights on the planet. As the American champion of that division, he was following in the footsteps of the likes of Sugar Ray Leonard, Thomas Hearns and Don Curry, so his pedigree was indisputable. Eddie Fisher was actually scheduled to share the ring with Mosley in the Irish capital that day, but Mickey Hawkins withdrew his charge as he feared a bad beating would hurt Fisher's chances in the upcoming national finals. Magee didn't need to be asked twice to fill the void and ensured the future three-weight world champion Hall-of-Famer did not make a wasted trip to the Emerald Isle.

'He was good,' Eamonn admits. 'Very good. Fast hands, strong, just a very good fighter. But I still reckon I beat him that day.'

The judges disagreed, however, awarding Mosley a 25–17 victory in a bout that remained highly competitive until the final bell. Despite privately disputing the decision, Eamonn for once took the positives from defeat.

Everyone knew Mosley was destined for greatness, yet this twenty-year-old, flame-haired tearaway from the Ardoyne pushed him all the way. The way Eamonn saw it, if he could mix it with the best in the world, the best in Ireland should not provide him with too many problems.

To be crowned the best amateur light welterweight in Ireland, he would have to beat three other contenders to the throne inside a week in the Irish capital's National Stadium. Located a couple of miles southwest of Dublin city centre, the National Stadium was the first purpose-built boxing arena in the world. It is a mini Irish amphitheatre with the ring sitting proudly in the heart of the room and shallow banks of seats spreading out from ringside to a ceiling so low you can practically touch it from the back row. It is a claustrophobic and atmospheric setting when 2,000 souls, high on bloodlust, cram in, particularly when a busload of Magee's nearest and dearest are positioned ringside.

In the amateur game, with the protective headguards and oversized 10oz gloves, elite-level boxers rarely blast one another out of the ring as can happen in the professional ranks. So it proved during the 1992 national finals as Eamonn put on a display of counter-punching, distance control and ring management that defied his tender years and earned three deserved points victories over vastly more experienced opponents. He negotiated fellow Belfast man Steven McCloskey in the quarter-finals before out-boxing Donore's Greg Ormond, uncle of future European lightweight champ Stephen, in the semis. The final, against the reigning champion, Neil Gough, was the toughest assignment of all, but after three closely fought rounds the Sacred Heart man's hand was raised in victory. Midway through his twentieth year on earth, Eamonn Magee had come of age in the boxing ring. He was the champion of Ireland and as his family and friends erupted inside the stadium, Eamonn scanned the crowd until he found Mary Doll, sat a few rows back with a huge grin on her face and an even bigger bump on her belly. A fortnight later, Áine Máire Magee was born.

Eamonn was on top of the world. He could see his life mapped out in front of him and he liked how it was looking. His own family was growing fast and he was about to go to the Barcelona Olympics as the Irish and Ulster champion. He would win a medal in Catalonia and return home to decide which big-money professional contract he would sign to begin making his millions in the paid ranks. Barney Eastwood was endorsing him in the press again, describing the light welterweight as 'the most professional-looking amateur of the championships' after he knocked out Cowan to win the Ulster final. But Eamonn couldn't help wondering – if Barney had been begging him to turn pro after a silver medal in the world amateur championships, imagine what the likes of Frank Warren, Barry Hearn or Mickey Duff would do to get an Olympic champion on their books. And few doubted his ability to both medal in Barcelona and make a successful transition to the pro game.

***

Nicolás Hernández Cruz, the Cuban coach who was so instrumental in revolutionising the training regime within Irish amateur boxing, was convinced that Eamonn and Wayne McCullough were the two best medal hopes Ireland had. He remembers the first time he met the seventeen-year-old Magee on the platform of Heuston Station in Dublin city. The team for the 1989 world junior championships was gathering for a training camp in Kerry but Eamonn stood removed from the other boys. He seemed older somehow, stronger. Not in physique necessarily, but he had a silent self-confidence and he was clever and he was hard. All the perfect attributes for a fighter, Cruz thought.

The two bonded over best-of-five table-tennis epics in the Kerry hotel. There was mutual respect between them because the Cuban treated Eamonn as an equal. He socialised with him, ate with him, spoke to him man to man and learned about Eamonn's life. When he caught him watching a risqué movie one night he sat down and watched with him. When he knew the boys would be on the prowl for girls, he asked if they had protection with them. It was about forging a strong enough personal relationship that they would respond to his strict and, at the time, unique methods in the gym but, with Eamonn at least, it was also entirely genuine. Cruz heard other members of the IABA describing Magee as wild, a lost cause beyond control, and he personally caught the Belfast boy drinking and smoking and breaking curfew plenty of times. But Nicolás saw a misunderstood kid, a good kid, one that only needed an arm around his shoulder every now and again to excel.

He also saw one hell of a boxer. One who could fight or box, who had great footwork and defence, who had a natural right hook from hell, who was determined and fearless in the ring. He saw a heart too big for his chest at times, a warrior who had survived bullets in his *barrio* and so would stop at nothing for victory in a mere boxing match. Magee was everything Cruz looked for in a young boxer and he couldn't wait to see him medal in Barcelona and then turn pro. Such was his opinion of Eamonn's capabilities that he believed he'd go on to surpass anything any Irish fighter had ever achieved as a professional.

Áine was barely out of the hospital when the shock news filtered through from Dublin. The IABA's Central Council had voted and decided that Magee must fight Gough again in a box-off to decide who was to go to the Olympic Games. Even the Ulster representatives failed to argue on their own fighters' behalf. The rationale was that the All-Ireland final between the pair had been so close that it would be unfair to choose the Olympian based on that contest alone. Although this was not without precedent, there were plenty of examples of similar situations in which no extra trial was demanded for Eamonn to choose from as he began his assault on the powers that be.

'How come they didn't give Paul McCullagh a trial before Seoul four years ago?' he angrily demanded. McCullagh had suffered a narrow and controversial loss to Kieran Joyce in the Irish senior final and yet Joyce was sent to South Korea, despite major struggles continuing to make the 75kg middleweight limit, with no further questions asked. 'I'm sick of the way we are treated as amateur boxers,' Magee continued. 'It's time everyone knew why these trials were called for. They're nothing but a political move by Dublin after seven out of twelve national titles ended up in the North. Frankly I'm disgusted. If they want this Olympic place for Gough, let them have it.' These were Eamonn's final words to the press on the matter.

To many commentators in the North, it was indeed nothing more than a cruel boardroom ploy from the Dublin hierarchy, driven by a resentment of the recent Ulster domination of the All-Ireland scene. Eamonn has always been convinced that it was personal as well. Put simply, he was not well liked in the corridors of power within the Irish amateur boxing set-up. Magee was, and always will be, as far from a company man as you will ever find. He is keen on telling people that he shoots from the hip, but only when you spend a little time in his company do you appreciate how often he fires and how deadly his aim is. His extra-curricular activities and extreme aversion to authority figures certainly did not help, but if this was punitive bias being shown towards him, it was an entirely disproportionate response to any trouble he caused as a teenage firebrand sneaking out to bars on an international trip abroad.

Art O'Brien, currently the national secretary of the IABA and a recent inductee into the Irish Amateur Boxing Hall of Fame for a lifetime of service to the sport, is the sole surviving member of the National Council from that period. He remembers only too well how difficult Eamonn was to manage but there is no anger or bitterness in his voice as he reminisces, and he baulks at the suggestion of an agenda against either Ulster or Magee. Like Cruz, O'Brien was blown away by the natural talent Eamonn possessed but, unlike Nicolás, he was never able to forge any meaningful relationship with the kid. Art recalls a young man carrying a lot of emotional baggage that he presumed derived from a troubled home life. According to O'Brien, Magee mistrusted everyone around him, particularly if they were perceived to be in a position of authority standing over him. He cites Felix Jones, the IABA president, as an example. Jones was Eamonn's biggest fan in the early days but, like the rest of the council, he grew to regard him as someone who couldn't be depended upon, as the kid who would always let you down on tour or in training camp.

Despite all those sentiments, however, O'Brien strongly denies that the personalities or reputations of the fighters involved influenced the council's decision. He is adamant that the demand for a box-off between Magee and Gough was the only sensible call to make after the close competitiveness of their recent All-Ireland final. And, rather than dislike, O'Brien believes that Eamonn's difficult character inspired nothing more than disappointment and a sense of frustration that they had a world-class fighter on their hands who appeared hell-bent on wasting his God-given talents.

To this day, Patsy McKenna finds that hard to believe. He is convinced that Dublin had been out to get his boy for years and points to a series of incidents that, when taken together, could suggest something of a campaign against the unruly kid from the Ardoyne. There was the blame for a £100 phone bill that another fighter had actually run up in a Canadian hotel. There was the Irish referee using a previously unknown European rule to deduct a point without warning from Eamonn when the gum shield slipped out of his mouth mid-round. There were the accusations of stealing beer at a tournament in East Kilbride when the beverages in question disappeared while Magee was boxing a local champion. There was the tip-off Patsy received upon registering at the national finals one year that the referees had discussed and agreed to disqualify Eamonn the first moment he spat in the ring, an admittedly unfortunate habit he had acquired since he upped his daily nicotine intake. Then there was the £4,000 grant from national-lottery funding that Eamonn was awarded to help cover his training expenses but never received.

It is still an emotive debate and common sense suggests that neither side is entirely blameless in the controversy. At the very least, it does appear that as time went on the IABA grew less inclined to throw any favours the Sacred Heart fighter's way. At the same time, Eamonn didn't make life any easier for himself with his attitude and some of his actions. But in his and Patsy's eyes, the IABA were attempting to deny Magee his dream, a punishment far too severe for whatever crimes he may have committed.

Regardless, most presumed Magee would back down, fight and beat Gough again, and conclude an exceptional amateur career in Barcelona. After all, the Olympic Games is the pinnacle of any amateur boxer's career. It is what every kid dreams of when they first lace up a glove and Eamonn was on record many times agreeing that it had always been his ultimate goal before he started earning money from the sport. This was his one and only chance of representing his country as an Olympian, so surely he would swallow his pride and box nine more minutes to achieve his dream.

All those who made that presumption simply didn't know Eamonn Magee very well. There is a bull-headed stubbornness within the man that borders on a mania. Even when he is wrong, he's right, and he will never be convinced otherwise. And when points of principle are at stake, he digs his heels in until the tops of his ankles are covered. It is a personality trait that wrecks friendships and relationships with wild abandon, but that, when managed correctly, drives individuals at the very top of their chosen professions. Professional sports probably contain more such characters than most walks of life and perhaps Roy Keane, the footballer who famously walked away from captaining his country at the 2002 World Cup in a dispute over training conditions, or Muhammad Ali, who sacrificed his peak years as the heavyweight champion of the world on account of a religion-inspired anti-war stance, can relate to this extreme obstinacy. Maybe they understood better than the rest of us Magee's mindset when he declared one last time on the eve of the planned box-off, 'I'll not box a trial with Gough or anybody else.'

And so he didn't. On the night the IABA expected him in Dublin for the contrived rematch, Magee was drinking with friends in the Shamrock.

Gough was immediately announced as the Irish Olympic squad's 63.5kg representative and Eamonn was instead included in a second team scheduled to fly out to Tenerife for an international meet with Spain. Such was his sense of anger and disillusionment, few thought Magee would turn up at the airport for the flight to the Canary Islands, but he was there, surprisingly chipper given the circumstances. His relative joviality masked the bitterness burning within him but no sooner had the flight taken off that the explanation for Magee's appearance became clear. He was drunk by the time the four-hour flight touched down in Santa Cruz and he barely sobered up for the duration of the tournament. Each morning when Nicolás Cruz gathered the men together to begin training and counted the bodies in front of him, there was always one missing.

'It's Magee,' one of the other boxers would say. 'Shall I go and get him up?'

'Forget it,' Cruz would reply before beginning the early morning run without the team's star man.

Cruz had a lot of sympathy for Eamonn after the Olympic snub and he also knew there would be no reasoning with him in this mood. Magee was not on this island to box, he was here on an IABA-funded holiday. As long as Eamonn could keep his eyes open that week, he was drinking. He actually turned up for one of his designated bouts and was foolishly allowed in the ring. In the opening seconds Magee sank his teeth into an unsuspecting Spaniard's neck and was disqualified as the poor man squealed in terror. Eamonn headed straight back to the bar without even showering. He was in full free-fall mode. Boxing, the only thing that had kept him vaguely near the rails over the past decade, had now conspired to send him careering off the track and into the dark unknown. The following night he was propping up the bar in a club in the early hours when a fellow fighter started fidgeting with the drawstring of his shorts. Eamonn looked on with interest as he finally coaxed a small white tablet from the elastic around his waist.

'What's that?' Magee asked.

He was handed the pill. 'Just take it,' the other boxer advised. 'You won't be disappointed.'

That ecstasy tablet was the first hard drug Magee ever took. As a kid in the Bone Hills that rise up alongside the Ardoyne, he'd tried a joint but quickly decided he preferred the buzz that alcohol gave him. Later, sitting in the abandoned Flax Street mill, listening to rebel music under the British snipers in their watchtower, he learned to love the relaxing effect of marijuana, but witnessing friends hallucinating on glue, rolling about in garbage believing it to be gold coins, or hurling imaginary fireballs at one another, had been enough to put him off any further experimentation with narcotics. The risk of being tested and found with something in his system at a major boxing championships had been another deterrent, but by this point he just didn't care.

The fighter was right; Eamonn wasn't disappointed. The ecstasy removed him from life just like the booze did, but the tablet placed him in an altogether different reality. Whereas alcohol exacerbated the darker thoughts that swirled around his head and rendered him heavy and sluggish as the night wore on, MDMA lifted his spirits and propelled him forward at breakneck speed into the small hours where mayhem resided.

As soon as he returned home to Belfast he threw himself into his new habit with the same single-mindedness with which he attacked everything in life. The early-1990s rave culture was in full effect in north Belfast and illegal pills to keep the party going were easy to find – particularly as Eamonn was now working the door of a city-centre bar frequented by the likes of Mickey 'Moneybags' Mooney, Paul 'Saul' Devine, Brendan 'Speedy' Fegan and Brendan 'Bap' Campbell, some of the most prominent drug dealers in Belfast. Magee's naturally sharp business mind immediately noted the ample supply available and limitless demand that existed on the street and in the clubs. Within weeks he was tapping into the market.

The twenty-fifth Summer Olympics commenced in Barcelona on 25

July. Eamonn pretended he didn't give a fuck, that he wasn't paying the games any attention. But he sat in Rosapenna Street with Mary, two-year-old Francis and six-month-old Áine and watched every round of it. Three of his closest friends in boxing competed. Flyweight Paul Buttimer and featherweight Paul Griffin lost their first round encounters but Wayne McCullough blasted his way to the bantamweight final where he was defeated 16–8 by the exceptional Cuban Joel Casamayor. Welterweight Michael Carruth went one better than McCullough and claimed Ireland's first-ever Olympic boxing gold medal when he edged out the formidable Juan Hernández Sierra 13–10. The fifth and final member of the team, heavyweight Paul Douglas, lost a quarter-final to Arnold Vanderlyde in a division in which the legendary Felix Savon marched to the first of his three Olympic golds. Two out of five fighters from a small country like Ireland medalling at the Olympic Games was an outstanding achievement, and while Magee was happy for his teammates, their successes deepened the bitter resentfulness that swallowed him whole when he sobered up enough to let his mind wander into the realm of what could have been. Success breeds success. One member of a team winning creates a momentum that can sweep others along to their own glory. To this day Eamonn is convinced he would have returned from Spain with a medal. The fact that Neil Gough, the man chosen in his place, had fallen at the first hurdle of a pre-qualifying tournament in Italy and failed to make the final Olympic team rubbed further salt into the raw, seeping wound.

Fuck the IABA, he said to himself. *Fuck the Ulster Council. Fuck Patsy even. Fuck them all. I'm through with boxing. I'm a drug taker and a drug dealer now.*

***

The IRA didn't like drug dealers operating in their districts. For most of the year they had been monitoring the influx of ecstasy into the working-class nationalist neighbourhoods and gathering intelligence on those responsible. The IRA didn't like the Irish People's Liberation Organisation (IPLO) either. Despite the grand title, this small, republican paramilitary group was more involved in drugs, prostitution, racketeering and internal feuds than in any campaign to free the Irish from 800 years of British oppression. They sprang forth from a split in the Irish National Liberation Army (INLA) in the mid-1980s and by the early 1990s the IRA had decided that their propensity for intra-republican violence, and the fact they operated outside the control of the Provos, meant it would be better for the overall republican movement if the IPLO ceased to exist.

It became known as the IRA's version of the Nazis' Night of the Long Knives. A few days before, they publicly warned locals in the areas concerned that a purge would soon take place. Isobel was sitting in the Shamrock with a couple of friends when a pair of balaclava-clad IRA volunteers entered the bar and read a statement to that effect. She had no idea her youngest son was on their list.

The operation was planned for Halloween night so that the sounds of firecrackers exploding would obscure the hollower crack of gunshots. One hundred IRA members were involved across the city and it began when Gerard 'Jock' Davison walked into St Matthew's Social Club in the Short Strand area of central Belfast and assassinated the IPLO's second-in-command, Sammy Ward. Throughout the night, over a dozen other men were taken out of pubs, clubs and houses across Belfast and received a bullet behind each kneecap. How many of these other victims were actually members of the IPLO is still debated to this day. Authorities declared the shootings the result of an IRA–IPLO feud, and it is true that the Provos soon ordered remaining members of the IPLO to hand over their weapons and leave the country. But the facts suggest it really was primarily a republican drive to eliminate local drug dealing. That the IRA also managed to forcibly disband the already weakened IPLO in one bloody night of violence was, it appears, more an unexpected bonus than the ultimate goal of the synchronised attacks.

Certainly, Eamonn Magee never had any involvement with the IPLO. He was also not in any of the usual drinking dens or houses that the IRA called upon that night as they sought to admonish him for his recent dalliance in the drugs trade. When he woke to the bloody carnage around him, he went straight to his father. Doc attempted to reason with the top rank of the Ardoyne IRA, but his son was guilty as charged and there was nothing Terrence could do to change that. With a heavy heart he told his youngest child that he would have to take a bullet. Eamonn accepted his fate and that decision saved his boxing career. The local OC offered a degree of leniency if Eamonn was waiting for the knock on the door the following evening and promised the bullet would rip through flesh rather than shatter bone in the fighter's leg.

Eamonn was waiting, sitting in the silence of his mother's kitchen in Holmdene Gardens, drinking a beer alongside Isobel, Terrence, Noel and Patrick. Mary stayed at home in Rosapenna Street with the two babies. When the rap was heard on the back door at 6 p.m., Eamonn rose on his own and left the house as his mother tried to hide her tears. Solemnly, he walked a pace ahead of his foreboding companion along the alleyway that lies parallel to Holmdene Gardens, took a left onto Berwick Road, crossed Brompton Park and stopped a few paces into a narrow entry that runs alongside his old primary school and into Old Ardoyne. A second man, this one masked, appeared and quietly instructed Eamonn to place his hands on the wall and spread his legs. With no warning, the shooter bent down so the muzzle of the gun was practically touching his quarry's trouser leg and fired a bullet through the left calf. The two Provos then walked away without another word spoken.

Noel and Terrence heard the shot as they sat in Noel's car on Holmdene. That was their cue and they immediately took off to the designated meeting point. It was a new Ford Escort, Noel's pride and joy, so he had meticulously lined the rear seats and floor with plastic bin-liners so none of his brother's blood would stain the upholstery. For his part, Eamonn had worn a pair of old trousers that he didn't care would now have a bullet-shaped hole in them. It all added to the macabre sense of surrealism of this prearranged and carefully managed maiming of the youngest member of their family.

By now, Eamonn had limped onto Brompton Park and was waiting by the kerb. Blood flowed freely from the gunshot wound but he was remarkably calm as his father applied pressure with flannels and his brother drove to the Mater Hospital. Shock does tend to numb most physical pains.

The incident had a profound effect on the entire family. Terrence, who had effectively negotiated the shooting of his own son, slipped further into himself and the bottle. Noel and Patrick went back to their families outside the Ardoyne but were tormented by the memories of having to sit idly by when a man came to their family home and took their baby brother away to be shot. Isobel's heart was broken. She has since forgiven every bad deed Eamonn has ever committed, but his involvement in drugs was the toughest for her to get over. She was also most conscious of the stigma attached to dealing and how attitudes towards a family in the district could be forever altered by one member's involvement in the life-wrecking trade. Sitting in the back of a black taxi on the way to visit her son the next morning, she listened in silence while the driver, unaware of who his fare was, chatted freely about no cab being willing to pick the drug-dealing scumbags up from the hospitals when they shuffled out on crutches and knee braces. Eamonn's mother was too hurt to speak up on behalf of her boy that day.

For Eamonn himself, positives could be taken out of the harrowing incident. He didn't stop using, but he ended his dealing days at the cost of a flesh wound. He looks back now and realises it was a small price to pay to keep breathing. Before the new millennium dawned, Mooney, who let Eamonn off a thousand-pound debt after his shooting, Devine, Fegan and Campbell, had all received bullets from which they never walked away.

Eamonn also reconsidered his decision to never fight again. His dad had put his neck on the line to save his son from a life-altering, crippling injury. Dozens of limbs have been amputated in Belfast after punishment shootings and doctors estimate that one in five suffer some form of permanent debilitating injury. Terrence had argued that Eamonn was one of the best amateur boxers in the country, the pride of the district, and he would one day be a great professional champion. He owed it to his father to get back in the gym.

The Ulster senior finals arrived too soon for him to defend his title, but Patsy was working him hard to ensure they'd be in Dublin for the national championships at the end of January. Magee hadn't boxed for over half a year, but such was his class you would never have recognised that fact. In a repeat of the 1992 semi-final, he met Greg Ormond in the quarters this time and emerged a comfortable 19–12 victor. Wary of having to fight three times against elite opposition in a short space of time, and unsure of his stamina having been out of action for so long, Eamonn was happy to do just enough to keep himself ahead and out of range until the final bell. In the semi-final he met Fergal Carruth, younger brother of the gold-medal-sporting Michael, and, as big brother looked on in the National Stadium, Fergal was totally outclassed in a 16–8 defeat to Sacred Heart's finest. Only Billy Walsh stood between Magee and his attempt to retain his crown as the best amateur light welterweight in Ireland, and Eamonn put on a masterclass of aggressive counter-punching to dominate the bout from the opening bell. Midway through the second round, the bullet wound on his calf, which he had carefully bandaged and hidden beneath white socks pulled up to his knee, began to open. As he boxed he could feel the warmth of the blood seeping out and a small red spot on his sock slowly grew as the fight went on. But Eamonn fought with such a focus that night that you could have put a bullet in his other leg and he still wouldn't have missed a beat. At the end of the third round of a high-scoring fight, his hand was raised aloft in a 29–16 victory.

It was the beginning of a great run for Magee. In February 1993 he knocked out Jamie Scanlon inside forty-five seconds as Team Ireland claimed a famous victory over Great Britain in Dublin. In March he was part of a three-week, eight-state, boxing odyssey around the US, in which he was once again voted fighter of the tour.

But it seemed like Eamonn managed to taint every boxing success abroad with his ill-discipline outside the ring. The Irish team were treated like kings in New York, even given their own float to take part in the famous St Patrick's Day parade. Eamonn found himself caught short and was forced to urinate off the back as it cruised through the Big Apple, the sheer quantity of beer he had necked prolonging the ordeal for what seemed like three or four blocks. The mayor's office also provided a high-spec RV, usually reserved for the families of visiting dignitaries, for the boxers to use. This time the whole team were guilty of excess and a famous photo depicts a line of Irish boxing's bright young hopes pissing up against the mayor's prized vehicle.

One day Magee, Griffin and John Erskine decided to jump in a yellow cab and instructed the driver to take them to a McDonald's drive-thru, at the time still a novelty for anyone from Northern Ireland. Not being used to the menu or system, they were taking a little longer than expected to make their order when the car behind decided to hurry them along with a horn blast and bumper-to-bumper jolt. Then, as the boys sat eating in the cab in an empty car park, the same car provocatively parked right beside them and glared in. The taxi driver hurled verbal abuse out the window, but his bark was clearly worse than his bite so Eamonn decided it was up to him to teach today's lesson. After Magee gave Griffin and Erskine their instructions, the trio bounded out of the cab, pulled open the doors of the neighbouring vehicle, and proceeded to give the occupants a kicking severe enough to ensure they'd have more patience the next time they were in line behind a group of Irish tourists at a fast-food joint.

At the airport at the end of the tour the team were told that Muhammad Ali was sitting around the corner in the terminal and Eamonn shadow-boxed with the Greatest while they waited for their delayed flight and then received a signed prayer card that he still treasures to this day.

His good form continued the following month when he went to Denmark and beat a local favourite 31–4 in as one-sided a contest as you will ever see in the boxing ring. But his ill-discipline also continued. In the 1993 world amateur championships in Tampere, Finland, a fellow boxer was on the other end of Magee's bare, wrathful fists. Eamonn was hosting a drunken hotel-room party when an inebriated Russian heavyweight thumped on the bedroom door and demanded entry. Once inside, the 200-pounder began throwing his Vodka-soaked weight around and putting others on edge. A few tried to ease the non-English-speaking big man out the door but Eamonn did not have their patience and the Russian was soon knocked unconscious and then dragged out onto the carpeted hallway. The next morning when the lift doors opened as Magee waited to descend to the breakfast room, his heart skipped a beat when his victim gingerly stepped out accompanied by two Finnish policemen. Thankfully the Russian was either too hungover or concussed to recognise his attacker. Or perhaps he was just too embarrassed to admit that a light welterweight had stretched him out.

Through it all, the lure of these alcohol and drugs binges was pulling him back into the life he could not afford to be living. Even away at boxing tournaments, he was soon out in search of dope to smoke and take the edge off the day when the sun went down. On that US trip, for example, he found himself lost in Hell's Kitchen after taking advice from some less than savoury street characters he approached for directions. On European ventures, he had more success, after striking up a friendship with a like-minded fighter who tended to arrive with his own supply. Eamonn was only too happy to be his most loyal customer.

***

He rattles the letter and numbers off as you might your date of birth.

'A9918.'

We are driving up the Crumlin Road, passing the Mater Hospital on our right and the grand but derelict courthouse on our left.

'Sorry?' I reply, slow to catch Eamonn's meaning.

'A9918. My prison number in the Crum,' he clarifies and, looking out my window, I see the old four-fingered jailhouse next to the hospital.

***

Eamonn Junior had been born in April 1993, but the new arrival did little to calm the wild heart that continued to propel his father towards the pursuit of extremes. In August he was sentenced to three months in prison, suspended for two years, following a conviction for common assault. He had badly beaten an old primary school classmate behind the Shamrock one night in what Eamonn had regarded as a fair fight between two men settling their differences as men should. In November he was pulled over by police for speeding erratically down the Crumlin Road. High as a kite, he refused to provide the arresting officers with a specimen and so resisting the police was added to the charges. He already had a long list of driving offences on his record, including driving with no licence, no insurance, no lights, obstructing the police and providing a false name and address. A raft of fines and disqualifications was the judge's verdict. Twenty-five years, and many more driving offences later, he still doesn't have a valid licence and claims the only car accident he ever had was deliberately crashing into a wall in Rosapenna Street in frustration after enduring an earful from Mary for the duration of the journey home.

It was these traffic violations that first put Magee behind bars. 'Just doing fines,' is how he terms it, enduring a few days inside in lieu of paying what the state had decreed he owed them. In doing time in Crumlin Road Gaol, he was also following in the footsteps of more illustrious prisoners such as Éamon de Valera, Ian Paisley, Martin McGuinness, Bobby Sands and Michael Stone. Built in the 1840s, it was a grim place with its harsh

Victorian austerity basically untouched until late twentieth-century renovations converted it into a now popular tourist attraction. With two men in cramped cells, inadequate and inedible meals, and just one hour of social time per day, prisoners in the Crum certainly knew they were in jail. It begs the question why Eamonn didn't just find a way to pay the fines, but short-term incarceration was such a normalised state for males from his district that he didn't bat an eyelid when his time arrived.

During this period he was only sporadically calling in on Mary and the kids, preferring to party all night and sleep off the excesses in another woman's bed or on the floor of some desolate flat the following day. When he did arrive home, he'd wander about in a drunken fugue state or sit spaced out on ecstasy pills staring at the television until *The Hitman and Her* came on and he'd bounce about like he was there in the nightclub with Pete Waterman and Michaela Strachan. Mary grew to prefer him staying away at these times, particularly when he became prone to opening the family's doors to anyone even vaguely connected to his core gang of drink-and-drugs buddies.

Naturally, his boxing suffered. He lost 13–3 to a future professional opponent and world champion, Oktay Urkal, in the 1993 world championships in Finland. He'd never been on the receiving end of such a comprehensive decision. Then a Georgian by the name of Kahaber Chikvinidze beat him in their preliminary stage bout at the European championships in Turkey. He returned to training in time for the 1994 Ulster senior championships but, while he gave it all in the gym as usual, it was never going to be enough to paper over the unseen cracks that a wild lifestyle will leave in a fighter's armour.

Antrim's Mark Winters was a good boxer, good enough to win the All-Ireland lightweight title in 1993 and a silver medal in the 1994 Commonwealth Games in Canada. As a pro he would win a British title and mix it with the likes of Ricky Hatton, Junior Witter and Graham Earl. But even if it is not immediately apparent in the comparison of records on pieces of paper, there are distinct levels in boxing and Winters shouldn't have been able to lay a glove on Magee. Instead, he forced the pace throughout the three rounds of the 1994 Ulster final, bullying a notably lacklustre Magee at times and regularly catching him with shots the Ardoyne man would normally slip in his sleep. By the third stanza, a trickle of blood escaped from Eamonn's nostril and his mouth hung open as his lungs gasped for oxygen. There were no complaints from Magee or Patsy in his corner when Winters was announced the winner by twelve points to eight.

Half an hour later, Patrick Magee found his brother sitting on the ground with his head in his hands in a dark and empty corridor of the Ulster Hall. Paddy couldn't see the tears fall but he sensed they were there. He had just watched a shadow of his younger brother bossed about the ring by someone a prime Eamonn could have dealt with one-handed.

'Are you all right?' he finally asked.

'No,' came the muffled reply. Eamonn then raised his head and gazed up at Patrick through tear-reddened eyes. 'What the fuck was that out there?'

What could Patrick say? They both knew it was a rhetorical question. *That out there* was a most public exhibition of a wasted talent, of a man falling apart. Aside from the drug and alcohol abuse that was neutralising the God-given physical gifts he was born with, there was a constant, sneering voice in his head that prevented him from committing to a path and trusting where it led. *You should have gone to the Olympics*, the voice said. *You'd have won a medal*, it teased. *You ought to be a pro making millions and fighting in stadiums rather than this amateur shite in front of a couple of hundred in the Ulster Hall.*

Patsy phoned him a week later. 'The Ulster Council have called for a box-off between you and Winters to see who goes to the Commonwealth Games,' he relayed.

'Fuck off,' Eamonn immediately replied. 'He won, he's Ulster champion, he goes.'

'I thought you'd say that,' Patsy sighed. 'Okay son, I'll be round to pick you up tomorrow morning. I've lined up some sparring for you across town so we can make sure we're ready for the All-Irelands.'

'All right, Patsy.'

The next day Patsy was met at the door by one of Eamonn's heavy-drinking pals. It was a bad sign but he was invited into the living room and told that Eamonn was just getting ready and would be down in a minute.

'Can I get you a glass of water, mister?' he was asked in a suspiciously and comically polite tone by his startled and drunken host, who was still clearly trying to get a handle on the situation.

'I'm not a fucking invalid,' Patsy retorted as his notoriously brittle patience snapped. 'I know where the bloody taps are, I'll get it myself.'

He rose and walked to the kitchen but when he pushed open the door, his heart sank at the sound of the empty beer cans scraping across the linoleum floor. It then almost broke when he saw a semi-conscious Eamonn lying amongst the remains of an all-nighter in a drunken stupor.

'That's it,' Patsy said with a sad shake of his head. 'We're through, son.'

And so they were. The next time Eamonn entered the ring it would be as a bare-chested professional, twenty-one months later.

Aged three at my auntie and
uncle's wedding.

Primary one school photo with Patrick.

Holier than thou for my
First Communion.

A young teen practising for the riots!

Terry, me and Noel.

With Eamonn Maguire (*left*) and Patsy McKenna on our way back from the
1989 World Junior Championships in Puerto Rico.

Showing my silver medal to the family.

Claiming gold at the 1989 Gaelic Games in Canada.

Another victory, and boxer of the tournament award, in the US.

'Kneecapping' Paul Griffin in
America!

Meeting the great Muhammad Ali.

Training with the Irish senior squad on Bettystown beach.

A family drink with grandad Emanuel Quinn in the middle.

The whole family together.

Team meeting with Mike Callahan (*left*) and John Breen.

Another session with Hamill.

A packed ring before the Neary fight: Vinty McGurk, Tommy Kelly, Bo Cameron and John Connolly all present.

On holiday with Francis, Áine and Eamonn Jr.

4

EXILE

Without boxing, Eamonn was hopelessly and dangerously lost. The drinking and drug abuse flourished in the absence of any semblance of sporting discipline. He had Mary and three young children to care for but he couldn't even begin to look after himself. In some ways life to that point had rendered him old beyond his years, but in terms of the faculties a man must develop for responsible fatherhood, he was still a frightened, immature, twenty-two-year-old kid.

When he turned his back on boxing, he also walked away from the only remaining male figure who was capable of exerting a positive influence on his life. Terry had fled to Wales, Nipper had died, alcohol and depression had stolen his father, and now he'd pushed Patsy away. Eamonn was always his own man but if anyone could handle him it was Patsy McKenna. Even today when Eamonn is in his presence, there is a subtle subservience in operation that contrasts starkly with his attitude towards every other human being on the planet. Patsy's is the only house I ever entered with Eamonn in which he didn't either carry in his own beer or immediately ask for one from the host before we had a chance to sit down. When Patsy talks, whatever he says, Eamonn listens and at the very least feigns attention. He is hesitant to interrupt his old coach in full flow, to the point that the shake in his hand from a lack of fresh alcohol must begin before he contemplates making excuses and chasing down a drink. Look closely at the pair together today, and you'll catch glimpses of a five-year-old Eamonn on his first day in Sacred Heart gym, following Patsy's bawled orders to a tee.

Not boxing also meant the final nail in the coffin of the master plan

Magee had envisioned upon winning his first Irish senior title in 1992. He should have been a dozen fights into his professional career by now. He should have already won an Irish title and perhaps even the British or Commonwealth. The purses would have been ratcheting up nicely as he approached world level and he'd now have been due a new contract from Warren or Hearn or Duff, one that would have set him up for life. That had been the plan, anyway.

He was probably never wired for a regular nine-to-five job but with beer and ecstasy now in total control, an honest day's work was out of the question. The closest he came was doing the doors of bars and clubs all over Belfast and beyond. He had his first gig aged just sixteen, bouncing his dad's old drinking haunt, the Jamaica Inn. They paid him forty quid a night, proper money for an Ardoyne teenager in 1987. Certainly enough to become an associate member of the Shamrock two years earlier than the norm and enjoy games of quoits and pints for as little as forty pence. By the mid-nineties the hourly rate had barely increased, however, and he now had serious addictions to fund and a family at home to feed. More cash was needed and Eamonn was naturally drawn to illicit means to secure it as fast as possible.

At times his doorman work presented opportunities too good to turn down. One night when he was working in the Thompson's Garage Club next to the city hall, the owner of a nearby clothes store offered to double his wages if he did security for a private all-night party raging above his shop. Eamonn accepted the generous offer and supplemented the pay by surreptitiously stuffing the street bins outside the front doors with the best designer gear he could pluck off the hangers and shelves without being noticed. He even swiped the device to remove the ink security tags so there would be no messing about once he got home and set to work flogging the merchandise.

On another occasion, the cash in hand arrived even more quickly. East Belfast's Ray Close was fighting his rematch with the World Boxing

Organisation (WBO) super middleweight champion, Chris Eubank, in the King's Hall. Close, who stopped Terry Magee in seven rounds for the Irish title in 1991, had somewhat fortunately drawn with the champion in Scotland the year before, but now on home ground he had high hopes of inflicting a first defeat on the Englishman. As it turned out he was unlucky to be on the wrong side of a split decision but that was neither here nor there to Eamonn, who left the arena a very happy man regardless. Part of his good mood was due to his brother Noel beating John J. Cooke on the undercard, but it was Noel's trainer, John Breen, who really made his night. Breen arranged the security for the event and, on Noel's recommendation, hired the youngest Magee without having ever met him. That in itself was not necessarily a problem, but Breen then made the mistake of placing Eamonn on the front doors. There, he was quick to offer punters who arrived without a ticket a discount if they slipped their notes into his pocket rather than the till at the official box office. He added over 300 pounds to his pay cheque that night.

Drugs swirled around the lifestyle Eamonn was living and while the bullet scar on his left calf was all the reminder he needed not to slip back into dealing, he was opportunistic enough not to look a gift horse in the mouth if the odds were weighted overwhelmingly in his favour. When a friend introduced him to a total unknown looking for two kilos of soap bar hash one morning, Eamonn couldn't help himself.

'No bother, mate,' he assured his pigeon. 'Meet me this afternoon at two o'clock in Morrison's.'

Morrison's Bar is still a fixture on the Belfast drinking circuit and part of its charm back then was the adjoining doorway which led into the Superbowl, a ten-pin bowling alley situated at the corner of Bedford Street and Clarence Street just behind the city hall. It was having this choice of exit, each leading towards distinct areas of the city, which made it the perfect spot for Eamonn to execute his plan.

On his way back from the gym he bought sixteen bars of Lifebuoy soap in the local Poundstretcher. Back in his kitchen he weighed it up, shaved a little off the sides, and wrapped exactly two kilos worth of the cleaning product in brown paper. *If this clown wants soap bar, I'll give him fucking soap bar*, he laughed to himself.

When they made the exchange under a table in Morrison's and the unsuspecting customer motioned as if about to slice open his parcel and sample the goods, Eamonn urged caution.

'Not here mate,' he hissed. 'Go out through the Superbowl and into the car park if you want to take a look.'

As soon as the stooge left through the bowling alley exit and into the Clarence Street car park, Eamonn calmly walked through Morrison's, out the pub's front doors and up the Dublin Road to lose himself in the crowds of Orangemen marching to celebrate the Twelfth of July. When the disappointed, but presumably clean-handed, buyer called later he was told in no uncertain terms: 'You asked for soap and that's what you got – now fuck off!'

Drug users probably paid the vast majority of Eamonn's wages in those days in one way or another. At times he simply provided a service: organising buses to Kelly's nightclub in Portrush and then selling over-priced tins of cider to the dehydrated pill-poppers who stumbled out into the car park at 3 a.m., or arranging an all-night, ecstasy-fuelled rave in a property on the Cliftonville Road and charging a tenner to enter. At other times, however, it was a downright swindle.

One of his favourite scams was to march up to an unsuspecting punter in a bar or club, quickly flash a fake police badge, declare himself an undercover drug-squad officer and invite the target outside to be searched. Eamonn's trained eye for spotting a dealer generally ensured a small bag of pills ended up in his possession nine times out of ten. Once, the victim panicked and ran, hurling two bags from his person as he fled. Magee scooped them up and let him go. That haul netted over 300 ecstasy tablets and guaranteed one hell of a weekend.

Another hustle was even more opportunistic. At a rave in Maysfield Leisure Centre one night, Eamonn quickly ascertained that there was huge demand and almost no supply on the premises. He raced to the nearest shop and cleaned them out of Anadin painkillers. He then sat around the corner and diligently sucked each tablet smooth until the A for Anadin had vanished. Inside Eamonn made a fortune, flogging the aspirins for twenty pound a pop with the cheeky guarantee of no headaches the following morning.

It was a big enough score to catch the attention of the IRA and they weren't long in paying Eamonn a visit, this time escorting him out of his grandmother's wake at the Kickhams GAA Club for a quiet word. He tried to make light of the situation, laughing that they were just headache tablets and all he was doing was ripping off a few teenagers who should have known better, but he knew he was on thin ice after his previous drug-related indiscretions. He had also recently had a first-hand reminder of the repercussions for breaking the local Provos' rules when he came across Sean Dunlop lying in an Ardoyne alleyway like a broken crab on the beach at low tide. Dunlop's crime was persistent joyriding and he had been beaten about the knees and elbows with bats, hammers and metal bars. Eamonn ran from bar to bar, asking to use the phone to call an ambulance, but all the proprietors had been pre-warned by the RA not to allow it. They wanted Dunlop's suffering to be prolonged for as long as possible.

Magee's other main source of income in those days were the fruit machines. He didn't play them – although the early flutterings of a destructive gambling problem were stirring inside his compulsive, addictive mind – but instead took to emptying the slots regardless of the configuration of spinning lemons, grapes and cherries. He had several modes of attack to clean out the machines. With any old knife he could slip the lock in seconds, as he did one famous day in Blackpool, which ensured the Ulster amateur boxing team returned home with their pockets filled with loose change. A claw hammer could be wedged into the panel joints to lever the side away and open the back just as easily. But the most inventive form of robbing them entailed a sawn-off Piezo igniter more commonly used to spark gas stoves into flame. He removed the metal casing of the lighter so that the electric charge generated by each click of the button could be applied to the metal-plated collection gutter into which the winnings of lucky punters tumbled. Eamonn didn't understand the science, but all he knew was that the spark sent the fruit machine haywire and caused it to regurgitate pound coins like there was no tomorrow.

These petty thefts were his bread and butter, but every now and again a more prosperous heist presented itself. Looking out the window of a friend's house in the Bone one afternoon, he watched with interest as kitchen units were hauled into the new builds then springing up behind Glenview Street. That night, with help, he removed one of those kitchens in its entirety, piece by piece. It was soon sold on and the proceeds financed a two- or three-day bender.

Unfortunately, it was a job just big enough to alert the all-seeing IRA, who took a dim view of any thieving on their turf that did not have their direct authorisation. They told him to get out of the district, that he was no longer welcome. He didn't have to ask what the alternative was.

Despite being painfully aware of the risks, Magee defied the Provos. He may not have been seen as much on the streets of the Ardoyne or the Bone for the next nine months, but he was there, holed up in the house in Rosapenna Street. He had no attic to hunker down in, but the parallels with Doc's ordeal were striking. Along with his mother and the local parish priest, he met with the IRA top rank in the church sacristy one evening to plead his case, but it was decided he was not reformed and, as such, still not welcome.

After nine months in supposed exile, he tentatively started showing his face in Ta Locky's Bar and other Ardoyne night spots again. No official word had come from the RA but he gambled that he'd served enough punishment for his crime. One night he felt a tap on his shoulder at the bar and he turned to find himself face to face with the man who had walked him from his mother's house to the alleyway off Brompton Park a couple of years before. That man was now the OC of the district.

'What the fuck are you doing here?' the Provo growled.

Eamonn nearly shit himself on the spot as he began a stuttering response.

The Provo then burst out laughing and slapped him on the back. 'Don't worry wee man,' he said. 'I think you're all right to be back now.'

His status as persona grata didn't last long, however. Within days he and Connolly got into a fight outside a chippy on Ardoyne Avenue that resulted in a connected guy losing part of his finger. In truth, Connolly was the main aggressor on this occasion but Magee was guilty by both association and reputation. He prayed it would blow over, but deep down he knew the consequences.

At around 6 p.m. two nights later there was a knock at the door in Rosapenna Street and Mary eased it open a couple of inches, just far enough to see the caller and respond that Eamonn wasn't there. She presumed it was someone looking for drugs or a drinking partner and was not in the mood to be sociable. Before she could get the door closed, however, a foot wedged itself in.

'This is the Irish Republican Army,' the man declared. 'We're taking over the house.'

Mary was ushered into the living room where Áine sat playing with baby Eamonn. Her mother had taken Francis across to Andersonstown to visit a stepsister who had just moved back from Canada. Eamonn had in actual fact just left to work the door of the Belfast Bar in the city centre. As it was a Monday night, Mary knew he wouldn't be too late home but she still had until around midnight to think of a plan.

'Listen, you're wasting your time,' she said as men came and went, in and out the back door, throughout the night. 'He won't be coming back here tonight. God knows where he is or what he's doing.'

There were nine or ten different faces in total. Some carried baseball bats. Others metal bars. One had a wooden club with the sharp end of four-inch nails protruding from it. Around 9 p.m., Mary's heart sank as she heard the front door open, but it was only her mother returning with Francis. They too were directed into the living room to wait it out. As midnight neared, Mary knew she had to act.

'This is ridiculous,' she began. 'And my kitchen is still a mess from dinner. Can I at least go in and do the dishes?'

Permission was granted, as was a quick trip to the bathroom. There she tore off a piece of toilet paper and, using her eye-liner pencil, she scribbled: *RA IN HOUSE, RUN LIKE FUCK.* She folded it carefully, tucked it into her pocket and then went down the stairs to stand over the kitchen sink and wait for Eamonn to appear. The Provos were still milling in and out but as Tuesday approached they began to grudgingly accept that perhaps the man of the house really wasn't coming back and their number dwindled. Mary still needed a slice of luck in terms of timing, but if she could get that square of toilet paper out the window unseen, Eamonn might avoid his violent fate for one more night at least.

The moment of truth arrived around 12.30 a.m. when Eamonn stepped out of a taxi and walked towards the house. He saw the toilet paper flutter out the window and seconds later he was back in the taxi that had since performed a U-turn to rejoin the Oldpark Road. Half an hour after that, the IRA gave Mary, her mother and her kids their freedom back.

'I told you yous were wasting your time,' she plucked up the courage to say as they left.

The Provo turned and looked her in the eye. 'He's a lucky man,' he replied. 'He wouldn't have walked again had we got him tonight.'

Eamonn fled west this time and when he did venture back towards north Belfast he often stayed away from Rosapenna Street. Part of that decision was a fear of the IRA returning one night, but the rows with Mary had grown so fierce and frequent that she was actually happy not to see him for a while. Mary liked a drink herself in those days and the two were a combustible partnership, prone to violent bust-ups over matters big or small and long since forgotten. But she was also a committed mother to her kids and she expected the same commitment from Eamonn. Mary was in her thirties at this point and although she could still party with the best of them at the weekend, during the week she wanted her partner to be there to help out with three children under the age of four. Eamonn, in his early twenties, just wasn't there yet.

***

James Gerard Hamill was born in 1963. Even by Ardoyne standards, his childhood was particularly tough. He never knew his father and before he could bond with his mother she left for Australia and never came back. He was raised a stray in various orphanages and homes and refugee camps in the north and south of Ireland. Somehow he fell between the gaps and just never really went to school. He was around Terry Magee Junior's age and in his early teens he tried to befriend Eamonn's eldest brother. But then Terry left too. People were always leaving Hamill. He always felt alone.

In his late teens he started drinking in the Jamaica Inn on the frontier where the Ardoyne becomes the Bone. He sat alone with his pints until Terrence Magee Senior took a shine to him. Doc liked the kid and Hamill loved being seen with Doc and the other big men of the district. Soon he was sent for carry-outs and allowed to sit in on the drinking sessions that pressed on through to the break of dawn in Terrence's house on Eskdale. Soon Hamill was an alcoholic too.

The drink rotted his brain quicker than most, to the point that no one was sure if Hamill was all there in the head. He was never allowed to join the Fianna or the IRA but the Provos would store weapons in his council flat. A tout revealed this once and an army raid unearthed a 9mm behind some pans in his kitchen cupboard. He was facing ten years inside before an RUC officer took the stand and described Hamill as harmless, nothing more than the village idiot. Hamill walked after several months on remand.

Then Eamonn grew up and got to know him. He knew he'd been close to his father so he automatically took to the little guy with the dodgy eye and faltering hearing. He'd tease him relentlessly, calling him Ham & Eggs or Hamilton, a largely Protestant variation of his surname, but he always looked out for James.

Once Eamonn walked into the 32 Degrees North pub on the Crumlin Road and noticed Hamill perched at the bar, three sheets to the wind. He sat a little away and observed as his little friend continued drunkenly antagonising a big fella standing beside him. The guy was connected, but he had left the Ardoyne when the loyalist mobs were burning Butler Street in 1971. Hamill was no fighter but he didn't know any better as he kept needling away at the man. When Hamill tottered towards the bathroom to relieve himself, the big man followed. Even from a distance, Eamonn could read the situation like a book. He rose and walked to the toilets as well, just in time to see Hamill take a blow to the back of the head that left him lying dazed on the floor between two urinals. His attacker's foot then rose and prepared to stamp the life out of his victim as Hamill turned and looked up from the piss-stained tiles.

'Hey!' Eamonn shouted and then knocked the man out cold with the sort of clean punch only a trained boxer can throw. He dragged the unconscious body into the cubicle and propped it up. He lifted Hamill, splashed water over his face, walked him back to his stool at the bar and instructed him to continue his pint and say nothing. Eamonn then sat down at his table and waited. Thirty minutes later the guy appeared, walking zombie-like, still on queer street. He weaved his way to Hamill, leant against the bar and rubbed his big, hazy head. He suspected something strange had just happened but he couldn't piece it all together. He looked at little, drunken, harmless James Hamill and then walked out the door.

Eamonn started drinking in Hamill's flat every Thursday night. When things got bad with Mary, he'd stay the night. When things got really bad with Mary, he moved in. Together over the coming years, Hamill and

Magee walked from one scrape to another with alarming frequency. One day they went to see a man about a dog in the Markets area of central Belfast. As they turned the corner the PIRA launched a rocket at an RUC Land Rover and killed the driver. The pair scurried into a house to take cover, but twenty minutes later the police kicked through the front door believing the murderers to be inside. They were held, interrogated and released before hurrying back to north Belfast to drink away the ordeal. The next morning Eamonn rose and looked out Hamill's front window, which had a view of the Sacred Heart Presbytery. As he was still intoxicated, it took a few seconds for his vision to defog and his brain to process the sight in front of him. 'C'mere Hamill. Quick!' he shouted with bewildered glee.

The two men stood watching Johnny 5 from the *Short Circuit* movies potter about the church steps. Up and round he went on his tracks, his camera peering over walls and around corners, his mechanical pincer probing at a suspicious-looking bag at the church door. From stage right, a big fat green soldier in an antique diving helmet waddled onto the scene. The men were tipsily mesmerised by the whole surreal performance. Eamonn moved to reach for a beer to better enjoy the show and immediately the soldier in the protective, oversized suit spun around. When he saw Magee and Hamill at the window his eyes widened and his arms began flapping.

'Get down,' he roared. 'Away from the window!'

One controlled explosion later, an RUC officer knocked on the door. 'Fuck sake, Eamonn,' he said. 'The whole street was evacuated – what the fuck were you playing at?'

They knew him by name by now. It wasn't the first time they'd knocked on that door. Sometimes they didn't bother with that formality. As much as the IRA liked to believe that they represented law and order in the district, the regular cops kept an eye on incidents like entire kitchens going walkabout as well. The RUC were determined to pin something substantial on Eamonn and raids on Hamill's flat when Magee was lodging became a regular occurrence. And well aware of his fistic reputation, they tended to come in heavy-handed, a full squad in riot gear storming up the narrow staircase into the first-floor dwelling.

Early one morning a strange pressure on Hamill's chest roused him slowly and painfully from a drunken slumber. It was no succubus but a meaty police arm forcibly holding him down under a Perspex riot shield. In the background his small flat was quickly filling with the dark uniforms of the RUC.

'James Hamill,' he heard someone yell amidst the commotion, 'you're under arrest.'

Meanwhile in the spare room, Eamonn was just back from the bathroom and wondering what all the fuss was about. *Brits wanting an up-to-date photo for their collection?* he wondered with a smirk to himself.

'Get up, Magee,' someone commanded. 'On your feet.'

Eamonn obliged, wearing nothing but a cocky grin, unashamed of his total nakedness. Behind him on the bed lay a blonde who was not Mary, equally unclothed but slightly more alarmed and abashed by the goings-on. He dressed and was cuffed. Outside on the landing he bumped into a dazed and confused Hamill still trying to make sense of the situation.

'Go sit down and relax, James Gerard Hamilton,' Eamonn teased. 'These gentlemen are only here for me.'

'Actually,' one of the RUC interrupted, 'we're here for Mr Hamill as well this time.'

It turned out they were struggling for justification to launch a fresh raid on the property to grab Magee when some bright spark at the station stumbled upon Hamill's unpaid, eighty-pound drunk and disorderly fine from a few years back. An arrest warrant for fall-guy Hamill was swiftly issued so the riot squad could kick in the front door and then, conveniently, pick up Eamonn in the process. Both men were bundled out the door and into separate cars, but while Magee was back in bed by lunchtime, poor Hamill spent a night in Maghaberry Prison as his beer-addled mind struggled to comprehend his latest unfortunate milieu.

But to Eamonn, the police were little more than a minor irritant. They could rarely find enough hard evidence to convict him of anything worth worrying about and he had a good lawyer to deal with the rest anyway. It was always the IRA that posed the more serious threat and they too were now well aware that he could more often than not be found in Glenview Street.

***

Magee, Hamill, Connolly and another man, Martin Clarke, had watched them gather on the street below all evening and it didn't look good. When the Provos believed they had a critical mass large enough to contain any physical violence from Eamonn and his pals, they crossed the street, climbed the stairs and entered into the flat.

'What's this all about, for fuck sake?' Hamill began pleadingly but he was immediately pushed against the wall.

'I'm fucking warning you, Hamill,' he was told, 'keep your mouth shut or I'll put a bullet in you.' All the uninvited guests were armed and not with replicas.

They separated Clarkey and Eamonn from the group and pushed them into the spare bedroom at the back of the property. There the pair racked their brains, frantically trying to second-guess what the RA were doing here and align their alibis accordingly. At one point Eamonn opened the window and considered the drop. It was a guaranteed broken ankle at best but that might be better than what the Provos had in store. Soon, however, Magee was hauled out and placed with Connolly and Hamill in the living room.

'Do you hear that?' Connolly suddenly asked about ten minutes later.

They all stood still and listened to the nothingness.

'They're gone.'

The paramilitaries were indeed gone, but they had taken Clarkey with them, bound, hooded and driven into the night. An hour later the hood was removed and he found himself tied to a chair in an unknown location. There, he was beaten with fists and sticks and kicked with steel-toed boots until he was recorded telling the Provos what they wanted to hear. They then put a bullet in his leg and dumped him on Jamaica Street.

The RA later played Doc the tape before they dealt with his son. In amongst the squeals and thuds and yelps, Clarkey was heard to reveal how Magee and others had stripped a derelict house and sold the valuable fireplace that was contained within. It was the Provos' house.

'They've got you banged to rights, son,' Doc said to Eamonn. 'You'll need to go with them. Clarkey was singing like a canary. You may need to teach him to keep his mouth shut – he wouldn't fucking stop talking!'

Kneecapping or forced expatriation off the island of Ireland were the options on the table this time and there wasn't a lawyer on the planet who could get these charges dismissed. Like his father before him, Eamonn wisely chose exile. The next morning, he was sat in the back of a taxi heading to the City Airport beside one of the others involved in the theft, when he suddenly broke the sullen silence to tell the driver to turn around.

'We need to make a quick stop at the Royal, mate,' he said. 'We're leaving because that fat bastard Clarkey touted on us. The least we can do is stop in and say our goodbyes.'

In the hospital lift as it rose to his friend's ward, Eamonn issued the orders. 'Don't even look at him. Just find where he was shot and start punching. Don't stop until I say so.'

They found Clarkey in his bed, lying alongside a dozen other convalescing trauma victims. Without saying a word, Magee drew the pale-blue curtain that circumnavigated the bed and turned on his startled target. For a full ten seconds, the two men laid into the man they blamed for the next untold months or years they would have to spend away from family and friends in a foreign land. Magee bludgeoned his face repeatedly while the other man focused on the wounded leg as instructed. Then, as suddenly as the attack had begun, it ended. Magee parted the curtain and walked away. Throughout the entire savage assault, not one word had been spoken between the three men.

'Don't run,' Eamonn whispered. 'Let's just walk out of here as calmly as we walked in.'

As they exited the ward they heard Clarkey shout out between agonised sobs, 'You're two mad bastards!'

Years later, the Provo who signed off on the decision to exile the pair was standing beside Eamonn at the Shamrock bar. 'You did the right thing calling in at the hospital, by the way,' he said out of the blue. 'I'd have done exactly the same thing.'

∗∗∗

The pair flew to London where Isobel's brother Charlie lived and ran a demolition business. Long since back home in the Ardoyne, Charlie remembers the nine months with his nephew in the English capital with that common mixture of mirth and exasperation that Eamonn so easily inspires. He immediately put the pair to work knocking down walls and hauling rubble. His own blood was a useful pair of hands to have on site but Eamonn's partner in crime rarely pulled his substantial weight. They slept on Charlie's floor for the first few weeks until a couple of pay packets were earned and they could move into their own spartan digs above the Blackstock Pub at the southern tip of Finsbury Park. It was a handy place to live for that is where the wages were both distributed on a Friday afternoon and pissed up against the wall by the following Monday morning. On their first night above the bar the landlord naively told them to help themselves in the kitchen if they needed a bite to eat to keep them going until they could pay the supermarket a visit. He meant to make a slice of toast and a cup of tea. Eamonn polished off four sirloin steaks and the kind invitation was immediately revoked.

The two young men hated every minute they were in London with a passion. Though they were barely a one-hour flight from Northern

Ireland, it was as if they had stepped off the plane onto a different planet. It was also, in many respects, a hostile planet. It may have been a decade removed from *No Irish, No Blacks, No Dogs* signs hanging on pub doors and shop windows, but an early 1990s surge in IRA attacks on the British mainland guaranteed criminals from north Belfast were not the most welcome of immigrants in 1994 and Eamonn's combative nature did the rest. Pub by pub they found themselves barred from establishments up and down the Seven Sisters Road as one or the other took offence to the tone of a local interlocutor and took the matter into their own fists. It wasn't long before they were more or less restricted to doing the vast majority of their boozing in the Blackstock itself. There, just a flight of stairs away from where they slept, they could relax and the regulars knew enough not to provoke them.

Plenty of the punters were from the large Afro-Caribbean community that resided in north London, but back then it was a rarity to see blacks and whites sitting together drinking a pint. Not accustomed to encountering skin any darker than what a pale Irishman can present after a fortnight on the Costa del Sol, Eamonn was blind to the unspoken and voluntary segregation that took place in the pub. Soon, when the black guys came in, he would throw his money on the table and join in the marathon dominos sessions that carried on until last orders.

But all Eamonn really wanted was to go home. At the end of 1994 he ventured back for Christmas and sent tentative feelers out to gauge how a permanent return would be received. To his surprise, there appeared to be no major opposition to him moving back into the district. Perhaps the IRA were more preoccupied with matters of vastly greater importance than wild Eamonn Magee and his tearaway friends. Sinn Féin were now fully engaged in peace talks with the British government and in August the Provos had announced a ceasefire. There were still several rocky years ahead before Northern Ireland could claim to enjoy anything resembling bona fide peace, but it was a hugely important step towards that Holy

Grail. In light of the history being made in the halls of Stormont and Westminster, Magee was given a pass.

Eamonn went straight home to Mary Doll and the kids, but any hopes she had that he had turned over a new leaf and was ready to settle down into fatherhood were soon dashed. Welcome-home drinks led to welcome-home drugs and within days he fell back into the same old routine. At a total loss, Mary looked to Isobel and Eamonn's brothers for help and at the beginning of 1995 a family meeting was called in Holmdene Gardens. Noel came up from Newcastle, Patrick from Ligoniel, and even Terrence sobered up enough to contribute. Though they didn't term it as such at the time, it was effectively an intervention to attempt to save Eamonn from himself.

One by one they tried reasoning with him. *Where is your life headed?* they asked. *The drink and especially the drugs are destroying you. The police are going to catch up with you if the RA don't get to you first. Mary needs a stable partner and your three kids need a present father.*

Eamonn erupted. Already destabilised by all the alcohol and pills in his system, he now felt backed into a corner and attacked by those closest to him. Consumed by paranoia, he lashed out both verbally and physically. Insults were hurled and furniture sent flying across the room until his brothers moved to restrain him.

'You can all fuck off and leave me alone,' he roared as he struggled free and slammed the door off its hinges on the way out.

In his devastating wake the family sat in a shell-shocked silence. There was no Plan B and no one wanted to be the first to speak. Finally Noel rose, got into his Ford Escort and drove back to Newcastle. On the journey home he continually looked at his back seats in the rear-view mirror and could still see his wee brother lying there with his red blood flowing from a freshly made bullet hole in his left calf. *It'll probably be more than a flesh wound next time*, he thought.

That evening, Noel couldn't bring himself to answer when his wife asked how it had gone. He went to bed but couldn't sleep as visions of the whole depressing charade in Holmdene kept buzzing about his head. After a couple of hours he got up, found a pen and paper, and sat down to write his first ever letter to his brother. All the things it was impossibly difficult to say to Eamonn's face, Noel poured onto the page in a heartfelt stream of consciousness. He expressed his love, his fear, his pride, his worry, his admiration and his hope for his baby brother.

It's boxing, Eamonn, he wrote. *You have to get back in the gym.*

At that time Noel was in his tenth year as a pro and he knew there was not much left of his own career. His most recent win, over John J. Cooke, had taken place before Eamonn's exile and had led to nothing. He didn't know what was around the corner but he wanted to bring his brother into the Belfast professional boxing fraternity before he himself had thrown his last punch in anger.

Come with me to speak with John Breen and Barney Eastwood before it's too late, he concluded his plea.

The next morning he drove back to Belfast and knocked on the front door in Rosapenna Street. Mary let him in and showed him up the stairs. He'd hoped to read the letter through with Eamonn there and then but, finding him comatose after an all-nighter, he merely tossed the folded page on top of his unconscious brother and hoped for the best.

Three days later, Noel answered the phone in Newcastle.

'Let's go and see Breen then,' he heard that unmistakeable, gruff voice say.

***

Born and raised in west Belfast during the 1950s, John Breen is the most successful professional boxing trainer in Irish history. As is so often the case in the noble art, he learned how to teach the hard way: by taking a beating himself between the ropes. He was first known as a decent amateur, winning multiple Ulster titles fighting out of the Immaculata Club based in the basement of the infamous republican tower blocks known as the

Divis Flats. In 1975 he turned pro and was trundling along fine until he ran into future world-title challenger Tony Sibson and then came out on the short end of a trilogy with the less-distinguished Peter Mullins. Those defeats bestowed a middleweight-journeyman status on Breen and he spent the next four years losing far more than he won in leisure centres and town halls across the UK. He made his final stand in Beechmount sports centre in Belfast in November 1979 and battled to a respectable eight-round draw with Dennis Pryce. It was as good a way to bow out as any.

After retirement, John spent a few years helping kids in the amateur game until Barney Eastwood came calling in the late 1980s. Eastwood was the undisputed Don of Irish boxing at that time, having spent most of the decade putting the sport back on the Northern Irish map as he guided Barry McGuigan through his illustrious career. That relationship soured in the searing heat of a Las Vegas car park, but Barney soon had new prospective champions coming through and he wanted Breen to train them in his Castle Street gym in Belfast city centre. Big John didn't let anyone down.

Under Breen's tutelage, Dave 'Boy' McAuley became International Boxing Federation (IBF) flyweight world champion, Fabrice Benichou the IBF super bantamweight champion, Paul Hodkinson the WBC featherweight champion, Crisanto España the World Boxing Association (WBA) welterweight champion and Victor Cordoba the WBA super middleweight king. It was a remarkable run of success but, of course, it couldn't last forever. In 1992 McAuley, Cordoba and Benichou all lost their world titles. Hodkinson's slipped away the following year and when Ike Quartey stopped España in the eleventh round in 1994, Eastwood's gym was suddenly without a champion again. By 1995 McAuley, España, Cordoba and Hodkinson had all retired, while Benichou, outclassed by Wayne McCullough in Dublin at the end of 1994, was back in France and happy to see out his career at a lower level.

Sam Storey, Oscar Checa and Noel Magee were Eastwood and Breen's only established regulars at this point and so they were in the market for fresh blood on the day Noel brought his little brother along to the gym. Barney had been eager to sign up Eamonn as a teen with a world amateur silver medal in his pocket but now, five years later, he wasn't so sure. After a brief meeting in the corner of the gym, Eastwood instructed Breen to find out as much as he could about the kid before any decision was made. A week later, the trainer reported back with his findings.

'I asked about forty people about him, Barney, and they all said the exact same thing,' he began. 'There is no doubt the guy is one hell of a fighter. But there is even less doubt that he's a complete asshole.'

That was all Eastwood needed to hear. As a highly successful gambling man, he knew all about weighing up risk versus reward and he could see no value in this punt. He invited Eamonn in to see him and rather than simply say thanks but no thanks, he presented an offer: £500 for ten wins. To the betting man, Eamonn was like a 10,000-to-1 shot and this was the equivalent of wagering a pound just for a laugh. It was so derisory that Barney knew there wasn't a chance in hell that Eamonn would go for it and there was no surprise when the contract was thrown back in his face with an aggressively novel suggestion about where it could be filed away.

On the one hand Breen was relieved. He didn't want to waste his time on someone who didn't live the required life and from whom he would never receive 100 per cent in the gym. But at the same time he was intrigued by the stories of Magee's frightening natural talent that spouted from the mouths of people who had no time for the Ardoyne man whatsoever. He also had Noel, nibbling away at him every day, begging him to give his brother a chance. So John began letting Eamonn into the gym to work out while Noel was training. After a few weeks, permission was granted for him to start using the speed and heavy bags as well. Finally, if there was time while Noel warmed down, he'd take the youngest Magee on the pads for a couple of rounds to see what he had. A guy like John Breen recognises ability when he sees it and it wasn't long before he started to think that maybe it was worth taking a chance on the boy after all. There was one remaining avenue open to a Belfast fighter hoping to break into the professional big time and Breen decided to explore it.

In his last hurrah in Beechmount Leisure Centre, Breen had been distracted throughout the eight rounds by a particularly insistent voice at ringside cheering on his opponent. When the final bell rang and his trainer was towelling him down, he asked where all the noise had been coming from. 'Some blonde over there,' he was told, and looking through the ropes he spied the most beautiful woman he had even seen at a boxing match on the other side of the ring. But in all the milling around that precedes a professional bout, he lost her in the crowd and thought no more about it.

A couple of months later, he was upstairs in the office of one of the nightclubs that he arranged security for when a burly bouncer knocked on the door to say there was a group of women downstairs insisting that they be allowed in.

'If we're full, we're full,' John replied. 'Tell them to come earlier next weekend.'

'One of them is saying she's Mike Callahan's daughter,' came the doorman's reply.

John shook his head and sighed. He considered repeating his initial response, but at the last second decided he'd go down and take a look himself. Once at the door he saw a group of four young women and most prominent amongst them was the blonde who had been screaming out for Dennis Pryce as the Englishman tried to take John's head off in Beechmount. Being the gentleman he is, there were no hard feelings from Breen, so he let the ladies in. One thing led to another, and John and Laura Breen, née Callahan, remain happily married to this day.

***

Mike Callahan fell in love with boxing when he stood on Distillery Football Club's Grosvenor Park pitch to watch Al Little and Patsy Quinn battle for fifteen rounds in 1938. Years later he would stage his own show there when Mick Leahy beat Boswell St Louis, but not before he had made his name as a matchmaker for the legendary English boxing promoter of the 1950s and 1960s, Jack Solomons. He put together the bills for such historic nights as when Randolph Turpin beat the great Sugar Ray Robinson in the Earl's Court Arena in 1951, and Henry Cooper's first crack at a young Cassius Clay in Wembley Stadium in 1963. During the latter event Mike became firm friends with the millionaire businessman and boxing promoter Jarvis Astaire. Astaire, who guided the careers of the likes of Frank Bruno and Terry Downes, described Callahan as the most intelligent man he had ever met and was convinced Mike would make himself a fortune within weeks if he moved to London where opportunities for men with his sharp business acumen were everywhere to be found.

But Mike loved his wife, he loved his kids and he loved his city. Taking what he learned from Solomons, Astaire and the rest, he began promoting his own shows in Belfast, introducing a young Barney Eastwood to the sport along the way. In the late 1960s he was packing out the Ulster Hall every three months, but when the Troubles flared up in the early 1970s, professional boxing was one of the many industries in Northern Ireland that was forced to practically shut down for a couple of decades. Visiting fighters are happy to assume the inherent risks that exist once they climb between the ropes, but they are less keen on taking chances with bombs and bullets on the streets as they make their way to the ring. Mike drifted away from an active role in the sport but, now he was approaching his seventieth birthday, there remained an itch he found harder and harder to resist scratching.

One night over dinner, John decided to mention Eamonn to his father-in-law. 'Noel Magee keeps talking about getting his brother into the game,' he began.

'And?' was Mike's typically forthright response.

'Barney's not interested.'

'Why not?'

'Eamonn has a bad reputation. He's a wild man. Drink, drugs, been shot and exiled by the Provos. He's got a big ugly scar on his neck from a street fight as a kid.'

'And what's your feeling?'

'I'm not sure.'

'Well, can he box?'

'Oh, he can box all right. He has talent to burn.'

They finished their dinner and Mike retired to his armchair with a glass of wine to mull it over. Just before he went to sleep he looked in on his son-in-law.

'Set up a meeting with young Magee.'

***

Callahan was physically small in stature but he more than made up for that with the sheer force of his personality. They called him a gangster, but more from affection than fear. More than anything he was a great talker. 'Horses' balls are lemons,' was one of his favourite sayings. 'If you can convince someone that a horse's balls are lemons you've got them just where you want them.' He was a throwback, the type of sharp, fast-talking besuited gent that would have fit right in on Jacobs Beach in the 1940s. He was close with all the current big-hitters this side of the pond. Barney Eastwood, Frank Warren, Barry Hearn, Mickey Duff, Frank Maloney – they all liked Mike, but more importantly they respected him. He was perfect for the boxing world and, as it turned out, perfect for Eamonn Magee.

Despite the forty-five-year age gap, the pair immediately hit it off. Eamonn loved how Mike carried himself and went about his business, treating men like men and taking no shit from anyone. He liked the thinking-man's-gangster reputation that Callahan had cultivated and knew he had the connections to start making him some money. There were no deals or written contracts and the financial side of things was not discussed in any great detail in that first meeting. Mike just said he wouldn't take a penny from Eamonn's purses until the Ardoyne man had earned over five grand. They departed with a handshake and an unspoken agreement that they were now fighter and manager. Or, as Eamonn always put it, fighter and *the Boss*.

Magee was eager to get his professional career up and running as soon as possible. After nine months of training six days a week with Breen – an extended probationary period to prove his commitment to this toughest of sports – he felt he had earned the right to fight. He had also been inspired by the opportunity to watch his big brother in action during the most eventful six months of his career. In March 1995 Noel was stopped in four rounds by the great Frenchman Fabrice Tiozzo. Three months later Tiozzo out-boxed the legendary Mike McCallum to claim the WBC world light heavyweight crown and he went on to win two further world titles, so Noel took heart from sharing the ring with such quality. He carried that momentum forward into May and the opportunity to realise the goal he had set himself when he turned pro a decade earlier: to win the British Commonwealth title.

Standing in his way was the champion Garry Delaney, an unbeaten light heavyweight from London. Noel would have to do it the hard way and win in Delaney's back yard, so the whole family set sail for Essex to offer their support. During the ringwalks, some of the Magee party took exception to unnecessarily aggressive heckling a couple of rows behind them and, as the temperature rose, Isobel slipped from her seat and snuck off to the toilets. Nervous but strong, when her boys were fighting, the nerves dominated. In the bathroom she met a glamorous young woman touching up her makeup. Isobel was pacing up and down, scrunching the life out of a tissue in her small fist, and finally the woman asked her if she was all right.

'Oh, I'll be fine when it's all over,' Isobel replied. 'My son is fighting now but I prefer not to watch.'

'Don't worry,' came the response. 'It always looks worse than it really is. I'm sure your son will be okay.'

By now a third lady had come out of a cubicle and was drying her hands as Mrs Magee thanked the kind young woman now making her way out to watch the fight.

'Do you not know who that was?' she asked Isobel when the noise of the hand dryer had ceased.

Isobel merely looked back with a puzzled expression.

'That was Jodie Marsh, Garry Delaney's girlfriend!'

Twenty minutes later, Isobel's daughter-in-law came charging into the toilets to find her, screaming that Garry had quit on his stool and Noel was the new champion. Isobel ran out and wiped away the tears to see her son standing in the ring with the Commonwealth belt held aloft over his head and his wife near strangling him in a congratulatory embrace. Looking to ringside she then found her other boxing son gazing up at his big brother in a wash of joy and pride and exhilaration. The party back in the hotel room, fuelled by the cases of beer the boys had left chilling in the bathtub in anticipation of a celebration, carried on through the night.

Noel's reign was short and sweet, however. Four months later he lost to Welshman Nicky Piper in Cardiff Arms Park as the main support to Naseem Hamed defeating local hero Steve Robinson to claim his first world title. Eamonn carried his brother's belt in front of 16,000 that night and as he looked around and soaked in the atmosphere during the long walk to the ring, he thought to himself, *I could get used to this.*

He only had two more months to wait.

5

ROBBERY AND REVENGE

'I want to finish him, John. I want the stoppage.'

'Just box, son. There's no rush in this game, you get paid the same either way.'

'I want the knockout.'

Eamonn rose to commence the fourth round of his pro debut on a Steve Collins undercard in the Point Theatre, Dublin, on 25 November 1995. In the opposite corner, Pete Roberts stood up and walked to the centre of the ring for the customary touching of gloves to signify that the final round is nigh. Roberts was out of his depth of course. The Hull man had been fighting for eight years but he was currently caught in the riptide of a five-fight losing streak that would soon see him hang up his gloves for good. He was actually victorious in his first bout back in 1988, but when he lost his next three against novices, the short, stocky super lightweight accepted the role of journeyman on the boxing food chain. When a prospect came along with real potential, Roberts was the type of guy the matchmakers called upon to provide a minimal risk workout for a promoter's latest golden egg.

There was never any doubt that Magee was going to win, and he had comfortably controlled the first three rounds to emphasise that point, but, this being his inaugural appearance in the professional ring, Eamonn was determined to make a statement. On the eve of the fight he had spoken of his style being tailor-made for the pro game. He liked to plant his feet and let his shots go. He was going to adapt easily and become European champion at the very least. Such big words needed a big performance. Pete Roberts couldn't be allowed to hear the final bell.

As the seconds ticked away, Magee began throwing his combinations with a little more spite. He made it personal in his head, shouting to himself that this guy wasn't going to take the shine off his debut, that he wasn't going the distance with him. He believed he would disappoint the family and friends who had travelled south to watch him begin his career if points, rather than submission or unconsciousness, determined his victory. Needing a referee's scorecard to confirm his superiority seemed like an insult to his ability as he whaled on a faltering adversary who attempted to hold on for dear life. Simply hearing the timbre of the final bell would be Roberts' victory.

And the journeyman looked like he was going to make it too. But with the end fast approaching, Eamonn wrestled himself free from Roberts' smothering embrace before taking a stride back into range and throwing a forceful uppercut into his man's body. His left glove rammed into Roberts' torso, just below the bottom rib, and the Englishman gasped before deflating onto the canvas floor. There he knelt and listened in breathless pain as the referee's count arrived at ten. There were just five seconds left on the clock.

Magee raised that dangerous gloved fist above his head and reached out to salute his fans, but they were nowhere to be seen. A full coach-load had set off from Belfast but got delayed along the way and ended up missing the entire bout.

As the arena gradually filled for the Celtic Warrior in the main event, Eamonn hung around to watch the rest of the supporting acts. As always within the tight-knit world of Irish boxing, there were connections, friend and foe, in nearly every match-up. His good pal Paul Griffin was impressive as he moved to 4 and 0. One of the Carruth brothers, the golden boy Michael, was less so as he plodded to his own victory. Paschal Collins then dealt handily with a limited journeyman to keep his own fledgling, unbeaten career on track before his brother was dragged down to his opponent's level in the main event and laboured to an unspectacular decision.

Mark Winters, the man who beat Eamonn in his last amateur bout, stopped John O'Johnson in the evening's other welterweight bout but Magee was unimpressed. A rivalry, fuelled by Magee's inability to digest the loss in the 1994 Ulster final and his paranoid belief that Winters lorded it over him, was festering between the two 147 pounders.

'Get me in the ring with that bastard,' he said to Breen as they looked on. 'I'd beat him tomorrow.'

Just after midnight, in a virtually empty arena, local boy Jim Rock made his own professional bow in a super welterweight contest. It was of interest to Magee because the Pink Panther, as Rock was known, was also a Mike Callahan and John Breen fighter. He was a ticket seller like Eamonn and Callahan planned to bring them along together until they were headlining their own shows. The two were Mike's entire stable at this point in time, their potential the sole reason for his re-entry into the boxing business. He placed a lot of faith in both young men and, luckily enough, the pair immediately hit it off and had no problem training, travelling and fighting alongside one another.

In March 1996 both appeared on the undercard of Steve Collins' next defence of his WBO super middleweight title against Neville Brown in Millstreet, Co. Cork. Jim beat the unheralded Peter Mitchell on points while Carruth, Winters and Griffin were again present and victorious. Magee was matched with Steve McGovern from the Isle of Wight. McGovern was on a bad run of form but he had lost only one of his first twelve outings and he knew his way around the ring. As an opponent for a second fight, he was certainly no easy touch. McGovern had the added attraction of having toed the line with Michael Carruth the previous year. Something about the Carruth boxing dynasty in the amateurs had always needled Magee. He was convinced that any deal he ever received from the IABA was as raw as steak tartare, while the powers that be prioritised the careers of a chosen few like Michael Carruth and his siblings. How much truth there ever was in Eamonn's perception is open to debate, but it was real in his own mind and it had spurred him on in the 1993 Irish seniors semi-final when he outclassed Michael's brother Fergal. Now, just a fight into his pro career, he was gunning for the Olympic golden boy, telling the *Belfast Telegraph* that he'd love to take Michael on in an Irish title fight. McGovern had lasted until two minutes and fifty-eight seconds of the fourth round against Carruth in what was the Olympian's ninth bout, so Magee had his target.

From the opening bell, Eamonn went for the kill. He stalked his man around the ring, jabbing him into position from his southpaw stance and then loading up on shots in an effort to blast the Englishman out in the first stanza. But McGovern was cute and knew how to squirm out of danger and survive. As a light puncher he offered practically no offensive threat and it was soon clear that his sole objective was to go the distance in the scheduled four-rounder. Magee grew more frantic as the rounds went on, so determined was he to better Carruth. In his own head it was probably the Dubliner he was fighting rather than the game McGovern. In the end he wanted it too much, he forced it when he should have let it flow. The final bell chimed and, though he had won every round by a distance, to Eamonn it almost felt like a defeat.

In contrast to Magee's glass-half-empty outlook, Callahan was delighted with how the first four months had gone. Mike, who had helped make the legendary battle between John Caldwell and the Ardoyne's Freddie Gilroy in 1962, had witnessed first-hand all the great Irish post-war boxers. He saw in Eamonn the same qualities that Jimmy Warnock, Tommy Armour and John Kelly, three southpaws regarded as the best the island of Ireland has ever produced, had possessed. Callahan was also fully aware that, like that famous trio, Magee was big at the box office. He and Rock had sold more tickets than the rest of the undercards combined in Dublin and Cork, and Callahan couldn't wait to bring Eamonn home to Belfast. The Steve Collins shows were staged by Frank Warren's Queensberry Promotions but now Barry Hearn of Matchroom Boxing had taken note of Magee's talent and the level of support he commanded. Hearn was putting on a show in the Ulster Hall in a couple of months and was soon on the phone to Callahan offering Eamonn a spot on the bill.

By now he had been handed the boxing moniker 'Terminator' by the local boxing reporter David Kelly. Eamonn had no say in the nickname and it was never one with which he was entirely enamoured. Taken from James Cameron's sci-fi movie franchise, it conjured up images of Arnold Schwarzenegger's relentless, unstoppable, genocidal android, which were totally at odds with Magee's slick but aggressive counter-punching approach in the ring. But with neither Eamonn nor anyone else offering a usable alternative, 'Terminator' stuck with him for the remainder of his career.

Callahan accepted Hearn's offer and on 28 May 1996 Eamonn returned to the Ulster Hall for the first time since the 1994 Ulster final. It was the first of Matchroom Boxing's Belfast Fight Nights and although Neil Sinclair, now also managed by Callahan, and Darren Corbett's names appeared in a larger font on the advertising posters, it was Magee who stole the show. He was matched with John Stovin, a tall and rangy fellow southpaw from Hull. The Englishman had a distinct reach advantage but Magee proved he was the stronger man in the early clinches and caught Stovin with cuffing lead left hooks, almost at will. With barely a minute gone in the first session, the local fighter followed one of those hooks with a quick right straight down the pipe that put Stovin on the seat of his satin shorts. He rose quickly, too quickly, and with a distressed and stunned look in his eyes he wandered towards his corner on unsteady pins. Magee scented blood and, as the capacity crowd roared that atavistic boxing-crowd roar, he bludgeoned Stovin from one side of the ring to the other and back again before the man from Hull dropped to a knee for refuge. Most believed that was that, but to Stovin's eternal credit he made full use of a nine-count to recalibrate his battered equipment. He then rose to see out the round, much as a piece of flotsam might survive a force-ten gale on the high seas. But it was just a temporary respite and when yet another ferocious left connected thirty seconds into the second round, referee David Irving saved the brave Stovin from himself.

Sitting at ringside next to Callahan, Barry Hearn leapt from his seat to applaud Magee as the ref waved it off. He followed the victor to his dressing room and congratulated him on both his performance and, tellingly, the ease with which he had sold almost 300 tickets. Speaking to reporters later, the London promoter was effusive in his praise for Eamonn, words like 'sensational' and 'world class' rolling off his tongue.

'He really stood out,' Hearn told the *Belfast Telegraph*. 'I want to do a deal with Mike Callahan because Eamonn can play a key role in future Ulster Hall shows. At this stage it is not who you are beating but the way you do it and Magee clearly has great potential.' The pure business mind of the qualified accountant then came to the fore when he added, 'The atmosphere when Magee was fighting couldn't be ignored. He sold a lot of tickets and that's another reason why I would like to work with him and Mike.'

Callahan, as shrewd as any of the big-hitters in control of British and Irish boxing, knew to keep his cards close to his chest. 'I found Hearn a very pleasant man to deal with,' he responded diplomatically when asked about the interest in his young boxer, 'and he was very impressed by Eamonn. But then again, so was Frank Warren.'

Hearn had made his substantial offer to promote Eamonn before he left the arena that night, but Mike kept his cool and told the Matchroom supremo that he would consider it along with the others currently on the table. He welcomed the praise and attention from such a prominent player, but professional boxing is a minefield and Callahan was canny enough to tread carefully, regardless of how much of a sure thing a path appeared to be.

Magee's performance had undoubtedly made him the talk of the town, however. Despite Corbett scoring a first-round knockout in the headline fight and Sinclair clinically dispatching a decent opponent inside five as the main support, it was Eamonn who woke up to all the plaudits in the following morning's press. Crisanto España, the former world welterweight champion, led the eulogies.

'A blind man could see the class this guy has,' the Belfast-based Venezuelan enthused. 'Magee looked the best of the boys tonight and he can go a very long way. He moves very well and even though it is only his third fight he looks like a very good professional. The way he went about beating his opponent impressed me a great deal.'

Hearn, chasing Magee's signature above all others, also confirmed what everyone in boxing circles had long suspected: Eamonn was already the biggest draw in Northern Irish boxing. That fact made him the obvious man to call out when fellow light welterweights were interviewed by local hacks. Within a week, both Winters and Paddy Loughran, younger brother of Eamonn, the recently deposed and retired WBO welterweight champion of the world, had made noises in the papers about fighting Magee. But Eamonn instinctively understood his latent worth and he knew that, despite his relative inexperience, he was the man in a position to call the shots. Loughran had already dilly-dallied over the chance to face him and would do nothing to boost Eamonn's ranking anyway, so he was sliding out of the equation. Winters was personal, due to that amateur defeat, but Magee doubted the Antrim man genuinely wanted the rematch and insisted he was not losing any sleep over the fight being made or not.

Underlying everything was Magee's belief that they needed him and not the other way around. 'I'm the one the fans are coming to see,' he told David Kelly. 'I would like to top my own show soon, but really I'm doing that anyway because I'm the biggest ticket seller. I know I'm a special fighter.'

It was a risky swagger for a three-fight novice, but nobody could refute the confident words. And when Dubliner Ray Kane, a recent addition to the Eastwood gym, pulled out of his Irish cruiserweight title fight with

Darren Corbett just two days before the bout in September, Magee's fight against Manchester's Kevin McKillan was the obvious choice to be bumped up to headliner status.

The Mancunian made all the right noises at the pre-fight weigh-in. He had no fear of Magee's street-fighting, hard-man reputation, claiming he was a son of Ardoyne himself. In fact, his parents had left the district for mainland Britain when McKillan was still a toddler, but he hoped the fact would spare him the worst of the vitriol from the crowd under the bright lights of the Ulster Hall. He also boasted a winning record after twenty-seven fights and believed his greater professional experience would give him a chance of the upset. It didn't and a befuddled McKillan was out-classed before being stopped midway through the fifth. In just his fourth professional bout, Eamonn was a winning headliner in a fight-mad city.

***

Hearn and Callahan wanted to keep Magee as busy as possible and, so long as he kept making short work of his opponents, there was no reason why he couldn't fight every couple of months. Just days after the McKillan victory, Eamonn was back in the gym with John Breen, keeping in shape and ready for the call when it came.

As far as Breen and Callahan knew, Eamonn was living the life of a disciplined professional boxer at this stage. John diligently kept track of his prospect's comings and goings in a ledger and was proud to say that young Magee hadn't been marked down as absent since he came on board. He was out of the house at 7.30 a.m. for a five-mile run before relaxing and arriving fresh at the Castle Street gym at 1 p.m. on the dot. There, in the claustrophobic sweat-box where the temperature remained tropical thanks to an array of gas heaters on full blast, he'd warm up intensely for twenty minutes before sparring four, six or eight rounds with Rock or whoever was on hand to give him an honest workout. Breen then took him on the pads for a few rounds to work on the speed and accuracy of his punches. A stint on the heavy bag helped build up his power, bench exercises strengthened his core, and a prolonged skipping routine then quickened and lightened his feet. Throughout the daily two- or three-hour session, the sweat lashed off Magee's features and no one who witnessed the torture he put his body through could doubt that he was giving it his all. The problem for Eamonn was always what happened when he walked out the gym doors, turned the corner and was out of sight.

Part of the issue was that these early four-round contests against second- or third-rate opponents were no real challenge to Magee. He knew he could get through them without putting in any more effort than had been required ahead of a tournament at elite amateur level. That meant if he gave it his all in the gym for a couple of hours each day, he could get away with giving even more in the bars and clubs and bedrooms of Belfast when the sun went down.

Even moving away from the Ardoyne failed to tame Eamonn. With all the top promoters in the UK buttering him up, he was earning decent money from the first bell, much more than a novice pro starting off today could expect. He took a chunk of it and moved his family out of Rosapenna Street and eight miles down the M1 motorway to the newly built Lagmore estate on the fringes of west Belfast. Breen and Callahan took it as a further sign that the wild man was settling down, but in truth he was just going undercover.

Cocaine was now on the table to supplement the alcohol and pills, and a few lines of charlie never resulted in an early night. Mary would still accompany her man on occasion at the weekend, but she and the kids were already resigned to daddy not being home for a few days if a midweek session took off. There was always a bed for him in Hamill's and, unbeknown to Mary, always a woman, any woman, to share it with.

Perhaps subconsciously frustrated by the lack of genuine physical threat inside the ring, Eamonn continued to find violence on the street with alarming frequency. The presence of the British Army in Belfast had gradually diminished in line with the reduced threat from the IRA, but the Queen's men still patrolled perceived high-risk districts like the Ardoyne and still found themselves in contact with Magee. He and Hamill bumped into a squaddie separated from his pack one night as they rounded the corner of the entry between the Shamrock and the Flax Centre shops.

'You're the boxer, ain't ya?' the armed soldier said in a tone he left open to interpretation as the two men sought to walk on by.

'Yeah that's right, you're the local hard man,' the Brit continued, quickly warming to his task of dispelling the boredom of his routine by antagonising a civilian.

Eamonn paused and turned to look at the man while an anxious Hamill tugged at his sleeve and urged him to walk on. Despite being on his own, the soldier was somehow emboldened and obviously keen to engage with the fighter.

'I remember your old man, Magee,' he said, talking of Doc as if he was already gone, ramping up the provocation.

Hamill's non-confrontational heart sank.

'What the fuck did you say?' Eamonn replied, approaching the smirking soldier now.

'You'll end up just like him.'

In a blink of the eye, the man with the gun and army fatigues was on his back and Magee and Hamill were sprinting down Ardoyne Avenue towards the Oldpark Road.

'You're a mad bastard, Eamonn!' little Hamill yelled under his faltering breath as he struggled to keep up with the fleeing boxer and his stinging knuckles.

Neither the army nor the police nor any other representative of the crown ever caught up with Magee for that incident but on other occasions he was not so fortunate. One morning he bumped into a group of his mates as he walked down Castle Street. They still reeked of the previous night's excesses and were on their way to keep the party going while they watched the Old Firm game between Glasgow Celtic and Glasgow Rangers. Eamonn had also been out the night before but he had a fight in a few weeks and Breen was expecting him in the gym.

'I've to go train here, lads,' he said, almost apologetically.

'No bother, Eamonn. Come and find us in Robinson's when you're done.'

'That'll do,' he said. 'And have your money ready for those fight tickets cos I can't be fucked with chasing yous the day before as usual.'

'Aye, all right then,' came the shouted reply as the group laughed their way out of the city centre in the direction of Robinson's Bar, the grand old Great Victoria Street establishment that had stood proudly alongside the Crown Saloon for over 100 years.

Three hours later, when Eamonn entered the pub in search of his friends, he heard them before he saw them. Sectarian tensions are always high in Belfast on Old Firm day, but it was actually a racial insult directed at Magee's friend, Tommy Hillman, that sparked the confrontation on this occasion. The fact that one side were dressed in the blue of Rangers and the other in the green and white of Celtic merely ensured that violence would be used to settle the dispute.

It was real Wild West stuff as other patrons unconnected to the main protagonists scattered for cover. Pint glasses shattered over heads and walls, while haymakers were swung randomly at whoever was sucked into the vicinity of the maelstrom. Eamonn arrived to find a mountain of a man stomping on Connolly and he immediately picked up a bar stool and crashed it down on the attacker's back to stymie the assault. Bouncers soon waded in and began bundling the brawlers out onto the street where Eamonn tried to calm things down by shepherding his group away from the scene. He was the only sober one and his instinct, at this point, was to defuse rather than inflame the situation.

But neither side had sated their thirst for violence and the ruckus sparked back into life as soon as a few sectarian jibes hit their intended nerves. Conscious he was due in the ring in a matter of weeks, Magee was still attempting to be the voice of reason but, seeing another friend getting a doing-over, he felt forced to intervene. A CCTV camera picked him up directing a stray boot at a body on the floor and that was all the police needed to charge him with affray. He was released until his case could be heard, but warned that a custodial sentence was a genuine possibility.

Before that court date arrived, however, a separate charge of causing grievous bodily harm made it onto the burgeoning Magee rap sheet. As Eamonn was working security for John in the Arena nightclub in Armagh one night, a punter on the dance floor was identified as a known drug dealer. When the bouncers stepped in to lead him away, they found him aggressive and high as a kite. A scuffle ensued and the dealer ended up on the floor with a broken jaw. Despite his profession, he was happy to take his chances with the police. He pressed charges against Eamonn, earning the boxer 240 hours of community service, and successfully pursued the Arena for compensation. A couple of years later, the man walked past Magee and Breen working the door of the Beaten Docket bar opposite the Europa Hotel.

'No hard feelings, Eamonn,' he said with a lopsided grin. 'I got twelve grand thanks to that left hook of yours!'

***

It was either testament to his mental fortitude, or a sad indictment of how accustomed he was to court cases hanging over his head, that Eamonn would be back in the gym the morning after such incidents as if nothing had happened. And what's more, he continued to reel off victories in the ring regardless of the troubles he faced when he stepped back out between the ropes.

Shaun Stokes was another opponent with a winning record, but Magee took less than five minutes to end his challenge in a bloody swarm of punches. To be fair to Stokes, he was on a hiding to nothing coming in as a late replacement after Paddy Loughran pulled out a couple of weeks ahead of the showdown. That was to be Loughran's final chance to face Magee, who dismissed the Ballymena man and his more illustrious older brother once and for all.

'Paddy Loughran or Eamonn Loughran, what's the difference?' Eamonn spat. 'I could beat the two of them but they haven't got the bottle to fight me.'

It was revealed after the fight that Magee had chipped a bone in his right foot during training and doctors had advised he rest up until it healed. But with his hundreds of tickets already bought and paid for, he didn't even contemplate withdrawing and disappointing his followers. He went on to describe the devastating performance as a message to the rest of the light welters in Britain and Callahan was quick to pick up the theme.

'When you've got a talent as hot as this there's no point hanging around,' declared the consummate salesman. 'He's only had five fights but he's proved yet again that there's nobody in Britain as explosive as Eamonn.'

In January 1997 he was handed a tougher assignment against a forty-eight fight, professional journeyman who once beat the three-time world champion Dingaan Thobela and fought for the British lightweight crown. Karl Taylor would also dance with world champions such as Kell Brook, Ricky Hatton, Junior Witter, Joshua Clottey and Anatoly Alexandrov before finally hanging up his gloves after an astonishing 165 contests. He was a nuisance in the ring, an expert in frustrating opponents who were invariably more accomplished than he was. He was the test every prospect needs to pass to learn a little of the dark arts of the professional game after so long in the clean-cut world of amateur boxing.

Taylor was also more than three inches shorter than Magee and exacerbated the differential by crouching and bending low to offer little more than the back of his head and the temptation of an illegal rabbit punch for the Irishman to work with. His favoured mode of attack was an ungainly charge in which his hard head had much more chance of doing damage to Magee's chin than his gloved fists did.

'Stand up you bastard!' Magee roared midway through the fight, but Taylor merely grinned back in response.

As Eamonn's frustration grew, he took to throwing lead uppercuts at Taylor in an attempt to force his quarry upright and so become a more traditional target. But Taylor kept boring in head first, launching wild, wishful right hands and then holding on for dear life, forcing referee Barney Wilson to personally rip the Englishman's arms from around Magee's waist. If the clinch lasted, he'd jolt his head to ensure contact with Eamonn's jaw and when they separated he'd leer and laugh and goad Magee into desperation.

'How the fuck am I supposed to fight this eejit!?' Eamonn demanded in exasperation when he sat on his stool at the end of the first.

Breen instinctively knew that his only job that night was to ensure his fighter kept calm, to prevent the rage that was boiling inside him from erupting in the ring. 'You're doing fine, son,' he said. 'Just box him, jab his head off, win on points and we all go home happy.'

For the most part, Eamonn did keep his cool, but at one point his composure briefly abandoned him. As he bustled about Taylor, his foe simply turned his back and leaned against the ropes, forcing the ref to intervene. Before the official got a chance, however, Eamonn fired in a couple of hooks to the kidneys as punishment for the continued spoiling tactics.

Big Barney Wilson, a heavyweight brawler back in the 1960s, knew he had to do something. But as a Belfast man, he was also keenly aware of what side his bread was buttered on. There is an unspoken expectation in boxing that refs will look after home fighters as much as possible, but after such a flagrant breach of the Marquess of Queensberry rules the third man in the ring had to be at least seen to act on it.

Grabbing Eamonn by the wrist, Barney yelled in the fighter's face as an irate father might to his misbehaving son. 'You see that door?' he roared rhetorically. 'If you ever do that again in my ring I'll throw you out that fucking door myself!'

Even to those as close as the front row, it appeared as genuine a dressing down as was ever delivered in a prize ring and Magee played his part admirably, nodding and apologising profusely for the indiscretion. Only Barney and Eamonn, able to read the truth in each other's eyes, were party to the charade.

Taylor did his job and went the distance and, even as the fight progressed, Magee matured enough to appreciate that it was a worthwhile and successful exercise. 'It was a good learning fight,' was how he described it to reporters at ringside immediately afterwards. 'He was ranked higher than me and is a good pro. I would have liked to have stopped him but I never lost a round and you can't ask for more than that.'

The blossoming boxing maturity was a welcome sign, but at that time you could have asked ten boxing insiders for reasons to be optimistic about Magee's future and you would have received ten distinct, yet totally valid, answers. Sean Canavan, the respected stalwart of Irish amateur boxing from 1970 until he retired from his post of IABA vice-president in 2015, described Eamonn as having the best hands in Irish boxing. Dennie Mancini, the great cornerman who worked with the likes of Nigel Benn, Chris Eubank, Richie Woodhall and Sven Ottke also waxed lyrical on Magee after working his corner for the Taylor fight. 'He can box and punch, which is rare in today's game,' he said. 'But Magee also showed great temperament and that's very important because if you can't control yourself, you can't control your opponent.' Jack Magowan, meanwhile, highlighted the forcefulness of Eamonn's determination. 'Eamonn's strength is his confidence,' he said in his editorial in the *Ireland's Saturday Night* sports paper. 'The conviction that he has the animal authority to dominate anybody they put in front of him.'

Certainly, Eamonn backed himself to beat any domestic light welterweight, despite his relative inexperience. Irish champion Malcolm Melvin talked a good game before crying off when an April date was presented, but Magee was already dismissing that calibre of fighter as an irrelevance in the grand scheme of things. He was looking further up the rankings and claimed he'd walk through the likes of Bernard Paul and Paul Ryan. But with domestic match-ups proving difficult to secure, a surprise call from the US had Magee packing his bags for a trip across the Atlantic.

It was his old friend Wayne McCullough who set the wheels in motion. The Pocket Rocket had turned pro after claiming a silver medal at the 1992 Olympic Games and moved to Las Vegas to be trained by the legendary Eddie Futch. He was North American Boxing Federation bantamweight champion within a year, and in his seventeenth fight he beat Yasuei Yakushiji in Japan to become the WBC's world champion. His manager throughout the journey had been the American Mat Tinley, but when Wayne dropped a split decision to Daniel Zaragoza at the beginning of 1997, his wife Cheryl began handling his affairs. Tinley was turning his focus to promoting via his ultimately ill-fated America Presents vehicle anyway and as a parting gift McCullough gave him a recommendation of an Irish fighter who was destined to become a star.

Tinley watched some tapes and was immediately sold. He tried to coax Eamonn to move to America and sign a lucrative, long-term promotional deal, but with Mike steering the ship, a more circumspect approach was taken. Matchroom were still heavily invested in Magee's career and there was also a reluctance to abandon the Belfast support that had proved to be so passionately behind him from day one. A one-fight deal was agreed and Team Magee set sail for Fort Worth, Texas at the end of February 1997.

The Lone Star state may not have as much Irish blood coursing through its veins as the likes of Boston and New York, but Eamonn still caused quite a stir when he went on local television. In his broad Belfast accent, he stated his intention to knock the rugged Tony Townsend out early and show the American public what a true fighting Irishman can do. The bullish cameo caused phones in the America Presents box office to ring off the hook and, despite the bout being broadcast live coast-to-coast on Fox television, around 400 Irish-Americans snapped up the remaining tickets and headed down to the Texas Music Hall to ensure that Magee's reception was more raucous than that which his Austin-born opponent received.

The venue was packed when the first bell sounded, and Eamonn didn't disappoint his newfound fans. He came out loose and relaxed, used his jab to get into range and landed punishing blows every time an opening appeared in Townsend's guard. Pure boxers can rely on timing to generate power and that is exactly what Magee did when a textbook left caught his man flush on the chin and sent him tumbling to the canvas floor. It may have been waved off there and then by a lot of referees, but American boxing is a bloodthirsty arena and the hapless Townsend was forced to rise and endure a ferocious flurry of punches that left him slumped on the bottom rope before this referee decided he had seen enough.

The American plaudits were immediate. 'Boston, New York, Chicago – the world is his oyster,' insisted the legendary MC Jimmy Lennon Junior. The Hall of Fame promoter Dan Goossen was equally effusive. 'This kid is something special,' he said. 'He's got a big future.'

Tinley was beside himself. 'This was a spectacular performance,' he announced in front of the cameras before comparing Eamonn to IBF welterweight king Felix Trinidad. 'Magee can be a big attraction in America,' he continued. 'I don't hang about with wasters. Eamonn Magee will be a world champion and that's why I want to sign him.'

It was all music to Mike Callahan's ears, but he was not going to rush into any multi-fight deals just yet. *Join the queue, Mat*, he thought to himself, *right alongside Frank Warren, Barry Hearn and the rest*. Instead, a second one-fight contract was signed to bring Eamonn to Boston for another televised America Presents bill at the end of March.

Eamonn arrived early to the spiritual American home of the Irish diaspora and immediately endeared himself to the natives. In O'Malley's Gym he sparred with Ray Oliveira, who had twice fought for light welterweight world titles, and 'Irish' Micky Ward (immortalised in the

2010 film, *The Fighter*), who was in preparation for his own shot at the IBF crown and would go on to fight a legendary trilogy with the late Arturo Gatti. Neutral observers came away from both sessions amazed that the young Irishman had clearly got the better of the two more illustrious names.

Another promoter involved in the show, Rich Cappiello, was equally impressed by the workouts but even more taken aback by the crowds that gathered in O'Hagan's Irish bar when Magee went in for a publicity pint. Tinley may have been in pole position to sign Eamonn up and keep him busy in the US, but he was far from being the only interested party. However, the key to the whole arrangement was Magee winning and Cappiello was quick to issue a warning that the Jamaican-born Teddy Reid would provide a tough test for any welterweight in the world.

'Eamonn will not be facing any pushover in Reid, who has four first-round stoppages and has only lost once on points,' Cappiello told the travelling Irish press corps. 'It's a clash of two very heavy hitters.'

Cappiello's words proved to be prophetic. With the benefit of hindsight, it was dangerously gung-ho matchmaking to put these two men between the ropes together at this early stage of their careers. 'Two Gun' Reid went on to win three different North American titles and challenge Kermit Cintron for the WBO interim crown. As a heavy-handed knockout artist, he was not the type of fighter a seven-fight novice wanted to face 3,000 miles from home. Reid also climbed into the ring that March night with a distinct, and unfair, weight advantage. At the previous day's weigh-in, the American arrived over two hours late and then tipped the scales a ridiculous six and a half pounds over the agreed limit. Callahan went ballistic.

'He goes away and sheds some of that excess and weighs in again at the contracted weight or there is no fight,' he raged at the rival camp.

Reid's trainer had other ideas, however. Pepe Correa had seen it all in boxing, and then watched the repeats. Having worked with the likes of

Sugar Ray Leonard, Roberto Duran, Lennox Lewis and Hector Camacho, the Puerto Rican knew all the angles and just how to exploit them.

'These boys have come a long way to get here, Teddy,' he whispered to his charge. 'A long and expensive way. If you don't get in that ring tomorrow, none of them boys get paid. Don't you worry about a thing, Teddy.'

Reid made no effort whatsoever to lose the extra half-stone and, just as his wily old trainer had assured him would happen, the visitors backed down and the bout went ahead in The Roxy. Towering three inches over Magee, Reid looked massive for a supposed light welterweight and he sought to bully the fight from the opening bell. The American-based Jamaican landed several telling blows, including a right hook that caused Callahan to later remark to Eamonn, 'at least we now know you've got a chin'. But Magee was composed throughout, fought cleverly off the back foot, continually countered to effect and raised his arms in victory at the final bell. Unfortunately, only one of the ringside scorers agreed with his judgement and the home fighter was announced the victor on a split decision.

Eamonn hung his head under a white towel in the dressing rooms and choked back the tears. He could have blamed the travelling, the matchmaking, the weight controversy or the skewed home decision, but all he felt inside was anger at himself. Suddenly he was seven years old again, crying in the toilets of Beechmount Leisure Centre, cursing himself for allowing the judges to award the fight to his opponent. But this time it was worse. He was fighting for his livelihood these days. He was fighting to feed, clothe and shelter his family. He viewed these first ten fights as nothing more than an apprenticeship, an opportunity to learn the vagaries of the professional business on the job before his career really began, and now he was back to square one. Worse even, for he had a loss to his name. How were Hearn and Warren and the rest going to sell him to the British audience now without easy access to that prized boxing adjective, *unbeaten*? For two or three days, it was the end of the world.

But Callahan and Breen quickly snapped him out of it. While Mike played up the gamesmanship over the weight issues and the sad predictability of losing a close fight away from home, John reminded Eamonn how good he looked toying with Micky Ward and giving Ray Oliveira all he could handle in the gym. But the trainer had a subtle way of giving it to his fighter straight as well.

'You deserved the victory, Eamonn, no doubt about that,' he said. 'But I watched you throw too many single shots in Boston. Reid was good and when you box his class of fighter you have to do more, you have to up the work rate. It takes combinations, not one-off punches, to beat this standard now.'

Eamonn nodded silently. He knew John was right. He also told his manager to get him back in the ring as soon as possible. Callahan obliged and within a month, Magee appeared at the Ulster Hall on the undercard of his brother Noel's last hurrah, a forlorn shot at Darren Corbett's Irish cruiserweight belt. Three weeks out from the fight, Eamonn's opponent was named as Dave Brazil. Two weeks out, it changed to Tony Swift. A week before the bout, Tommy James was the man. By the time the first bell rang, Peter Nightingale stood in the opposite corner. The uncertainty didn't matter a jot. Nightingale was outclassed and refused to answer the call for the third round. Eamonn barely needed a shower before he watched Noel in the main event.

A month later it was the familiar face of Kevin McKillan who squared up to Magee, but this time the Mancunian lasted a round less, beaten into submission midway through the third. Eamonn was on a mission. Now aged twenty-six, he knew it was time to start winning some titles.

Malcolm Melvin had held the Irish light welterweight strap since he claimed it the day before the feast of St Patrick in 1993 and had defended it a grand total of zero times since. Magee called him out repeatedly, but due to a combination of Melvin's reluctance to face him, his manager Pat Cowdell's intransigence throughout negotiations, and the Boxing Union of Ireland's (BUI) infuriating reluctance to force the issue, a prospective showdown between the pair appeared destined to remain just that – prospective.

In October Mark Winters claimed the vacant British title in a hard-fought twelve rounder with Carl Wright in Sheffield. On his journey back to his native Liverpool, Wright slipped into a coma and needed emergency surgery to remove a blood clot from his brain. Thankfully he survived, and made as full a recovery as the doctors could have expected, but it was one of those near-tragic incidents that the fight game throws up every year to remind all involved of what is at stake. Life must go on, however, and Winters and Magee were soon back trading jibes in the press. Eamonn wanted to fight the Antrim man immediately, while Mark claimed that the flame-haired southpaw needed to beat someone with a top-ten ranking before he deserved a shot at a British title.

Barry Hearn was meanwhile teasing Magee with the carrot of Bernard Paul's Commonwealth title. Paul had taken Jonathan Thaxton the distance in challenging for the WBO inter-continental crown and edged the previously undefeated Zambian Felix Bwalya to win the Commonwealth belt. But Eamonn wasn't impressed, describing the prospect of facing Paul as a 'chance to show off as well as take the title'.

It was a period of uncertainty as far as Eamonn's boxing career was concerned. Alongside the interest from Hearn and Warren, the Americans were still keen for a piece of the Irishman and US promoters proposed various foes throughout the summer and autumn of 1997 to lure Magee back to the States and continue his progression there.

It was also towards the end of that year that Barney Eastwood decided to call time on his long and distinguished participation in the sweet science. After promoting over seventy championship fights, managing six world champions, and keeping boxing alive throughout the darkest days of the Troubles, Eastwood closed the famous Castle Street gym in order to focus completely on his betting-shop empire. As a pure business move measured in dollars and cents it was undoubtedly a wise decision: ten years later he would sell those fifty-four bookies to Ladbrokes for £135 million. But for Northern Irish boxing there was a real fear that Eastwood's departure might rip the heart out of the sport in the country.

Breen and Callahan were determined not to let that happen, however. While Mike busied himself securing match-ups for the fighters and exploring the possibility of promoting his own shows, John sought out new premises within which he could mould a new generation of champions. He soon got lucky when local businessman Tony Diver offered up a space above his Monico Bar on Winecellar's Entry in Belfast's city centre. Breen's Gym was opened by the deputy lord mayor in October 1997 and would be home to John and his fighters for the next seventeen years. Seventeen years in which Diver never took so much as a penny in rent.

In the end the promise of the Commonwealth title proved too enticing to ignore and that is the route Team Magee decided to take. But when Paul Burke beat Bernard Paul on points in August 1997, the Preston man became the Terminator's target. Callahan also pulled a surprise by eschewing the advances of Matchroom, Queensberry and America and signing his prized fighter up with the London-based Panix Promotions. Panix was bankrolled by the businessman Panos Eliades and spearheaded by Frank Maloney, the trainer-cum-manager-cum-promoter who had made his name alongside Warren before an acrimonious split in the late 1980s. Panix controlled the career of Lennox Lewis and Mike decided if it was good enough for the then WBC heavyweight champion of the world, it was good enough for Eamonn Magee.

1998 began with a straightforward demolition of the over-matched Dennis Griffin in London, before two more competitive contests in Belfast Crown Court and Armagh Magistrates Court. Magee pleaded guilty to the charges of affray and assault causing both actual and grievous bodily harm, and picked up a £750 fine and 100 hours of community service for his trouble. He then set his sights on becoming the Commonwealth light welterweight champion.

First up was a final eliminator against Darlington's Allan Hall. Hall, with a 17–2 record, was a decent and experienced boxer but he had been out of the ring for almost three years and it was clear from the opening exchanges that Magee was operating at a different level. The end mercifully arrived in the seventh stanza when Eamonn spied the muscles in Hall's left shoulder tense in anticipation of throwing a jab and countered with his own lightning right hook over the oncoming glove and onto the Englishman's chin. The speed of the punch belied its power and for an instant it appeared that Hall's senses couldn't quite believe that they'd been rattled. He froze and the world stood still while the message travelled south and turned his legs to jelly. Referee Keith Garner stepped in between the two men to end the contest before Hall could be badly damaged.

Referees are trained to treat each second in the ring on its individual merit, but it is understandable why Garner would have been less inclined than normal to let an obviously beaten fighter hang on in there for an extra torturous minute or two. The mid-1990s was one of those dark and uncertain periods in boxing history that follows high-profile fatalities in the ring. The deaths from brain injuries of Bradley Stone in 1994 and James Murray in 1995 had devastated British boxing, and in 1997 Paul Burke found himself caught up in a new tragedy when he travelled to Zambia to defend his Commonwealth title against Felix Bwalya.

Burke actually lost the fight in Lusaka in highly controversial circumstances, but nine days later the Zambian was dead. Bwalya had built up a sizeable points advantage for the first nine rounds of the bout but, as he faded and Burke came on strong, the Zambian was dropped three times and was lying on his back when the final bell sounded, at least two minutes early according to Burke's corner. There was no doctor at ringside and a young medical student had to stitch up a cut over Burke's eye in the dressing room. Looking back, the Englishman must be thankful that was all the attention he needed after twelve brutal rounds. It turned out that the challenger had been allowed to fight despite having recently contracted malaria. When awarded the dubious victory, he embarked on a forty-eight-hour celebratory drinking binge that resulted in his admission to hospital complaining of severe headaches. There, Bwalya lapsed into a coma and, seven days later, passed away.

Burke would later reason that it was the sorry combination of being allowed to fight with malaria, not having a doctor immediately check him out after thirty-six minutes of boxing and three knockdowns, and then mixing vast amounts of alcohol with the medication in his system that killed Felix Bwalya. But the tragedy naturally stung the Englishman and it was ten long months before he stepped back between the ropes. He stopped Tony Swift five minutes into his return and then confirmed that he would be in Manchester in November to vie with Magee to reclaim the now-vacant Commonwealth light welterweight title.

Eamonn was ringside to watch Burke's destruction of Swift and expressed indifference towards his rival's prowess. Indeed, he spoke of him as little more than a stepping stone towards World Boxing Union (WBU) champion Shea Neary, with whom he was already trading barbs in the press. But if there was any genuine complacency lurking within Magee, Callahan and Breen immediately set about eliminating it. They whisked him away to a remote Crumlin farm owned by Fra McCullough from the BUI and kept him isolated there for six weeks, far away from trouble and temptation. He was up, chopping wood and running across the cold Stonyford hills, at seven each morning and the closest he ever got to the city lights was a visit to the Immaculata Gym for circuits and Breen's Gym for eight or ten hard rounds of sparring. It was a level of dedication that the twenty-seven-year-old's body hadn't witnessed before and by fight week he was as fit as he had been back in 1989 when he won silver at the World Juniors.

At the Bowlers Exhibition Centre in Manchester on 30 November 1998, Magee emerged with brand-new boxing garb in honour of his first major title fight. Up until this point in his twelve-fight career, his get-up had been a rather understated ensemble of white robe and white shorts, both sporting a matching trim of green on the shoulder or down the thigh. Now the main support act, challenging for the Commonwealth title, live on Sky Sports, he felt it was time to commission a look uniquely representative of Eamonn Magee from the Ardoyne. The boxing apparel specialists Carletti were tasked with creating the outfit according to Magee's precise specifications: the green and white were to stay, but this time with the addition of some glitter to catch the lights and a large splash of orange, the final colour of the Irish tricolour. The result was a zip-up satin robe that effectively doubled as an Irish flag, and a green, white and orange Hawaiian grass hula skirt stitched into the waist of the original white shorts.

Magee's sartorial preferences caused a stir in the hyper-sensitive, post-conflict world in which Northern Irish society was still taking its first, tentative steps. Symbols, especially those representing a particular nationality or faith, take on a highly exaggerated importance within divided communities. Colours, flags or any other visible emblems that can differentiate one side of the same coin from the other are quickly hijacked and exploited by those seeking to maintain or widen the division. It is a lamentable state of affairs, laughable in many instances, but everyone in Northern Ireland is only too aware of the very real dangers involved.

To the Protestant, unionist and British half of the country, green, white and orange are the colours of a Catholic, nationalist and Irish culture that they fear is seeking to replace their own. Just as loyalists use the red, white and blue of the Union Jack to paint the kerbstones and identify their areas as such, republicans demarcate their own districts with the three Irish colours. Likewise, the murals on the walls of each neighbourhood that glorify one side's fighting men over the other. The fact that the orange third of the Irish national flag, first flown when the Easter rebels hoisted it above Dublin's General Post Office in 1916, was actually inserted to represent the Protestant community on the island, with the white tranche in the middle a gesture of peace after the green third of Gaelic tradition, has long become an irrelevance: symbols assume whatever meaning the people choose to attach.

The political minefield is why the likes of Barry McGuigan and Wayne McCullough opted out of it altogether and chose colours that could only be construed as neutral: as much as anything, it simply guaranteed a slightly easier and quieter life for themselves. Eamonn's subconscious desire for conflict ensured he rarely selected the safest route through life, but on this matter he is adamant that he simply followed his heart and had no intention of provoking a reaction, good or bad, from either community in Northern Ireland.

***

I raised the subject when I saw his ID documents on his kitchen table. Despite a youth in the Fianna and a career decked out in the three shades of the Irish tricolour, Eamonn now holds a British passport. Drawing attention to the royal coat of arms on the cover, I teased him, calling him a traitor to the cause.

'You know I don't give a fuck about all that crap,' he replied as he dunked my teabag in a cup of boiling water. 'I can't remember but it was probably just quicker or cheaper to get the Brit one this time.'

When we settled on his living room sofa I continued the conversation, asking what it was all about then, the Irish tricolours everywhere when he fought.

'Listen,' he said in an even tone. 'It's not anyone's fault where their da puts his cock, is it?'

The logic, bluntly put, is hard to dispute. But I push back that he knew fine rightly that nailing his colours so vigorously to the mast in the 1990s was always going to be interpreted as a sign of provocation. Why not just follow the lead of McCullough and remove himself totally from the political arena by donning colours with no special relevance in Northern Irish life?

'To this day, I can't do anything about how people want to interpret my actions. You mention Wayne there, a Protestant from the Shankill, one of my best mates from the first time we met as kids boxing in small hall shows all over the city. Like I've told you before, I have nothing against Protestants or unionists or whatever you want to call them in Northern Ireland. But I'm Irish. I was born in Ireland. I'm very proud of where I come from. I'm proud to be Irish. If I was English, I'd probably have worn a St George's Cross. If I was Scottish, their Saltire. Welsh, a dragon or whatever. You know what I mean? I've nothing against anybody, but I'm Irish and you won't take that away from me or stop me showing it.'

With that he downed the remainder of his breakfast beer and I know that, in his head, Eamonn will never accept the situation to be more nuanced than his monochrome depiction.

'Anyway,' he suddenly continued with a renewed light in his eye, 'I never wore the Irish colours against Burke in that first fight. I was dressed head to toe in the fucking Ivory Coast flag!'

***

Re-watching the old fight tapes, I saw it to be true. The tailors at Carletti had got the colours right but the order wrong and the result was technically a representation of Côte d'Ivoire's national flag rather than that of the Emerald Isle. They also forgot to add glitter to the robe and the skirt strands and, sitting backstage, Magee had been nothing short of disgusted.

'A simple fucking job,' he muttered to himself as he worked up a sweat, throwing at his own shadow on the dressing-room wall all the punches he planned to unleash on Burke. He'd have to make his performance sparkle under the television lights to make up for his plain old, West African outfit clearly not being up to the task.

The fight has gone down in British boxing annals as one of the great robberies in the history of the murky sport. The likes of Bradley versus Pacquiao, Holyfield versus Lewis or Chavez versus Whitaker may be more renowned on account of the global status of the robbers and victims involved, but the decision Paul Burke was awarded at Magee's expense in 1998 was no less of a shame-faced mugging than any of those famous crimes against boxing.

It is possible that Burke got the better of a cagey opening quarter in which a tight Magee had his nose bloodied, but after that there was only one winner. From round four onwards, Eamonn proved himself to be the stronger man, with the faster hands, the harder punch and the more astute boxing brain. At the clinches, Burke would simply hold and pray for referee John Keane's intervention, while Magee would bustle, force an inch of space and continue landing punches. If the ref still didn't split them, the Irishman would then spin and throw his rival away with disdain.

Burke, like a swarthy David Niven with his pencil-thin moustache, looked stunned and tentative throughout, doing little more than ineffectually reacting to the younger, fresher fighter who imposed his will on the fight as the only man landing hurtful blows. It looked like Burke touched his glove to the canvas while under assault in the sixth, but the referee declared no knockdown and, thus, no ten-eight round. Ian Darke on commentary opined that it certainly appeared to be a legitimate knockdown, 'but it doesn't matter much anyway'.

He was right with his first statement, but very painfully wrong with the second.

On three more occasions, Burke's knees touched the ring floor amidst flurries of punches, and three more times the referee merely waved the fight on. It was a disappointingly scrappy affair throughout and none of Burke's trips south were the result of particularly heavy punches, but to receive the benefit of the doubt four times on one night is fortunate to say the least.

A diaphanous slit appeared on Burke's forehead in the sixth and a stray elbow opened it into a bona fide gash in the ninth. As the tenth drew to a close, everyone watching had Burke well behind and in need of a knockout to win. 'It would be a brave man who would call Paul Burke the eventual winner from here,' Darke said on live television.

The Preston man did rally in the eleventh and twelfth when he knew he had to go for broke, but even giving him the tight rounds in the contest, he clearly lost the fight. When the final bell sounded, both boxers raised their arms aloft and turned to the referee: Magee in joyous expectation, Burke in forlorn hope. To the total shock of all who witnessed it, John Keane grabbed Burke's wrist and declared him the champion. In those days, the referee was the lone scorer of the contest and he'd deliver his verdict immediately by grabbing the victor's wrist and hoisting his fist aloft. Eamonn looked to plead his case before swiftly giving up. With his gloves on the top rope he looked out at his supporters with a pained and incredulous smile. He then walked laps of the ring, shaking his head every now and again, battling to keep his rage bottled up inside. The announcer confirmed that Keane had scored Burke the winner by a point while Darke declared the result a robbery and a mystery, and sympathised with 'poor Eamonn Magee'. Ringside scorer Glenn McCrory was generous to Burke but still had him losing by three rounds while McGuigan in the studio gave it to Magee by five. Alongside the Clones Cyclone, the recently retired Chris Eubank struggled to maintain a façade of diplomacy on his debut as a Sky Sports pundit.

'Someone should be hung, shot and quartered,' he began. 'I think it is plain for everyone to see, all the viewers at home to see that was … Listen, everyone has eyes to see and one and one makes two and, you know, this didn't add up tonight and that is not a controversial thing to say.'

'I thought I won that fight easy,' a shell-shocked Magee concurred on the ring apron immediately after. He then pushed the boundaries of political correctness to their limits by asking whether Stevie Wonder had scored the bout and suggesting that the mixed-race Burke would be red in embarrassment if his dark complexion allowed it to be seen. Burke half-heartedly defended the decision but his body language said it all: he knew how lucky he had been and, despite having the lion's share of the support in Manchester, he left the arena to boos and jeers of derision from a crowd who knew exactly what they had just witnessed.

***

While Mike faxed official complaints to the Commonwealth Council, and Burke insisted he'd fight a rematch anytime and anywhere if it was ordered, a shattered and disillusioned Magee attempted to drink and snort his pain away. He was volatile at the best of times, but the coke put him in a mood in which violent incidents became a given. In Hamill's one night, one of a group of revellers made the mistake of teasing Eamonn about the loss. He wasn't a regular within the gang and clearly failed to grasp the nature of the beast he was poking. Despite several warnings from Magee and others in the room, the tragically misguided joker just kept going.

'Beat by Burke,' he said. 'That's probably your level then, Magee. That's as high up the ladder as you'll get.'

Eamonn finally snapped and with his hand around his antagonist's throat he gave him one final chance to shut up.

'I'm just saying,' the apparently parasuicidal man continued as he made to descend back onto the sofa, 'you've gotta beat Burke if ...'

Bang. An uppercut detonated on his chin before he knew it was on its way. Where the guy's head had hovered a split second before, there was now just a noticeable imprint on the plasterboard wall. The rest of him was slouched unconscious on the sofa. Hamill looked on in muted horror as Magee then sat down and calmly resumed his beer. He knew the terrible damage Eamonn's fists could do and he didn't want to be disposing of a corpse the next morning. Hamill spent the next half an hour monitoring the sleeping fool on his sofa, slapping him gently every now and again, urging him to wake up in a whisper drenched in panic.

'I think he's dead,' he finally blurted out when his nerves couldn't take it any more. 'You've killed him Eamonn for fuck sake.'

'Sit down and finish your drink, James,' Magee replied coolly. 'The stupid cunt will be fine.'

The stupid cunt was fine, relatively speaking. When he finally came to, Eamonn walked him into the kitchen, splashed water on his face and cleaned him up. He walked away the next morning with just a very sore jaw and a more cautious tongue for his trouble, but others who crossed Magee in those months did not get off so lightly.

***

A phone call woke him early.

'Two bastards beat the shit out of Budgie a few hours ago,' a voice said by way of a good morning. 'They climbed through his window and did him as he slept on the sofa.'

'For what?'

'For fucking nothing.'

'Right, let's go to work. Come round and pick me up now.'

Eamonn rolled out of bed, cracked open a beer and got dressed. The last thing he did was lace his steel-toed boots tightly. Budgie had been friends with Eamonn since they were kids. Magee was back in primary school, dealing with a pair of bullies.

An agonising justice was administered swiftly that day. The two men knocked on the first culprit's door and forced their way in as soon as it was ajar. They kicked and punched him until he lay motionless on his hallway floor in a bloody mess.

They soon spied the second man on Ardoyne Avenue and dealt with him in a similar manner. Perhaps due to that beating taking place outdoors on a hard concrete street, where kerbs and walls could be used to accentuate the suffering, Eamonn felt inexplicably ill at ease as he sat later, drinking a can of beer.

'That wasn't fair,' Eamonn began to his friend's surprise, before elaborating on his train of thought. 'We really hammered that bastard outside there and it makes me think we let the other cunt off lightly on the comfort of his nice, carpeted hallway.'

He then necked his drink and stood up. 'C'mon, we're not done yet.'

They returned to their first target, still in his house licking his wounds, and launched into him once more with fists and boots until Eamonn was satisfied that both men had received fair and comparable punishment for their joint misdemeanour.

It was extremely rough justice, but this was how Ardoyne men handled disputes and disagreements and it all took place within a world in which the traditional bastions of law and order were never welcome. The two men did initially go to the police, but soon decided to drop the charges. The cops knew that victims of Eamonn's fists would never cooperate in enquiries, but they still kept a close eye on Magee. They were determined to one day catch him for something substantial, a crime that would yield a sentence long enough to provide some satisfaction to counter the frustration of knowing he often operated as if a law unto himself. On one of the many occasions he was lifted and taken for questioning, several officers had clearly made their mind up that the boxer was going to resist arrest regardless of the reality that unfolded. Disbanding the RUC was a key element within ongoing peace negotiations and some on the force perhaps felt time was running out to take Eamonn down. Cornering him as he walked back to Hamill's with a carry-out from the local off-licence, four or five approached the boxer with their batons out and raised. Eamonn dropped to his knees with his hands behind his head when instructed to do so, but he could see by the looks in the eyes that focused on him that this was not going to be a peaceful arrest. Only a passing pensioner saved him from a taste of his own rough-justice medicine that night.

'You leave him alone,' the old woman shouted from down the street. 'I've seen the whole thing and there's no need to be hitting anyone here tonight.'

***

Released without charge on that occasion, Eamonn decided he needed a break from Northern Ireland. Luckily enough, he was currently operating his own illicit travel agency alongside his other business interests: Magee Travels would soon arrange a couple of weeks with the sun on his back somewhere.

The enterprise was the dubious outcome of a partnership between Eamonn, a genuine but dodgy travel agent in England, and an even less scrupulous employee of a major high-street bank. When Magee sold a holiday at a too-good-to-be-true rate, the travel agent sorted out the logistics and the banker provided the credit card details of a particularly wealthy customer to finance the deal. Naturally, the three amigos running the scam took a cut for their efforts. The thinking was that the high-rollers whose accounts were chosen would not be the type of people to notice a couple of grand skimmed off a balance in the multi-millions. The idea was sound and at one time or another, Eamonn had half the Ardoyne in some exotic, far-flung location for the price of a B&B weekend in Donegal.

A group of five headed off to Tenerife. The festivities began in Belfast International Airport and the gang were all half cut by the time the plane was skirting the coast of Portugal a couple of hours later. Eamonn had angry words with one of his party and the matter, something insignificant and long since forgotten, was not resolved as they collected their luggage and walked through the arrivals hall. Magee was drunk and his alcohol-soaked fuse was even shorter than usual. A loose tongue lit it and he decked its owner with an overhand left. *Fuck sake*, he thought as he marched outside into the Canarian sun and towards the front of a line of waiting white taxis. The boot of the car in pole position was open in anticipation of a fare and he threw his bag in and jumped into the passenger seat. He'd barely sat down when he noted the steering wheel in front of him and realised his mistake. *This is Spain, they drive on the right, I'm in the fucking driver's seat.*

It was an honest error and he was about to alight and switch sides when the driver grabbed him aggressively by the shirt and pulled him out onto the road. He presumed this drunken Irish lout intended to steal his vehicle and with it his livelihood. The Latin blood in Spaniards ensures they are an emotional race, but those who face daily interaction with the lairy, foreign masses who invade their towns and beaches for a fortnight of debauchery are particularly prone to heated responses when cooler heads may just prevail.

Magee, drunk but thirsty for another, fresh from knocking out a friend in the terminal building, still internally raging over the Burke robbery, didn't hesitate. He dropped the *taxista* with one sharp left hand and then spun in his southpaw stance to handle his *compañeros*, who had been drawn to the commotion like a swarm of wasps to a jug of sangria. It was chaos as Eamonn took out as many as he could before they overwhelmed him through sheer weight of numbers. He managed to roll free from the boots that kicked and stomped him and grab a luggage trolley. He raised it up over his head and turned to launch it through the taxi's windscreen but the shift of his centre in gravity caught him by surprise and he toppled backwards with the trolley smashing down on top of him. With embarrassment now hurled into the potent mix of his emotions, he charged at the Spanish army of cabbies, pushing the baggage cart ahead like a free-wheeling metal battering ram.

Eamonn was single-handedly winning the war when his vision suddenly blurred and his eyes began stinging and weeping. Police had arrived and were corralling him into a corner with their aerosols full of choking CS gas. As he struggled to see and breathe, an intense whipping pain suddenly shot down the length of his thigh and he screamed out and fell from the shock as much as the hurt. Looking up he saw a cop raise a thin, telescopic, steel baton and lash him again in the other leg to quell any lingering sparks of resistance.

He was tossed in a cell for the night and appeared in court the next day, his eyes rubbed red raw and dried blood caking his face and hands and staining his clothes. He looked like he'd just been dragged from the rubble of an earthquake after three days of searching. Unseen behind his jeans, both his legs were bruised black from the knee to the top of his thigh thanks to the blows from the metal whip. The judge took one look at him and decided he wanted nothing to do with Eamonn Magee. After a meaningless slap on the wrist he was sent on his way.

He recovered in Lagmore and then made a second assault on Spanish shores, this time to Andalusia on business. An acquaintance known only as Al's My Pal had arranged this trip in order to smuggle cheap, tax-free cigarettes across the border from Gibraltar. Eamonn found the supplier on a luxury yacht and began taping bags of tobacco to his legs and torso. He then donned an unseasonable, full-length trench coat and set off on the long trek across the border under the punishing Mediterranean sun. Five times throughout the day he repeated the trip as temperatures hit the mid-thirties. On his final jaunt he met some like-minded souls who laughed at the sight of the sweat-drenched man covered in brown tape.

'Look,' one of the fellow smugglers said as he surreptitiously opened his coat an inch. 'Why the fuck didn't you just sew some pockets into the lining like this?'

That night Magee felt he deserved a few hard drinks. He'd earned a couple of grand for his endeavours but it had been as tough as cutting weight for a title fight. Beer was for once refused in order to get torn straight into a case of whiskey. He drank until he passed out, and slept until his morning flight was already halfway home without him. After a day in the airport and a night cuddled up with the local alcoholics who claimed a stretch of terminal for themselves each evening, he finally made it home the following morning.

***

Back in west Belfast, Eamonn was soon climbing the walls of his house in frustration. He was an old-school, disciplinarian father, the man to ensure the children sat down together to eat a healthy evening meal and then practised their instruments ahead of music classes he sent them to on the posh Malone Road. But his now frequent and prolonged absences from the family nucleus reduced his legitimacy for playing that role. The kids were growing fast: Francis eight, Áine just turned seven and Eamonn Junior approaching his sixth birthday, and they were now old enough to question and fear their dad's erratic behaviour. Mary still clung desperately to the memories of a sober and sane Eamonn, and attempted to banish darker times from her mind, but that self-coping mechanism was weakening as the dangerous, truculent, violent version of her man grew ever more dominant.

He needed to get back in a training camp, find a routine, fight for money and, most importantly, right the wrong of the Burke mugging. But boxing politics had other ideas. The rematch, ordered by the Commonwealth Council, was announced for March 1999, but Burke then withdrew as the date approached. The Englishman was still declaring in the press that he was happy to fight Magee, while at the same time gladly accepting smaller purses to face the likes of Bernard Paul and Alan Bosworth in easier, voluntary defences. It all served to further disillusion Eamonn, who knew in his head that he should be preparing to take Shea Neary's world title from him rather than fretting over getting another crack at Burke.

Callahan and Maloney sought to appease Magee by securing him an Irish title shot in the meantime, but Malcolm Melvin continued to live his charmed life. Then, having held the title, but not defended it, for six years, the elusive Brummie was finally nailed down to fight Eamonn on 22 May in Belfast on the undercard of Damaen Kelly's defence of his Commonwealth flyweight crown. Eamonn returned to the gym but he had barely broken a sweat when news of Melvin's inevitable withdrawal filtered through. The patience of the BUI finally snapped and Hartlepool's Alan Temple was chosen to go head to head with Magee for the vacant title now stripped from Melvin. At last, Magee had something to get his teeth into.

Then, on the eve of the bout, the Irish title was taken off the table. In farcical circumstances, Temple failed to produce a birth certificate or any other means of proving that he was indeed eligible to challenge for an Irish crown. Eamonn was by now past caring. He just wanted to get into the ring and hurt someone, and Temple was that unfortunate soul, regardless of his nationality or what was at stake. It was the most jarring knockout of Magee's pro career. Temple actually began well, perhaps earning the opening stanza on work rate alone, but Eamonn took control in the second and then moved in for the kill in the third. Just as the bell sounded to end the round, a left hand over the top and a right hook both landed clean and Temple was unconscious before his limp body came to rest on the canvas floor. The referee decided to complete one of the most futile counts in boxing history, but the Englishman wasn't recovering his senses anytime soon.

Once more Burke was forced to agree a date to rematch Magee, this time in July. Once more he cried off, claiming he needed more time to prepare. Instead, Eamonn flew to England to keep himself ticking over with a second fight against the durable journeyman Karl Taylor. Taylor had gone the six-round distance with Magee two and a half years before, but Eamonn was a different animal this night in London. He kept flicking a spiteful jab into his man's face from the opening bell and followed it with hurtful combinations every time the opportunity arose. The flesh around Taylor's peepers was puffed and tender by the end of the first. His nose was broken in the second. In the third he hit the deck and after a minute on his stool to consider the dire circumstances he found himself in, he didn't bother rising to meet the call for the fourth stanza. The inexplicably tough Taylor had just gone the distance with Oktay Urkal, Junior Witter and Jon Thaxton, but he couldn't live with Eamonn Magee that night.

Yet again, Burke agreed to the rematch, now in Bethnal Green's famous York Hall in September, and this time there were no more excuses to be found. Eamonn headed back to the farm, back to isolation and concentration. He was driven, not by any doubt that he would defeat Burke, but by a desire to punish and humiliate him. Years later he would reflect and acknowledge that Burke didn't actually deserve any personal ill-will. He hadn't robbed Eamonn, the referee's scorecard had. It was true that Burke had displayed no haste to grant Eamonn the rematch, but that was his own prerogative. He had a family to feed as well so why wouldn't he choose easier nights at the office to earn his wage? But at the time, Magee held the Lancashire man directly and solely responsible for the wasted year his career had spent treading water. He pinned a picture of a smiling Burke to his bedroom wall so it was the first image he saw each morning and the last before he closed his eyes to go to sleep. *Seeking Justice*, the fight posters screamed out. For Eamonn, it was more like vengeance.

'The ref will be redundant this time,' he told reporters. 'I'll walk right through him. Burke knows that I beat him last time and I'll do it again. There's no doubt in my mind that he'll get a hiding. The only way he'll beat me is if I have a heart attack.'

It was clear from the opening stanza that Magee had learned from the first encounter with Burke. That fight had been Eamonn's first twelve rounder and, believing himself to be in full control, he had been happy to keep nicking the rounds to go the distance and get the experience of boxing for thirty-six minutes straight. John Keane's bizarre scoring scuppered that plan, however, so this time he was determined to settle the contest himself. He wanted a brawl, a street fight. Every punch would be a venomous power shot, thrown with the worst intentions. From the opening bell, he sought to decimate the champion.

And in six one-sided, ill-tempered rounds in east London, that is exactly what he did, breaking Burke down and then stopping him in style. The first five rounds went the Irishman's way as Eamonn's brazen brutality appeared to intimidate the champion. Burke looked scared to step into range and, as a result, he absorbed three times as many punches as he landed. The beginning of the end then arrived in the sixth with a reaching left hand followed by a juddering right uppercut that drove into the bottom of the Englishman's mandible and snapped his jaw shut. As Burke dropped, Magee wheeled away throwing a flurry of celebratory uppercuts as he went. Turning within sight of the neutral corner as referee Dave Parris began his count, Eamonn shouted over to his stricken foe with spite in his voice, 'Get up you, I'm not finished just yet!'

Burke obliged and an almost carbon-copy knockdown followed, this time Parris needing to physically push the leering Magee away from the stunned, kneeling Burke. The champion bravely rose again, but when a further, almost dismissive, barrage of blows ordered him to the canvas for a third time in less than two minutes, it was all over and a half-crazed Irishman embarked on the most over-zealous celebration of his career. There was no need for the cruel triumphalism, and the referee told him so in a stern rebuke, but Eamonn had fought this fight with genuine hate in his heart.

'I went in there wanting to kill him,' he admitted in the post-fight press conference. 'It's a terrible thing to say but that's how I felt – I wanted to tear his head off.'

He soon acknowledged that such an extreme emotion was entirely misplaced. Misplaced in any ring against any opponent, but particularly against a good man like Paul Burke, who was guilty only of finding himself on the end of a fortuitous referee's decision. The pair met at a British Boxing Board of Control (BBBofC) champions' dinner a few years later and Magee apologised for his behaviour but, on the night itself, his adrenaline was pumping too hard and fast for rational thinking.

He was at least two years behind schedule, but he'd reached a major milestone in his career nevertheless: after sixteen professional contests, he had just become the first Irishman to hold the Commonwealth light welterweight title.

6

HATTON AND THE RA

Any novice with more than five minutes in the game will tell you that professional boxing is not a sport. It is in reality a business, the ultimate risk-versus-reward business. Up until this point in his career, the calibre of fighter Magee needed to face to progress up the rankings had viewed the Ardoyne man as all risk and precious little reward. Now, though still a dangerous proposition for any light welterweight on the planet, he at least had a coveted belt around his waist to attract potential suitors. Eamonn, his eyes firmly set on more titles and more money, immediately signed another four-fight deal with Panix and instructed Callahan and Maloney to sift through the options as they began crawling out of the woodwork within which they had been safely cocooned for years.

Mark Winters and the opportunity to finally settle that long-running domestic grudge match was one possibility, but Winters had lost his British title to Jason Rowland the previous year and followed that defeat with another to the young up-and-comer, Junior Witter. In truth, any spite between the old amateur rivals had largely dissipated over the years as well and when Winters could only eke out a draw with James Hare, the Antrim man ceased to be a serious figure in the reckoning.

Another blast from Eamonn's amateur past threw his hat in the ring when the unbeaten Danish European champion, Thomas Damgaard, claimed he was willing to take on the Terminator. Magee had comfortably outpointed Damgaard in Copenhagen a decade earlier in the Belfast man's first overseas trip representing Ireland and he was confident of doing even better now they were both mature professionals. But the Dane refused to fight outside his homeland and, not being a particularly big name in the division, a quick risk-versus-reward analysis determined he was not worth much consideration. It would be another seven years before Damgaard finally agreed to fight away from home, when he flew to Atlantic City to face Arturo Gatti and record the only defeat of his thirty-nine-fight career.

For his part, Maloney was keen to make a fight with an impressive Mancunian by the name of Ricky Hatton. The twenty-one-year-old WBO inter-continental champ and young fighter of the year had been walking through his opponents to date and when his promoter, Frank Warren, mooted a match-up with Magee, Maloney tried to convince Callahan that it was the best offer on the table. But Mike and Eamonn only had eyes for one opponent at this time, Liverpool's WBU champion of the world Shea Neary.

Neary, known as the Shamrock Express due to his Irish heritage, had been on Magee's radar for a while. When the Englishman fought Mike Griffith at the National Stadium in Dublin earlier in the year, Eamonn was not only ringside, but he also had 1,000 fliers printed and placed on the arena's seats, each one calling out Neary and attempting to embarrass him into a fight. Neary was an attractive prospective opponent, not just for the title he held, but on account of the huge following he had built up since winning the WBU strap in 1996. His success had drawn terrestrial television back to the sport, with ITV now broadcasting his fights to massive primetime UK audiences. He was also a name in the US, and HBO had secured the rights to broadcast his next defence live on American television. At the level Magee was now operating at, TV networks had to be a party to negotiations and if the executives could not be sold on a particular fight and persuaded to stump up the cash to fill the bout's purse, the clash had little chance of materialising.

Callahan fired the opening shots in the bartering while Magee was still struggling with his hangover from the Burke celebrations. He publicised the fact that he had a certified cheque for £50,000 made payable to Shea Neary sitting in a bank account as a guaranteed prize for the champion before he even considered his cut from TV income. That additional TV money, he added, would most likely need to come from Sky Sports as, in his opinion, this fight was just too big for ITV to afford.

Neary's manager, John Hyland, who had previously promised Magee a shot if he dealt with Burke in impressive fashion, was determined to play hardball, however. Emboldened by Frank Warren fancifully mentioning pay days as high as £150,000 for his man, he scoffed at Mike's fifty grand and turned his attention to America. A fight with Arturo Gatti was announced before the Italian-born, Canadian-raised, America-based warrior pulled out. In his place Micky Ward, the Bostonian who, like Neary, claimed he bled green, white and orange when cut, stepped up. Ward was happy to travel for his chance and the bout was made for London in March 2000.

Eamonn decided to keep busy while the negotiations rumbled on. A month after destroying Burke, he was back in the ring to stop the hopelessly over-matched Radoslav Gaidev inside a minute. Next up was a Commonwealth title defence against the Kenyan Joseph Miyumo in Peterborough.

'Who's that old boy?' Magee enquired at the weigh-in when he noticed a middle-aged-looking African staring at him from across the room.

'That's your opponent,' Mike replied.

'Fuck off!' Eamonn shouted as he stifled a laugh. 'That fella looks about forty-five!'

Despite the misgiving about his true age, Miyumo was actually expected to provide a decent test on the night. But a double left hand followed by a thunderous and sickening right hook ended the African's challenge forty-eight seconds in and caused Glenn McCrory in the commentary seat to wonder out loud whether he was a little older than his birth certificate claimed.

The prize for that win was to have been a big-money fight with the highly rated American Ivan Robinson in Madison Square Garden on the undercard of Lennox Lewis defending his heavyweight title against Michael Grant, but once more boxing politics conspired against Eamonn. Angered at having his purse cut by $25,000 and Panix sending him a poor-quality video of Magee in action, Robinson was easily convinced by Bob Arum to renege on his deal to face Magee and instead go in against future world-title challenger Antonio Diaz. Replacements were announced – Cesar Bazán, Ahmed Santos and Reggie Green among them – but none actually signed on the dotted line and a frustrated Callahan was forced to abandon the New York venture at the last minute.

The poor second prize was a spot on the undercard of Clinton Woods' European light heavyweight defence at Wembley Arena. Magee faced David Kirk, a tough journeyman who had been stopped only once in thirty-one previous fights and would share the ring with the likes of Kell Brook, Matthew Macklin, Brian Rose and Junior Witter before he retired after eighty-nine contests. Embittered by circumstances beyond his control, Eamonn beat poor Kirk from pillar to post, dropping him in the fourth, sixth and eighth stanzas before the referee decided he could witness the punishment no more.

Eamonn barely celebrated in the ring that night at Wembley. It was impossible to muster enthusiasm for defeating David Kirk in London when he had been getting ready for a Robinson or a Bazán in New York. To make matters worse, he had sat ringside at the Olympia a few weeks before and witnessed Micky Ward's vicious body shots end Shea Neary's three-and-a-half-year reign as WBU champion of the world. In fact, he had shared a hotel lift with Ward on the eve of the fight and advised the American that targeting the champion's body would see him return home with the belt. That shock result appeared to reduce Magee's chances of a big-money showdown with his domestic foe even further.

A couple of weeks later, it looked like the Irishman's fortunes were finally taking a turn for the better. With much local fanfare, Callahan announced that a deal had been struck for Eamonn to face Ward as the main support for Lennox Lewis versus Frans Botha in the London Arena on 15 July 2000. Eamonn was elated, describing the opportunity as a dream come true and the reason he first laced up a glove. Mike was just as pleased and he referenced his old champions, John Caldwell and Freddie Gilroy, when articulating how special this night would be.

Unfortunately there was no real foundation to the story and Ward's people dismissed it out of hand within twenty-four hours. To Eamonn, these blows were tougher to take than anything being thrown at him in the ring. Callahan scrambled to recover the situation and within a week he notified the press that his fighter was still appearing on the Lewis Botha bill and Shea Neary would be in the opposite corner. This time it was an acceptable second prize, but yet again fate blindsided Magee. A gold filling came loose during sparring and what he expected to be a routine trip to the dentist turned into a nightmare. The damage to his tooth was so extensive that the entire nerve needed removing, which left the southpaw in agony with swollen features resembling the elephant man. Training was out of the question and so the fight was put back to November with a new venue still to be confirmed.

This latest setback hit him hard. Beating Burke was supposed to have been the stepping stone to massive title fights and the money and accolades that came with them. Yet here he was a year later having completed just seven rounds against three nobodies for relatively insignificant purses. The inactivity bored him and a bored Eamonn was a dangerous Eamonn. It gave him more time for drink, more time for drugs, more time for trouble.

It marked the start of a wild summer of iniquity that blazed on un-hindered into early September. In fact, only a surprise call from Callahan arrested the flow of alcohol and cocaine and pills into his charge's bloodstream. Howard Eastman was defending his Commonwealth middleweight title against Sam Soliman on a Panix Promotions show at York Hall in six days' time and Panos Eliades was in desperate need of a last-minute support act. He had an unknown, and unbeaten, Russian by the name of Pavel Melnikov ready to go and he expected Mike to repay an old favour by convincing Eamonn to complete the match-up. There was also an intimation that scratching his Greek-Cypriot back now would increase Magee's chances of landing a shot at the formidable WBC champion Kostya Tszyu after the Neary fight.

Eamonn, out of shape but in need of cash, accepted in a heartbeat and headed to the gym for half a week's preparation. John Breen wasn't even there as he had made the most of a rare break in his schedule to go on holiday with his wife. Indeed, the trainer only returned on the Thursday before the fight and immediately repacked his bag to fly to London for the weigh-in. With Neary less than two months away, Breen was privately livid that everything was being put in jeopardy against an unknown quantity just to dig a promoter out of a hole, but he knew he just had to get on with it.

The eight-round fight proved a real struggle. Melnikov was strong and a decent technician, but the problems were caused more by Magee's lack of conditioning than anything his opponent did. He looked sluggish from the off and spent the final three rounds on the ropes, waiting for the Russian to come to him and hoping to land enough telling counters to sway the referee. He did just enough and Dave Parris handed the Irishman the verdict by 78 to 76.

Barry McGuigan, working as a pundit on the televised bout, was one of many who felt Eamonn was a little fortunate to get the nod. 'He was rusty and he got out-worked,' proclaimed the Clones Cyclone, before adding that Magee should be looking after number one and forgetting all about doing favours for promoters or managers. McGuigan certainly had a point and Magee, arguing that getting paid for eight hard rounds was always a good night's work, smacked of a spin doctor on full damage-limitation mode. In truth, perhaps the only positives from that night were Eamonn coming through unscathed and Melnikov, who would go on to fight for the WBU world welterweight and WBO inter-continental super welterweight titles in his next five contests, agreeing to act as chief sparring partner for the big Neary fight on 11 November.

This time, under no illusions as to the size of the task in hand, Eamonn made sure he got a full camp in at the Crumlin farmhouse that was becoming his cold, spartan home away from home. It was a true fifty-fifty match-up between two hard men operating at the elite level of their profession and the prospect was enticing enough for Sky Box Office to charge their subscribers £11.99 for the pleasure of watching. In a ground-breaking deal for a UK boxing event, a company called World Broadcasts also paid for the right to relay the fight live online around the world. Belfast's Waterfront Hall jumped at the chance of staging the show, the first championship boxing match to take place in the riverside auditorium. The 2,250 seats sold out fast.

It was clear that the fight needed little promotion to be a commercial success, but with one eye on the limitless potential of pay-per-view sales and the other on antagonising Neary, Eamonn did his bit to draw attention to the showdown regardless. Despite being born and bred in Liverpool, Neary was fiercely proud of his Irish ancestry and marched to the ring to the tune of 'The Irish Rover' in a blaze of green, white and orange. Though he was entitled to self-identify as he pleased, the Irish shtick jarred somewhat with the fact that Neary was an ex-British soldier and even served as an infantryman with the King's Regiment on the streets of Derry in the early 1990s. It was an open goal for Magee to attack and he gleefully labelled his opponent a Plastic Paddy and as Irish as Tony Cascarino, the recently retired Irish football player who just weeks before had admitted in an autobiography that he had no Irish blood whatsoever in his veins.

The taunts injected an added dose of enmity to the usual pre-fight she-nanigans that continued right up to the weigh-in. While Neary was forced to strip naked to scale two ounces under the limit, Magee arrived late, half a pound overweight, and swaggered around sporting a T-shirt with the logo *100% Irish* plastered across it. Neary's manager, John Hyland, was enraged and lambasted the Magee camp's perceived unprofessionalism, but Eamonn returned thirty minutes later, having shed the necessary excess with little fuss in a nearby sauna. Hyland was perhaps feeling the pressure, having allegedly made a £50,000 bet with Panos Eliades on the outcome of the fight.

As always, Magee was nervous but confident as the fight bell drew nearer. He welcomed the onset of fluttering butterfly wings in the pit of his stomach for it told him he was switched on and fully conscious of what was soon to come. This was the biggest fight of his career by a considerable distance. Neary was the best light welter in the British Isles, had been a world champion just seven months earlier, and the Liverpudlian was now the last barrier to Eamonn making the final assault to reach similar peaks. But in a rare in-depth interview in the week of the fight, Magee explained to Karl McGinty from the *Irish Independent* that the label of world champion meant nothing to him.

'I don't want to be a world champion,' he began, 'I want to be a millionaire. But you have to fight for world titles to earn that sort of money. If I won the lotto on Saturday night, you'd never see me in the ring again. It's as simple as that.'

It was classic Magee, the type of blunt and brutally honest statement in which he specialises. No one has ever accused him of being a romantic, but there was more to it than that. The Commonwealth title victory had raised his stock in boxing circles and with it arrived praise and the first saplings of genuine adulation from press and fans alike. The development unnerved Eamonn somewhat. He had become accustomed to a life of back-handed compliments, of plaudits with caveats. He felt more comfortable being told how great he could be in one breath and then condemned for his drinking and lack of dedication in the next. That kept expectations low and gave him an easy out. *Sure I'm just a lying, drunken scumbag – you know how this story ends.* But now people where envisioning a happy, Hollywood climax for him and that was a pressure he felt incapable of shouldering.

He wanted love and support from the boxing fraternity, the writers and the public, but he feared it too. Tactless statements about not caring about the sport or the glory of a belt kept that prospective, widespread approval in check. Claiming he was just in it to make some money then get out ensured he remained a dangerous outsider, never fully embraced by anyone beyond his close circle.

The fight was awarded the tagline 'Men of War'. While ostensibly a simple, clichéd nod to the two protagonists' highly physical profession, it carried added resonance given Eamonn and Shea's youthful pasts as Fianna petrol-bomber and British squaddie on the streets of Northern Ireland. The Waterfront Hall was packed to the rafters and a whole different noise to what the auditorium was used to hearing was generated as the two men made their way to the ring. Magee supporters were in the majority, of course, but busloads of Neary fans had made the trip from Liverpool and Dublin and, fuelled by a full day sampling the many bars Belfast has to offer, they were in fine voice as well.

Neary emerged to 'The Irish Rover', his head hooded in black to shield his eyes and hide his emotions. His party wielded three Irish tricolours which they waved vigorously in the ring while their fighter sat motionless on his corner stool and awaited his foe. A siren blast signalled Magee's arrival. He beat his yellow gloves together over his head and took a deep breath before descending towards the squared circle. In a deliberate move, his team went one better than the opposition and hoisted four Irish tricolours skywards while the crowd roared and drowned out Eamonn's walk-out tune, the Baha Men's 'Who Let the Dogs Out'. Adam Smith, commentating for Sky Box Office, struggled to make himself heard as well.

'Hard, moody, truculent and tough,' Smith began his introduction of Magee. 'Incredibly intimidating – and that comes from trainer John Breen. His face is a scowl that could freeze molten lava. A lifetime on the down-trodden Ardoyne estate in west [sic] Belfast has moulded Eamonn Magee into a very dark man.'

The authoritative Roy Francis, regarded as the best and most experienced British referee operating at that time, was the third man in the ring. When he called the two fighters together for final instructions and a touching of gloves, it was clear there was no love lost and any mutual respect had yet to be earned.

Magee began flawlessly, countering over the top of Neary's single jabs to land at will. In the second round, a short right hook as he spun off the ropes buzzed the Liverpudlian and Eamonn unleashed an unanswered thirty-punch flurry in search of an early stoppage. He couldn't land cleanly, however, and the fight then settled down into a predictable pattern. Southpaw Magee was content to stay on the outside, circle to his right, slip his foe's advances and land counters when he could. Neary, the bull, continued forcing the pace, marching his man down, throwing more leather, hoping to either land big or win rounds on work rate alone.

And as the fight wore on, into the eighth and ninth and tenth, Neary's greater volume of punches probably did earn him the rounds. This was always the risk Eamonn's style of boxing ran. As a counter-puncher, he rarely initiated exchanges and this left him open to accusations of coasting and attempting to nick rounds rather than grabbing a fight by the scruff of the neck and dominating it. But so long as a counter-puncher lands enough clean hits, and avoids the majority coming back at him, he should never be punished for his style. At that time, computerised statistics were coming into fashion and armchair experts and ringside commentators alike were easily blinded by the one-dimensional numbers. Many punches that were rendered harmless by a defensive glove or arm still registered as scoring blows, the alleged equal of sharp, truly damaging shots that zeroed in on their mark. Eamonn would have thrown and landed more punches than very few of his opponents, all of whom employed the tactic of pressuring and outworking the Terminator, but he still comfortably beat the vast majority of them.

Magee was also said to struggle with that needling seed of doubt that a lack of total dedication during camp could plant in the back of a boxer's mind. Could he afford to put everything into every round? Would he run out of gas in the second half? He claims today that he always finished his championship bouts the strongest, but that may have been more to do with holding back in the middle portion of the fight than with admirable fitness levels. Anyone can empty the tank when the finishing line is in sight, the real challenge is to begin the process when there are still many miles to run.

As he sat at ringside alongside his wife, Noel Magee's early satisfaction with his brother's performance had been replaced by an anxious foreboding that Eamonn was in danger of letting his title slip away. As the rounds passed, his anxiousness increased and though he shouted himself hoarse, he feared his messages were getting lost amongst the myriad yells of support and scorn that the crowd relentlessly poured into the ring. At the end of the ninth Noel could take it no more and left his seat to run around the side of the ring to Eamonn's corner. There, he gave his best Angelo Dundee impression: 'You're blowing it son, you're blowing it,' he screamed at his little brother.

Eamonn rarely absorbed any of the advice he received mid-bout. As far as he was concerned, he had the optimum boxing brain for his style of fighting and, as the only man actually in there hitting and getting hit, he was best placed to decide what action needed taking. He valued John Breen and the rest of his corner highly, but in his mind they were all there to get him ready and in the best shape possible to do what he does when the bell sounds for each new round. Noel was blood, however, and his voice stood out amidst the din. When he heard his big brother, Eamonn turned and looked him in the eye.

'You're behind, Eamonn,' Noel continued. 'You need to do more!'

Eamonn nodded almost imperceptibly and went out and won the championship rounds.

Jim Watt, working as a ringside scorer for Sky Sports on the night, had

Magee two points down going into the final three minutes, but general opinion was largely divided depending on whose team you were on. Neary had undoubtedly fought as the aggressor, but he never had Eamonn in any trouble and the Northern Irishman landed the vast majority of the cleaner punches. For whatever reason, Eamonn threw caution to the wind in the last and bossed Neary around the ring, firing first and forcing the challenger to grab and hold. His punches were wild but eye-catching and the commentators loved it, with Watt and Smith suddenly waxing lyrical on what they were seeing from the Belfast man.

But to Magee, that final three minutes was just ragged street fighting to please the crowd and he was confident his measured boxing had won the fight in the previous thirty-three minutes. Anyone could stand toe-to-toe and brawl, but the sweet science was in essence a game of chess, a test of who was the smartest, who could hit and not be hit. As far as Eamonn was concerned, he had already proved conclusively that he and not Shea Neary was that man. Micky Ward beat Neary up in a fight, but Eamonn Magee had set out to defeat him in a boxing match.

As soon as the final bell sounded, both men looked to referee Roy Francis, but it was Eamonn who strode towards him with a broad grin. Francis obliged and anointed Magee a two-point winner and still the light welterweight champion of the Commonwealth.

The inevitable boos from Neary's highly charged fans clashed with the roars of delight from the locals. Hyland was naturally convinced his man won and his paranoia over being on the wrong end of a home decision intensified when rumours circulated that the ref had been threatened before the bout. According to fellow umpire Mickey Vann, Francis told him he was warned he'd be stabbed if the local fighter didn't get the decision. The BBBofC duly investigated and ruled those controversial claims to be entirely baseless. According to Francis, threats on his person arrived after the fight and he presumed they came from drunken Neary fans less than enamoured with his decision.

Eamonn ignored the fuss. He was now on the cusp. Warren made an immediate £40,000 offer for him to face the new WBU champion Jason Rowland, with a guarantee of more money to then fight Hatton if he won, but Callahan dismissed the idea with typical gusto.

'Eamonn Magee doesn't box exhibitions,' he quipped, 'and that money is a joke.'

There did certainly seem to be bigger fish to fry across the pond with WBC champ Tszyu, IBF champ Zab Judah, WBA champ Sharmba Mitchell, and the box-office Arturo Gatti all apparently within reach. But Eliades was suddenly not so vocal about his alleged deal with Tszyu and when the Russian-born Australian announced a unification fight with Mitchell, those two names quietly slipped off the table. Judah and Gatti soon drifted out of Eamonn's range as well when the former agreed to face Reggie Green and the latter hit the mother lode by signing to fight the Golden Boy, Oscar de la Hoya. From declarations that Magee would not fight again unless it was for a world title, Panix and Callahan were suddenly resigned to making fights just to keep their man busy.

The result was 2001 not being the vintage year it could and perhaps should have been. It wasn't until mid-March that he was permitted to throw a punch in anger while stopping Alan Bosworth, an honest but unspectacular pro, inside five rounds in Plymouth. He returned to Devon two months later and took two rounds longer to knock out the South African Harrison Methula in the third defence of his Commonwealth crown. Defence number four followed soon after and another Springbok, this time Matthews Zulu, stood in the opposite corner. Zulu, a blown-up lightweight with a decidedly average resumé, wasn't in Magee's class and yet he lasted the full twelve rounds in what was a desperately disappointing spectacle. Eamonn was lethargic throughout and, though he won nearly every round, the performance did nothing for his stock in the light welterweight division. By the midway point, jeers of derision could already be heard from the crowd, while the fee-paying Sky TV viewers were struggling to stay awake on their sofas. When Eamonn's arm was raised by the referee to salute a unanimous-decision victory, his face displayed a vacant expression that hinted at a mind not totally on the job. A mind distracted by the constant turmoil of his chaotic life outside the ring.

***

Just three fights in a year afforded more free time than it was safe for a man like Eamonn Magee to have. Particularly when that sixty-seven minutes of action paid handsomely enough to indulge in the vices that Eamonn has always found impossible to ignore. Drink, drugs and infidelity were still a constant in his life and placed a devastating strain on his relationship with Mary and the kids. On occasion Mary inevitably lost it and the resulting rows would be ferocious and, at times, physical. In the aftermath, Eamonn would storm off and not be seen for days, leaving her to pick up the pieces and attempt to maintain at least a façade of normality for the children's sake.

Once, when Francis, Áine and Eamonn Jr had been left at the school gates, Mary returned home, packed all of Eamonn's clothes in black bin bags and deposited them in a charity shop on Castle Street in the centre of Belfast. A couple of days later, Eamonn was walking to the gym when he noticed the shop-window mannequin dressed from head to toe in what looked suspiciously like his own garb. Upon entering the store, a quick scan revealed his entire wardrobe for sale at knock-down prices. He bought it all back and returned home to an empty house where he proceeded to cut a chunk out of the side of every one of Mary's dresses. They'd later kiss and make up, and it never crossed Eamonn's mind that, one day, Mary would surely lose all patience and decide to be rid of him for good.

The abuse of various substances sparked much of the trouble Eamonn found, but, in truth, he was an extremely high-functioning alcoholic. He admits that a heavy night on cocaine left him less than 100 per cent the following morning, but he could put away any quantity of drink and pills and wake early the next day to hit the gym or go about his business with no ill-effects. This was a blessing at face value, but an undoubted curse in the long run. Mike and John did not know about the full extent of the drug problem, but they were well aware that their prized asset was overly fond of the drink. That was a large part of the reason for spiriting Eamonn away to isolated farmhouses in the countryside in the build-up to big fights. For added security, Callahan would leave handwritten notes behind the bars of any pubs he suspected Eamonn of frequenting, begging the staff not to serve the boxer if he had a fight in the coming weeks. Eamonn could be persuasive, however, and there were always new drinking establishments to explore anyway.

On top of the substance abuse, another demon had by now tightened its destructive grip on Eamonn. From the moment he had a few coins in his pocket as a kid, Eamonn loved the thrill of gambling. And from games of pitch and toss for a handful of loose change in the school yard, it wasn't long before local bookies became familiar with the flame-haired punter popping in and out throughout the day to bet on anything from horses and tennis to football and the GAA.

***

On the day I meet his brother Patrick, I drop Eamonn off at a local social club that offers cheap and early pints to pass the morning. In what is unlikely to be simply a happy coincidence, Sean Graham has a branch of his bookmakers next door. When I arrive after a couple of hours with Patrick, I bump into Eamonn dashing out the door with a grin on his face and a winning docket in his hand.

'Go on in and get a pint,' he shouts as he jogs out of the car park. 'I'll be back in a sec.'

It is a standard set-up inside the low-ceilinged club. A well-stocked bar, a well-used snooker table and large screens on the wall showing Sky

Sports news and the racing channel. Eamonn soon returns and picks up where he left off with the pint of Harp on the bar.

'How much did you win?' I ask him.

'Ah, a few quid,' he replies, before motioning up to the screen. 'It's all on the favourite now.'

Looking up I ask him what his horse is called, but he never pays any attention to the names. All he knows is it is number five and the wager and odds were good enough that it'll cover all our expenses for the day. He's an all-or-nothing type of guy so needless to say, he only ever bets on the nose. With pints in hand we watch the 15.10 at Ludlow commence. It turns out that number five is called Duke's Affair and he is going along nicely until number four, Minellacelebration, comes up the outside and beats him by a length.

'Fuck that then,' Eamonn mutters as he rips up the betting slip and tilts his empty glass towards his nephew working behind the bar to signal another pint is required. Easy come, easy go.

In the grand scheme of things he didn't lose much that day, but only because he didn't have much to lose. But back when boxing was paying Eamonn well, he became well known in gambling circles for regularly staking £20,000 on the outcome of a race or a match, and at times betting double that. He has plenty of winning stories but as usual it's the hard-luck tales that stick in the memory. There's the untimely last-minute point in an All-Ireland final that he had £40,000 riding on. There's the grand he lost when the jockey inexplicably slid off his horse when he cleared the last and was cantering home with nobody near him. There was the family weekend in Leopardstown when he lost every penny at the races and the police were called when he couldn't pay the B&B bill. In amongst those extremes there is a decade's worth of constant, if unremarkable, gambling that he now estimates saw close to a million pounds lost and won and lost again.

'A gambling addiction is a really terrible fucking thing,' he tells me as we drive out of the car park. 'It can control you every bit as bad as the drink and the gear. It can trick you into thinking that money grows on trees and so it doesn't matter if you lose, you'll get the money back again soon one way or another. And that's what I believed back then – that there was always another score, or another win, or another big purse just around the corner.'

I don't want to be a world champion, I want to be a millionaire, he said before the Neary fight. Accumulating that amount of money was more than a desire; it was a need. Each time he got in the ring and fought for a purse of money he was chasing the losses that were just around the corner.

✳✳✳

In terms of his career, 2001 was more notable for the machinations of making the fight between himself and Ricky Hatton than anything that transpired in the three bouts he fought on the canvas dance floor. Frank Warren offered a potential four-fight package that, if Magee kept winning after first facing Hatton, would have been worth half a million pounds. But one of the unacceptable caveats was that Eliades would be kept out of the picture and, with Callahan wanting a bigger purse up front for the Hatton fight anyway, the negotiations dragged on.

In March Sky Sports invited Eamonn, Mike and John to attend a Hatton fight and help keep the hype train chugging along. Magee took it as a plus-one-type deal and arrived at the dock early on the Saturday morning with an old pal, Bo Cameron. The pair hadn't been to bed and Bo felt as bad as Eamonn looked. Hatton knocked Jason Rowland out in the fourth stanza that night to claim the vacant WBU title, and when Eamonn was invited into the ring and introduced to the crowd he received the type of welcome Manchester sports fans normally reserve for visiting Scousers. 'Ricky's gonna kill you' rang out as Magee grinned and leered and lapped it all up.

On the way home the next day, Eamonn asked John to swing by Leyland, about thirty miles north of Manchester, to call in on his mother. Isobel, who had met an Englishman and was now living in Lancashire, prepared lunch and after the meal Eamonn decided that he and Bo would stick around for a few days. Then, with barely twenty quid between them, the two tourists headed for the nearest bookies to gather funds for their stay. For once, the luck of the Irish applied to Eamonn's gambling and he went on a streak that reaped in enough to convert a planned two-night sojourn into a fortnight's holiday. While there he struck up a romantic relationship with the daughter of Isobel's man and, sleeping in an adjacent room, he made sure his wannabe stepdad heard every bang of the headboard and squeal of his daughter as he vigorously consummated the affair.

When Magee returned to Manchester later in the year to fight Zulu on the Hatton–Pendleton undercard, the reception was even hotter. The Irishman was quoted in the programme as being confident of cutting Ricky to ribbons when they met and 20,000 lairy Mancs inside the MEN Arena didn't let him forget it throughout the twelve insipid rounds. It was all music to the ears of the promoters and TV executives, and by the end of the year a deal was verbally agreed, in principle at least: Eamonn would defend his Commonwealth title against Jonathan Thaxton as the chief support for Hatton–Krivolapov in February and, presuming both came through unharmed, the Hitman versus the Terminator would finally take place in early summer 2002.

Thaxton was no mug, however. A fellow southpaw, he was three years younger than Magee and had just given Hatton all he could handle over twelve tough rounds. Further down his resumé he had impressive wins over the likes of Paul Burke, Bernard Paul and Paul Ryan, as well as comfortable victories over old Magee adversaries Karl Taylor, David Kirk and Alan Temple. Eamonn knew he had a fight on his hands and it pushed him to put in what he regards as the most dedicated six weeks of preparation of his entire career.

This time Mike kept him cooped up in a tiny cottage on the outskirts of Loughinisland, a small village twenty-five miles south of Belfast. The area is known only for the 1994 massacre in which a UVF murder squad opened fire on a bar full of people watching the Ireland versus Italy World Cup match, killing six innocent men. A trusted associate, Michael Hughes, was installed as camp manager with strict instructions not to take his eyes off Magee, and Eamonn's brother Patrick also stayed and trained with him during that camp. But when Callahan dropped the trio at their accommodation on Boxing Day in the middle of an unforgiving winter, none of the group were particularly enamoured with what they encountered. Hurrying in out of the snow, they found the inside of the old, white cottage as cold as the barren fields that surrounded it. There were only two rooms, one with three dubious-looking single beds, and the other with a couple of beat-up sofas, a sink, a gas stove and a fireplace you could almost stand up straight in. The floor was paved with the type of concrete flagstones more commonly found on an outdoor patio, as if to ensure that absolutely no heat could be retained inside the building.

'You must be fucking joking!' Eamonn roared at Mike as his manager stood in the door, surveying the quasi-prehistoric scene in front of him.

'You need this after that display last time,' was Callahan's curt response and without further ado he strode to his car and settled in for the warm drive home.

After much effing and blinding, the two brothers and Hughes accepted their lot and began focusing on the task at hand. Each morning they'd rise at daybreak and Patrick would walk to the top of a long, steep hill and then instruct his younger sibling to sprint up after him. Eamonn made it about a quarter of the way at his first attempt, but that was fine, training for a boxing match is all about peaking at the right time. As soon as a breathless Eamonn did reach the summit, Patrick set off at a rapid pace and told his brother to try to catch him up before the eight-mile, undulating loop took them back to the cottage. Those runs were invariably through snow for much of the route, at times knee-deep. Wild deer and rabbits would scamper for cover when they heard the Ardoyne men coming. Back at the cottage Eamonn would beat a giant tractor tyre with a sledgehammer before chopping chunks of wood with a long-handled felling axe. It was real, old-school, brutal, Rocky-esque training, but it was exactly what Magee needed to torture his body into prime fighting condition. Five weeks in he was sprinting the whole way up that incline and flying past Patrick less than a mile down the road.

We drove past the area on the way to Newcastle to see his brother Noel, and Eamonn fondly pointed out the landmarks as we cruised by. The peaks and troughs of the hills he pounded for eight miles a day, every day. The petrol station where they'd steal bags of coal in an attempt to create a blaze big enough in the gaping fireplace to at least temporarily warm their stone-age living quarters. Finally the off-licence where he admitted to allowing himself six tins of lager each Saturday night as a reward for a week of relentlessly hard work. This was the most dedicated six weeks of preparation of his career, but there are no happy miracles when it comes to alcoholics and their poison.

Nevertheless, come fight week, Magee was primed for action. Back in Belfast he was packing his bag for the trip to Manchester when the phone rang: the news wasn't good. The night before, Mike was overcome with chest pains and rushed to the coronary unit of the Royal Victoria Hospital. He was stable, but the doctors were not letting him go anywhere for a few days and a journey across the Irish Sea to watch a prize fight was certainly out of the question. The news stunned Eamonn. Callahan bristled at the idea of sympathy and huffed and puffed about it all being an overreaction, but he was a seventy-five-year-old man still living at a thirty-year-old's pace, so everyone knew this was no joke. It was the most important bout of his life and Eamonn was forced to face up to the reality of his manager being absent from his corner for the first time in his career.

As John Coyle reiterated the standard fistic instructions in the centre of the ring, the difference in stature between the two fighters was stark. Thaxton, slightly shorter and much stockier, looked chiselled from granite as he flexed his muscles opposite the lithe and loose Magee. The Norwich fighter appeared a ball of intense, nervous energy as he bounced on the spot and then pushed his face to within millimetres of Eamonn's in an attempt to force a reaction. But Magee didn't bite. He appeared focused but relaxed. There was additional pressure for, although the Hatton fight was virtually agreed, he knew he had to not only win, but win in a style that would impress fans and TV execs alike to guarantee the contract got signed. Nevertheless, he seemed at peace and confident as the opening bell tolled.

From the off, Magee was on it. Thaxton had no chance of out-boxing the shrewd southpaw in front of him, so he bulldozed in, swinging hooks and attempting to be the bully in the ring. He enjoyed flashes of success in each of the first two stanzas, but nothing sufficient to guarantee him the round as Eamonn simply spun away from any incident that promised trouble or greeted Thaxton's charges with exquisitely timed counters.

In the third, Magee landed one with real intent. He faked a jab to the body and then launched a left hand over the top of Thaxton's own pawing jab and onto an exposed temple that put the Englishman down hard. The sheer speed of the blow belied its destructive power, but as Eamonn made to stroll to a neutral corner to watch his foe languish on the canvas, he suddenly stopped in his tracks. Thaxton had bounced back up instantaneously and looked impatient to get the mandatory eight count over and done with so they could get back to it. Magee wondered how the hell he had absorbed such a shot so well but there was no time to dwell over the mystery and he set about Thaxton with a barrage that kept referee John Coyle close and poised to jump in if one more devastating punch connected.

Thaxton survived and even leered at Magee when the bell chimed to provide him with a minute's respite, but the writing was on the wall. It is to the Englishman's credit that he came out and made the next two sessions the most competitive of the fight, but Magee was taking one of his infamous breathers and using the extra time on his hands to spy a fatal flaw in his opponent's technique. Eamonn tended to circle clockwise around the ring but he noticed that if he changed direction and forced Thaxton to do likewise, the Norwich man briefly crossed his legs as he sidestepped back into range. Against a boxing brain as sharp as Eamonn Magee's, that was a mistake that was destined to be punished.

The moment arrived around one minute into the sixth stanza. Moving to his right with his back against the ropes, Eamonn allowed Thaxton in and then detonated a chopping left hand on his chin. He instantly recognised that his rival was in dire straits and launched a hurtful tirade of rights and lefts, hooks, uppercuts and crosses that sent a buzzed Thaxton spinning into the centre of the ring. The brave and highly conditioned Englishman refused to visit the canvas again, but every other blow now penetrated his weakened guard and with nothing coming back in return, the referee stepped in. Just as all professional boxing referees should be, Coyle was brave enough to stop a fight one punch too early rather than let it go on one too late. There was a look of anguished protest on Thaxton's face, but few complaints from his own cornermen. Magee had stopped him spectacularly to silence any remaining doubters and rubber stamp the showdown with Hatton.

Manchester's finest did the business with a ninth-round stoppage of his game Russian challenger a little later, but Magee's was undoubtedly the performance of the night. Suddenly Hatton's biggest fans were wondering whether Eamonn was worth the risk after all. The Hitman's own trainer, Billy Graham, would later admit that he never wanted his charge anywhere near Magee, a telling statement in light of how negotiations for a fight that had seemed all but made twenty-four hours earlier somehow dragged on for another couple of months.

In the meantime, Magee sought distraction and he found it one night standing at a Belfast city-centre bar. As he sipped his pint he overheard a drinking acquaintance lamenting the fact that after nearly two years of fundraising, he had only managed to accumulate £350 towards kitting out his nephew, Blaise Hughes, with the custom-made wheelchair he needed to compete in the discus event at an upcoming championship for people with disabilities in the US.

'How much do you need?' Eamonn butted into the conversation.

'About two grand, Eamonn.'

'Two grand? Fuck sake, I'll have that for you by the end of the week.'

And he did. On one afternoon he walked the length of Blaise's native Falls Road, stopping in each watering hole along the way to wet his whistle and encourage fellow drinkers to throw a few quid into the kitty for west Belfast's future para-athlete. The cash came so easily that Eamonn decided not to stop there and set himself the target of raising enough to send as many members of Blaise's family as possible to America to support him.

Given his success, Magee decided that the next step would be to get sponsorship for some sort of challenge. Walking to the gym one day, he came up with the idea of jet-skiing across the Irish Sea from Scotland to Northern Ireland. Jim Rock and three other pals were soon roped in and a month later, off they set.

It didn't seem too bad as they cast off from Stranraer on Scotland's west coast. The day was clear, the sea appeared calm and it was around sixty miles as the crow flies to reach their destination in Belfast. Eamonn had been sure to pack provisions, twenty Regal Kingsize and four tins of Magners cider, so what could possibly go wrong?

From the moment they left Lough Ryan and moved out into open waters, it was evident that the sea was not as tranquil as it had appeared when they were still within touching distance of Scottish soil. And by the time they had made it about halfway across, ten-foot swells were sweeping the jet-skis up and releasing them to hurtle down the other side at a rate of knots none of the group was particularly comfortable with. Each man was tossed from his vehicle more than once and the salty water that clung to their clothes and skin served to exacerbate the wind chill and make life even more miserable. At one point the SeaCat – the high-speed catamaran ferry – breezed past, but so tensed were the bodies holding on for grim life that they couldn't even raise their arms to wave.

Then Magee hit a breaker at the wrong angle and was catapulted into the ocean. This time the collision had been so violent that the motor's key, attached to each rider's wrist with a rubber band, slipped over his hand and began to sink. Eamonn saw it and made to dive under but his life jacket refused to let him submerge. The key disappeared into the depths, and Eamonn was left alone in the water as his four mates disappeared into the distance.

It was a full ten minutes before Rock realised that five had become four and the flotilla turned back in search of the missing seaman. They found him, shivering on his drifting jet-ski, fag in his mouth and a half-drunk can of cider in his hand.

'Where the fuck have yous been?' he managed to yell through rattling teeth.

They gave Eamonn the spare key and all five were soon in sight of Irish landfall. Straight up Belfast Lough they proceeded until Mary and the kids could be seen next to the Odyssey Arena, screaming and shouting for their old man. Harbour police were soon on the scene and abruptly directed the unauthorised fleet to a more appropriate spot to disembark. Just over two hours after they bade farewell to Scotland, Magee's final thrust on the accelerator swept his motor onto the shore just as the last drop of petrol was consumed.

In was an eventful crossing but, by the standards of Magee's typically hectic adventures, a successful one. The money raised managed to send Blaise's parents and grandparents to the games to watch their champion in action.

Eamonn enjoyed making charitable gestures such as these. He was well aware of the reputation he had in many quarters and perhaps it was just to prove to himself that he was not as bad as some made him out to be. Those closest to him already knew the truth, of course. His heart was fundamentally good: the drink and drugs just had a habit of temporarily poisoning it. But in running the Belfast marathon for a hospice or painting an old boy's front room for nothing, Eamonn reminded himself of what he was beneath it all.

Back in the boxing world, the final obstacles to making the Hatton fight were falling away. After five successful defences, Magee vacated his Commonwealth title in order to avoid having to face a mandatory challenger. Manchester City's Maine Road Stadium had been mooted as a possible venue, but in the end both parties agreed that filling the MEN to its 20,000 capacity was the best bet. A date was then secured to keep both Sky Sports in the UK and Showtime in the US happy and the fight was finally announced for 1 June 2002.

***

Magee celebrated the news the only way he knew how: a few pints with mates in a north Belfast bar. They found themselves beginning the festivities in Chimney Corner, about eight miles up the Antrim Road from the Ardoyne. When they had just settled down with their opening drinks, a bouncer approached the table and asked them to quickly finish up and be on their way.

'It's in your own best interests,' he added ominously.

He didn't need to say any more. On a quiet Sunday evening in 2002, one of the most famous sportsmen in the country was warned that his religion made him an unwelcome visitor in that particular establishment. Northern Ireland may have come a long way since the dark days of the Troubles, but at that point it still had quite a distance to travel.

***

It was as big a domestic match-up as could be found on British or Irish shores at the beginning of the century. Frank Warren raised a few eyebrows when he compared it to the legendary Benn versus Eubank rivalry from a decade earlier, but it certainly felt like it had that potential. Not so much in the level of the personal vitriol between the two protagonists – although Eamonn certainly got under young Hatton's skin – but more in the prospect of what may unfold in the ring. Hatton, the unbeaten champion and darling of the British media, was the favourite, but few were willing to put too much money where their mouths were, particularly after Magee destroyed Thaxton, who had recently given Hatton all sorts of bother.

Callahan found a new training camp to house his most prized and troublesome asset, this time even further from home. A small, isolated farm with converted outhouses at the foot of the Mourne Mountains on the northern side of the border was chosen to keep Magee safe from the temptation of his city life. Once again, Mickey Hughes and Eamonn's brother Patrick were given the job of keeping an eye or four on the fighter, but this time it proved an entirely thankless task. In truth, Magee was not a man to be watched and managed and controlled. He had been his own boss since he could walk the streets of the Ardoyne and regardless of what Mike Callahan or John Breen or anyone else believed, he always did as he pleased. Something about the Thaxton challenge had motivated him, but now, on the threshold of the wealth, fame and adulation he craved, with one of the toughest light welterweights on the planet waiting for him, he couldn't find the spark. He couldn't muster up the flame of determination to fully sacrifice for six weeks and give himself a fighting chance.

Callahan had deposited Eamonn far enough away to make soirées into Belfast an impossibility, but unfortunately he overlooked the proximity of the bright lights of Newry, a town recently granted city status as part of the Queen's jubilee celebrations. Magee may not have toasted Her Majesty, but he certainly drank to everyone else's health but his own during that chaotic camp in south Armagh. Alcohol now effectively controlled him. He still woke each morning and did everything asked of him in terms of physical training throughout the day, but two or three times a week he was out in a bar or club, drinking heavily and returning to his quarters in the early hours with someone to keep him awake a little while longer.

Perhaps he subconsciously started believing his own hype. After a career in which he felt the media were either out to get him or wilfully underplaying his accomplishments, suddenly they were queueing up to praise his ability and hail him as a genuinely world-class operator. He had taken Thaxton apart with ease in half the time Hatton had spent struggling to keep his nose in front of the exact same foe. Eamonn couldn't help interpreting those two facts as confirmation that he would surely beat the champion. It is logic that rarely adds up with such simplicity within the confines of a fistic triumvirate, but for an alcoholic seeking to justify a binge it would do just fine.

Patrick and Mickey were cowed into silent complicity while Mike was kept in the dark altogether. Back in Belfast, John had his suspicions and would force extra rounds of sparring onto his charge if he caught a whiff of alcohol seeping from his fighter's pores, but he wouldn't know the full extent of the partying until years later. However, one man who was fully aware of Eamonn's behaviour at this time was the local IRA commander.

Magee had not exactly been discreet with his after-dark manoeuvres. He had use of a Range Rover jeep, branded from bonnet to boot with garish Hatton versus Magee advertising, for the duration of his stay and it wasn't long before everyone recognised the boxer's car approaching. So when a four-wheel drive vehicle started tearing through villages at all hours of the night, there was little doubt about who was behind the wheel. It was only a matter of time before someone paid the Belfast man a visit.

One night around midnight Eamonn was lying in bed in that fuzzy state between wakefulness and sleep when he heard a light scratching sound at the patio doors of his room. In an instant he was fully alert, with eyes wide open and ears pricked. The average man would have dismissed the noise as a cat or leaf, or some other of nature's night-time murmurs, but Magee has always had a justifiably suspicious mind. He could hear nothing else coming from outside on the patio, but he slipped out of bed and crossed the room to open his door and peer out in search of Patrick and Mickey downstairs. He took a bare-footed step towards them when a sudden thud on the front door obliterated the peaceful silence of the house.

'Get up here now!' Eamonn roared to his brother and friend, before stepping into Patrick's room.

'What the fuck!' Patrick screamed as he sprinted up the stairs to his brother against the backdrop of the front door being punctured by steel-toed boots intent on forcing entry.

When all three men were inside Patrick's bedroom, the other two froze in the centre of the room as Eamonn dragged a heavy chest of drawers across the door. By now a splintered hole had been booted into the wooden front door of the bungalow and three masked and armed men were standing in the hallway.

'Come out here now, Eamonn,' a south Armagh voice demanded. 'This is the Irish Republican Army and we need to have a word with you.'

Nobody in the bedroom moved a muscle or made a sound.

'Come on, Eamonn,' the paramilitary continued. 'We just want to talk.'

'Aye right!' Eamonn shouted back in reply. 'Just talk. I've heard that a million times before.'

The stand-off continued with a back and forth along similar lines conducted through the bedroom door for several minutes. Finally, Eamonn reached the conclusion that whatever these men had come for, they were in charge of the situation, and the last thing he wanted was to provoke a scenario in which Patrick or Mickey would unduly suffer.

'Okay,' he said. 'I'm coming out now on my own. Back away from the bedroom door and I'll talk to you.'

After hearing the boots tramp a few steps away, Eamonn pushed the chest of drawers aside and cracked the bedroom door so a line of light cut his face down the middle and he could peek out and see what he was dealing with. The three men stood there, each holding a gun in their right hand. But he had no choice, so with a deep breath he slipped out of the bedroom, closed the door behind him and walked towards the unwelcome guests.

'Hello, Eamonn.'

'What do yous want?'

'Just a word, like I said. I'm glad we found you here tonight. We've been round before and there was no sign of you.'

'I'm normally here.'

'No you're not. And that's the problem. Normally you're out in that fucking jeep. Driving around these roads pissed at all hours. Boozing and shagging all round you from what we hear.'

'What are you–'

'Shut up, Magee. Just fucking listen for once in your life. You don't come into our area and behave like that, understood?'

Eamonn nodded.

'Also, you're fighting Ricky fucking Hatton in less than a fortnight and you're drunk every other night. What the fuck are you playing at?'

'What?'

'This is the big one. Concentrate on training for a few fucking weeks and you could be set for life after it.'

'Okay. Jesus Christ. Message received.'

'We only want to help you, you know.'

'Help me? Fuck me lads. You think kicking my door through and marching in here with guns in your hands is helping me? Could you not just have sent me a fucking text message or something?'

'Watch yourself, Eamonn. You're the guest down here and we can very quickly put you out.'

With that they left and Eamonn, Patrick and Mickey looked blankly at one another for an instant and then each retired to their room.

The next morning Eamonn rose, drove into town and bought a wooden panel to mend the front door. In an adjacent shed he found a pot of the same blue paint that had been used on the bungalow and he was able to make the door look as good as new. He walked to the main farmhouse and told the owner that there had been a change in plan and they'd be returning to Belfast today. He paid the man in full, climbed into his jeep and never looked back. That was the end of his training camp for Ricky Hatton.

I've heard that story told on two separate occasions, once by Eamonn and once by Patrick. In terms of the detail, both relay almost identical tales. But in terms of the tone each man adopts as they retell it, there is a world of difference. For Patrick, it is like reliving a nightmare, more a post-trauma flashback than a simple recollection. He pauses to shake his head at various points, still a little stunned by the experience. For Eamonn, however, it is just another story, one of the countless number in his memory bank to laugh and joke about. He was only thirty years old but he had already seen it all. That granted him a macabre perspective on life, a twisted interpretation of the old maxim: whatever doesn't kill you only makes you stronger. He had developed a fatalistic view of the world and, as long as he physically walked away from a situation, that was good enough for him. Later in life he'd be haunted and tortured by past events preying on his mind, but back then at the height of his professional career his attitude was simple: fuck it all.

**

Magee gathered his team together for the fight of his life. A boxer is permitted a maximum of four seconds, with just one being allowed to climb between the ropes and face the fighter on his stool between rounds. Over the course of his professional career, Eamonn only ever employed nine different men in his corner. In the early days, the great Dennie Mancini acted as his cutman, a privilege derived from Mike Callahan's friendship with one of the most respected cornermen in British boxing. On the rare occasion Dennie was already contracted to an opponent, Mick

Williamson proved a more than capable substitute, and when Mancini hung up his Enswell and Vaseline for good, Oscar Checa took over the blood-stemming duties. The Panamanian had trained alongside Magee in Breen's Gym for years and Eamonn trusted the ex-super welterweight to deal with any nicks that opened. Head trainer John Breen was, of course, ever-present and Eamonn also liked to have his brother Patrick close at hand throughout a big contest. Dean Powell, a fixture in boxing circles for decades, having worked in various roles for the likes of Frank Bruno and Lennox Lewis, was another face that occasionally appeared in Magee's corner on headlining nights and old pal Jim Rock stepped in right at the end.

The final spot on the team always went to the chief gym helper, the guy that is in first and out last, opening up and locking the doors, turning the heat on and wiping up the blood, sweat and tears that flow throughout a session in a professional boxing gym. Young Tommy Kelly, christened 'Spit Bucket' by Eamonn, often played the part with enthusiastic aplomb, adding a very vocal cheerleading aspect to the role. But for the Hatton fight, Magee was determined to have old Fintan McGurk by his side. Vinty had been one of the founding members of the great Immaculata Amateur Boxing Club on the lower Falls Road and began working with Breen when Eastwood's gym closed in the mid-1990s. Aged eighty-two, he had never been on a plane and owned no passport or other photographic identification, but Eamonn insisted he make it to Manchester. A fake driving licence was soon secured and, much to everyone's amusement, Vinty nervously strapped himself in for his maiden flight.

For the first time in his career, Eamonn also wanted his three kids to be ringside with Mary to watch their old man fight. At the airport, ten-year-old Áine spotted the Irish boyband Westlife, then at the height of their global fame. Nicky Byrne, Brian McFadden and the boys were trying to keep a low profile, but when they spied Eamonn they approached for a chat and posed for photos with an openly elated Áine and a secretly delighted

Francis and Junior. The singers wished Eamonn all the best in the fight and arranged VIP tickets and backstage passes for their upcoming gig in the Odyssey Arena, a night which helped keep Magee in his daughter's good books for longer than usual.

Once in Manchester, however, the well-wishers were few and far between. Magee's questionable dedication to training made him a trainer's nightmare, but his innate ability to hit a raw nerve with a cutting sound-bite made him a promoter's dream. This time his role was public enemy number one, both to goad Team Hatton into a position where they could not refuse the fight, and to force an enmity between the men that would guarantee a sell-out at the MEN. Eamonn had played his part in the build-up admirably and saw no point in relenting on fight night. With the undercard in full swing, and Hatton's hardcore fans starting to stream in through the venue's front doors, Magee stood outside in a tracksuit smoking a fag and glaring at anyone foolish enough to hold his gaze. You would have to go pretty far back in history to find evidence of a boxer smoking a cigarette an hour before he fought in a title bout.

He maintained the spiteful, bad-boy act right up to and including the ringwalk. The fight had been christened 'Anarchy in the UK', with a Union Jack flag providing the backdrop to all the promotional material, and the atmosphere inside the arena as Eamonn waited to make his entrance was a hostile mix of hate and nationalistic pride. Never one to back down from confrontation or provocation, Magee fanned the flames further by adding a pair of novelty Irish tricolour sunglasses to his traditional green, white and orange garb. Below his surname on the back of his robe, *Ard Eoin*, the Gaelic spelling of Ardoyne, had been added.

Team Magee were called to leave the dressing room for the ringwalk but were kept waiting for what seemed like an age in one of the narrow corridors within the warren-like bowels of the MEN. Then they were urged forward and a curtain parted so the television cameras could focus in. Once more, however, they were told to wait, this time in full view of the

A post-fight drink with Hatton. © *Tom Casino. Courtesy of Paul Speak*

Backstage with Nicky from Westlife just after the Hatton fight.

In the changing rooms with Jimmy Vincent after our world title fight.

Posing with my WBU world title belt with Frankie McCann (*right*) and Patsy.

My proud dad with his world champion son.

Our proud mum wearing my WBU strap and Noel's Commonwealth version.

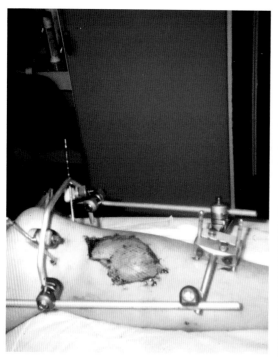

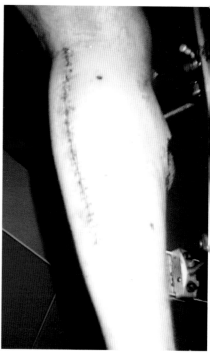

My leg when doctors wondered
if I'd walk again.

Post-surgery – just a few stitches!

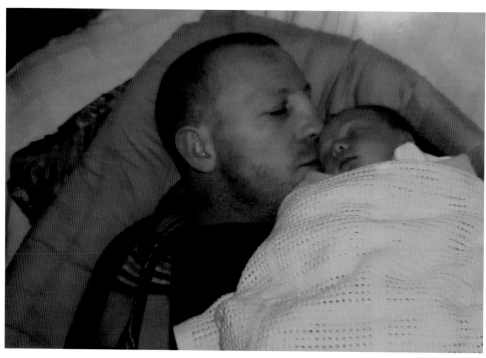

Baby Ethan.

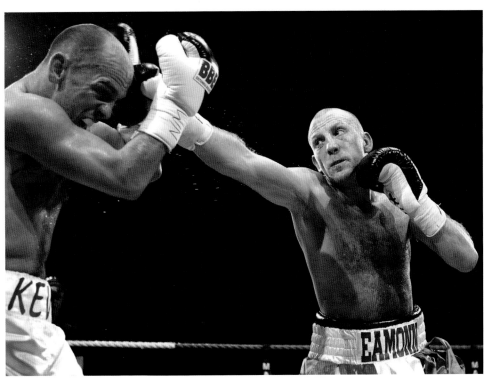

Landing a jab in my final bout against Kenny Anderson. © *Press Eye Ltd*

My brothers and I featuring prominently on the Ardoyne Avenue mural.
Courtesy of Extramural Activity

The four Magee boys after the Belfast marathon.

I couldn't have been happier to see Jr win my old Ulster intermediate light welterweight title.
© *Press Eye Ltd*

With my fiancée, Bronagh.
Courtesy of Michael Lowther

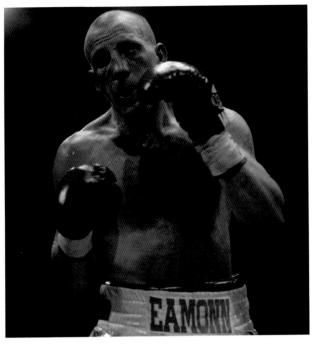

Waiting to knock out Allan Vester in my
comeback fight. © *Press Eye Ltd*

My youngest, Ethan,
getting bigger every day.

Advising my son, Jr, on the toughest of sports. © *Press Eye Ltd*

Carrying Jr's coffin. © *Press Eye Ltd*

The corner where my son took
his final breath.

With Áine, Francis and grandkids,
Cormac and Eamonn, at Jr's grave.

thousands of Hatton fans that surrounded that opening. Some of the more inebriated decided to greet the Irishman with vitriolic abuse and pints of beer and urine poured from above. Eamonn looked up menacingly while John Breen, wiping the liquid from his head, went ballistic and gestured to security to do something about the animals. Magee felt his temperature rising: he was getting angry, just as the Hatton camp would have wished. *It's all one big conspiracy*, he decided.

When word came from Sky TV to start the ringwalk, Eamonn refused to move. As Glenn McCrory wondered on live television whether he had forgotten his cue, Eamonn stood in defiance. His music began, a seven-minute recording of a traditional old Gaelic song about a lone warrior going into battle, and he was determined the English crowd would listen to every second of it.

Finally, led by Danny McAlinden, the ex-British and Commonwealth heavyweight champ who always cleared his path to the ring, Eamonn walked. Over 5,000 had made the crossing on boats and specially chartered planes to be in England and support Magee, but they were drowned out by the storm of jeers that rained down from Hatton's fabled followers in the bleachers. Eamonn's eyes were hidden behind the shades, but the rest of his countenance portrayed a sense of calm assurance. He knew his preparation had not been ideal, but he couldn't see anything other than his hand being raised in triumph at the end. Since the moment the Hatton fight was signed, he had asked himself the same rhetorical question more than a thousand times: *I'm a thirty-year-old man. How the fuck is a twenty-three-year-old kid going to beat me?*

He believed Hatton to be nothing more than a one-dimensional bully. An aggressive, come-forward, pressure fighter that charged around the ring for twelve rounds, throwing thumping hooks to the body, zapping his prey of energy until they dropped breathless to the canvas floor. But Eamonn had had John Breen beat his midriff mercilessly with a baseball bat at the end of each sparring session to toughen up any parts of his torso that his elbows and forearms would not protect. And he thrived on opponents that attempted to force the pace and march him down. He let them hurry into range on his own terms before punishing them with short, sharp counters, like the one which did for Thaxton in the same ring just four months before. While Supra's punked-up version of 'Blue Moon' sent 15,000 into raptures and propelled a hooded, gum-chewing Hatton between the ropes, Magee swaggered about his corner, his thin lips gently pursed as if in a knowing smile.

The first third of the contest belonged to the visitor. A fired-up Hatton emerged at the opening bell exactly as expected, all hustle and bustle, determined to walk his quarry down. Magee, anticipating just that, backed away and made himself comfortable on the ropes. He planned to spend the entire night there, veering and leaning and ducking out of harm's way, countering and awaiting the opportunity to land a big one. To everyone's surprise, that moment arrived after just forty-five seconds. Drawing the champion in, Eamonn bobbed, then weaved, then unleashed a short right hook as Hatton left the side of his face wide open while doubling up with his own hooks to the body. Not seeing the punch coming, Ricky dropped for the first time in his professional career. But walking across the ring to the neutral corner, it was Eamonn who cursed his luck.

'Fuck sake,' he snarled. 'Too fucking early.'

Hatton was back on his feet before the referee, Mickey Vann, had time to take up his mandatory eight count. Watching his recovery closely, Magee knew there was no point in going in for the kill just yet. *I got him once so I'll get him again*, he reasoned as he resumed his counter-punching stance. *A ten-eight round to open up will do me just fine.*

Hatton continued full steam ahead in the second. His style resembled that of a hungry front-row hooker on the rugby pitch, boring into a busy ruck in search of the ball. Close quarters was Ricky's territory, the space in which his hooks and uppercuts and sneaky elbows were most effective. As the shorter man, he was adept at burrowing into Eamonn's chest and, once he could taste the Irishman's sweat, he was not averse to jolting his cherubic head if there was the slightest chance of inflicting pain.

But Magee's hands were faster and his boxing brain a little sharper. Patience was beyond him on the street, but between the ropes Eamonn was blessed with composure and restraint and the capacity to bide his time for as long as it took. Again, quicker than expected, another moment arrived. Finding an inch of space, Magee exploited it to land a cuffing right hand that seriously buzzed Hatton. The Englishman immediately sought to hold and wrap his rival up, but Eamonn recognised Ricky's peril and desperately wrestled his arms free. It was still much earlier than he had planned for, but this time he was going to pour it on. Barely four minutes into the biggest fight of his life, he was going for the finish.

When he squirmed out of Hatton's faltering embrace, the champion turned and wobbled head down and head first into Magee's corner before turning involuntarily to face the challenger, now poised and ready to pounce. But as the Irishman cocked his right hand, Mickey Vann's own paws suddenly and inexplicably stretched out between the two fighters as if to separate a non-existent clinch.

'What the fuck are you stopping me for?' Eamonn cried with an almost plaintive look on his face as Vann sheepishly backed away out of shot.

This was Vann's seventh Hatton WBU title fight in a row and a suspicious Magee camp had lobbied hard to have a different face in charge of the proceedings. In one fell swoop, the Leeds-based arbiter had provided conspiracy theorists with all the ammunition they needed. It was a fleeting intervention, two seconds at the very most, but it was a vital repose for the home fighter. It was time enough for Hatton's haze to dispel and for Magee's momentum to stall. Vann had effectively slammed the tiny window of opportunity shut just before Eamonn could wedge his fingers into the gap. He commenced an attack anyway, but he knew the chance was gone and halted the assault halfway through for fear that, in the long run, he would suffer more than his foe from prolonging it.

It was a different Hatton after that second scare as he became a more circumspect fighter, bouncing in and out of range on nimble feet. Magee had trained to have a Manchester Pitbull on top of him for thirty-six minutes, but suddenly a wary, yet still dangerous, Doberman was sniping from distance. Reluctant to immediately accept the new order of things, Eamonn stuck close to his own corner for the next couple of rounds, occasionally attempting to provoke his opponent with a smile or a wave of the glove. But the champ was not for turning. Showing an adaptability and ring awareness with which he had not previously been credited, Hatton set out to rewrite the script, albeit with the same happy ending for himself.

But he needed time to settle into his new role, and in that time the challenger continued to rack up the points. The fourth was competitive but Magee landed the cleaner, crisper shots, including one straight, stabbing right hand that cut Hatton under his right eye. The uncharacteristically officious Vann intervened once more in bizarre circumstances, this time to rebuke the Irish corner for excessive instructions mid-round, but on the vast majority of neutral scorecards Eamonn was at least three points up after four sessions.

Magee stepped towards the centre of the ring to commence the fifth but was immediately drawn back to his corner as if tethered by a bungee cord. From that position he lashed out occasionally, but Hatton was now wiser to his opponent's counters and appeared more comfortable with each scoring raid he made into enemy territory. When the Manchester fighter did stick close and pump his arms like pistons while his head drove into Magee's chest, it was Eamonn who received a warning from Vann for pushing down on his attacker. It all served to increase the Irish camp's belief they were up against it in more ways than one. Regardless, it was Hatton's round.

As was the next, a stanza most notable for the ironic cheers that echoed around the arena as Eamonn finally left the small square foot of canvas by his own corner from which he had fought for the majority of the preceding nine minutes. The Irishman responded with a smile and a dance, skip and shuffle, but Ricky was the man who had found his rhythm. He was the one now dictating the beat.

Hatton continued on top throughout the seventh. It appeared that he was now in tune with the nuances of Magee's feints and weight shifts. Leaning in close, the champion sensed what was coming and when, and could adjust accordingly. With this subtle revelation, his confidence visibly soared. Suddenly, there were Tyson-esque bounds to either side to plant both feet and dig violent hooks in under Eamonn's ribs. Magee nodded in recognition at one such blow near the end of the round, as if acknowledging that this was an entirely different fight now.

The eighth was relatively quiet with neither boxer excelling. Perhaps both were slyly happy to rest up before the final third. The problem of such an approach for Magee, however, was that he was never going to be the beneficiary of any doubt in the ringside judges' minds when it came to marking each man out of ten. Eamonn was the counter-punching challenger, away from home, fighting on the back foot against a young, popular, aggressive, come-forward local champion. Ten to nine Hatton. Scores level on my card.

Magee returned to the close environs of his corner for the duration of the ninth. 'C'mon!' he beckoned to his foe before catching him with a solid left hook. An uppercut was also successful, as was a straight right hand as Hatton encroached, but some of the zip and spite had left Eamonn's punches now and the Englishman took the punishment in his stride. It was a much better three minutes from Magee, maybe even good enough to nick the round in the Waterfront or Ulster Hall. But this was the MEN.

He got on his bike in the next before parking it back in his corner for the eleventh, with the former approach causing Hatton to miss more than he scored. Glenn McCrory on commentary had the champion two rounds up going into the last, but in truth, rounds nine to eleven could have gone either way. Magee's heart believed he was leading, but his head computed the circumstances and accepted he was most likely behind. He clamped Ricky's outstretched glove between his own in a gesture of respect and latent friendship before pointing towards the Englishman for one final effort at provocation.

As was often his wont, Eamonn finished strong. He would twist that fact to convince himself he trained hard enough for the championship rounds but, again, he was merely burning fuel he had conserved by coasting through, and losing, earlier sessions. However, he certainly got the better of the last, buzzing Hatton again and forcing him to grab hold and buy a few seconds for his head to clear.

At the final bell the two warriors embraced, as everyone who looked on knew they would, before each began their hopeful celebrations. As Ricky climbed the corner ropes to salute his adoring masses, Magee drew the same public's wrath by parading on the top of Oscar Checa's shoulders and conducting the jeers with orchestral waves of his fists. Eamonn was convinced he had won, but was even surer he wouldn't get it. When Mickey Vann called the two men together for the verdict, his face betrayed the empty feeling of resignation that seeped into his consciousness and dulled his senses. He clapped the scores but, already, his mind was elsewhere.

7

THE SNOWMAN

There is a famous photo of Ricky with his arm around Eamonn in the dressing room immediately after their fight. Both faces are heavily battle-scarred and Magee is yet to wash Hatton's dried blood from his shoulders and matted chest hair. Boxers often embrace in such circumstances after twelve vicious rounds, but these two bonded more quickly and deeply than usual. They were cut from a similar cloth in many ways, with the subtle distinctions in the fabric accounting for the Englishman's ultimately more successful career. In his book, *The Hitman*, Hatton devotes a full chapter to Eamonn, describing their bout as one of the toughest he contested and the most useful in terms of how much he learned throughout the cut and thrust of those thirty-six minutes.

In the photo, Hatton is still kitted out in his shorts and gloves with the retained WBU belt positioned proudly around his waist. Magee has already stripped to his protective groin guard, his gloves and hand wraps long since ripped from his swollen paws. How else would he be able to grip the half-litre tin of Magners Irish cider that he raised towards the photographer's lens?

He was drunk by the time he left the MEN that night and any sense of sobriety did not return for the alcohol-sodden guts of a week. From Belfast International Airport he took a taxi directly to the Chester Bar on the Antrim Road, where an impromptu welcome-home party soon gathered pace with the help of a generous helping of cocaine. When the Chester finally kicked them out in the early hours of Monday morning, the party headed south into Belfast city centre and the familiar surrounds of Kelly's Cellars on Bank Street. There, the drink and drug-fuelled shindig raged on for days.

Built in 1720, Kelly's is Belfast's oldest and most historic pub. It was within its whitewashed stone walls, on the cold concrete floors in front of a blazing open fire, that Wolfe Tone, Henry Joy McCracken and other leaders of the United Irishmen met and plotted the 1798 rebellion against English rule. More than two centuries on it was Eamonn Magee's latest local, an eight-pint pit-stop he made between the gym and home after training every afternoon. Soon it was as if Eamonn owned the place.

The official legal owner at the time had a particularly laissez-faire approach to managing the business and he let Magee and his cohorts do as they pleased. At closing time, Eamonn would be left with the keys and free run of the bar until it was time to open up the following day. He would collect a tenner from everyone locked in the pub and stuff the kitty into the till: it was then a free for all as far as drinks were concerned. He befriended a young barman named Brian and after that his daily eight pints of cider were on the house. Brian loved having Magee around; he was good for business in that he both attracted customers and proved to be the greatest bouncer the bar could wish for, such was his ability to settle rowdy clients down with little more than a look or a quiet word in the ear.

Eamonn had never felt so at home in a pub outside the Ardoyne, but it still wasn't quite perfect. So he and some pals took a couple of sledgehammers to a side wall of the listed building and knocked it through to create their own little nook where they could truly feel at ease. One morning during that fuzzy week after the Hatton fight, the electric board called to cut the power due to unpaid bills. Magee and the gang didn't care: they lit a few candles, threw a few more blocks on the fire, and continued boozing in the near darkness.

It was in Kelly's that he first made the acquaintance of Alex 'Hurricane' Higgins, the two-time world snooker champion and another of Northern Ireland's extravagantly gifted and fatally flawed sporting figures. He was a hell-raiser on and off the table, and his genius on the baize was only exceeded by his capacity to drink, smoke and clash with authority off it. It was thus hardly a surprise when Alex and Eamonn struck up an immediate rapport. The Hurricane rarely left home without a couple of joints in his pocket, while the Terminator could be relied upon to carry a small bag of charlie, and once Guinness for the snooker player and Harp or cider for the boxer were hurled into the mix, nothing could stop the volatile duo.

Higgins was born and raised in the loyalist Sandy Row district of Belfast and once pushed his notoriety to extremes by threatening to have a fellow pro and countryman, the amicable and universally loved Dennis Taylor, murdered by the UVF. Such aberrations, coupled with frequent physical assaults on whoever he decided had crossed him, had made Higgins an even more controversial figure than Magee in Northern Ireland. Eamonn still recalls associates approaching him in the early days of his friendship with Alex, questioning what he was playing at hanging around with that 'Orange cunt Higgins'. They were always shocked when an angry Magee, clearly not sharing their sectarian prejudices, turned on them, promising his own physical retribution if another insult came Alex's way.

'Fuck all of them,' Eamonn told his new pal when the infamously confrontational Higgins looked a little wary for once in his troubled life. 'Come on, mate, we're going to the Ardoyne.'

A short black taxi ride into the republican heartland later, Magee was buying Alex pints in the Shamrock and the Glen Park, always keeping a menacing eye out to ensure no harm would befall his Protestant drinking partner. Before long he was welcome in the Magee home as well, even if his appearance sent young Áine scurrying away in squealing terror. The sight of his sickly pale and gaunt countenance under a black, wide-brimmed hat, as the throat cancer and accompanying radiotherapy emaciated his already frail frame and rid his mouth of teeth, startled adults and children alike in those days.

For years the partnership was strong and the pair kept each other company on bar stools all over Belfast. Alex's health gradually deteriorated (until his six-stone body was found lifeless in sheltered housing accommodation on the Donegall Road in 2010), but while he could still keep up with Eamonn he was only too happy to get involved in any escapades that came along. It was generally mischievous more than anything, a bit of friendly pool hustling or low-level shoplifting, but Magee imagined it helped Higgins feel he was still that exhilarating wild child, living life at a hundred miles an hour with two wheels hanging precariously over the edge. When a shifty-looking Hurricane blew tamely out of the Belfast Christmas market one brisk December afternoon, his long coat swaddled around both his painfully thin body and the two bottles of red wine he had just swiped from a nearby stall, Eamonn could only smile at the sight of how this one-of-a-kind, ex-millionaire was writing the last chapter of his life.

Magee paid for the goods he left the market with that day, but on occasion his fingers were just as light as Alex's. He has had a long and conflicted relationship with the less than noble art of theft. It dates back to his first offence, when he returned from a religious retreat to Mount Melleray grotto with more than he had when he arrived at the Co. Waterford holy site. He was only six years of age at the time, and the item in question was merely a cassette tape of the Irish rock band Bagatelle, but a feeling of guilt and regret bothered Eamonn for weeks.

In later life he adopted what he saw as a quasi-Robin Hood role, stealing from anyone perceived to be richer than him to sell the item or items at a knockdown rate to anyone poorer than the original owner. With that dubious motto he could justify snaffling sausage skins from the factory he worked in to flog to a local butcher, or pilfering plywood from a construction site behind his house to help furnish Breen's new gym.

By the time the twenty-first century had dawned, Magee was earning a handsome wage in the ring and had no pressing need to thieve. But somehow, he just couldn't help getting himself involved in an array of low-budget, and often comical, heists. One drunken night saw him break into a Lisburn Road bar to remove a six-foot replica Roman centurion. Local paramilitaries with an investment in the establishment soon put the word out that the statue was to be immediately returned. On another occasion he was drinking with a friend who knows his art, in the Botanic Inn close to Queen's University. Partly for the craic, and partly for the two grand his pal offered, Eamonn spent the evening loosening a painting on the wall before finally walking out the fire exit with the artwork stuffed inside a jumper. The next morning he was woken by a call from his solicitor.

'Were you in the Bot yesterday evening, Eamonn?' the lawyer began in lieu of pleasantries.

'I was yeah, why?' Eamonn responded tentatively.

'Did you leave through the emergency doors with something you shouldn't have?'

'How the fuck do you know that?'

'I've just had a call from my neighbour who also happens to own the Botanic Inn. He saw you on his cameras and he knows I represent you.'

'Fuck sake. Okay, what do we do?'

'As a favour to me he says he won't call the cops if you give the painting back today and never return to any of his bars again.'

'Okay, fine. Wait, what do you mean, *any* of his bars? How many does he fucking have?'

'Quite a few, Eamonn,' his brief laughed. 'Quite a few.'

It turned out his legal counsel's neighbour was the CEO of the Botanic Inns Group, who not only owned a large portfolio of drinking establishments in Northern Ireland, but appeared hell-bent on buying up any that weren't yet his. Over the next two or three years, Eamonn discovered he was barred from another new pub on an almost monthly basis.

At other times he was guilty of little more than going with the flow, or association with the likes of James Gerard Hamill. On a Magee Travels jaunt to America, Hamill decided to pinch a Salmanazar of champagne from a supermarket while Eamonn picked up snacks for the kids. As

235

alarms blared and the shop assistant flew out in search of the thief, Eamonn trudged outside, bracing himself for a trip to an American police station. There was only a massive car park and an open expanse outside the shop, nowhere to hide and too far to run for Hamill to have completed his getaway with nine litres of expensive champagne under his arm. Yet, as he surveyed the scene, the little man was nowhere to be found. The clerk wandered about for a minute, circling the concrete columns that supported a giant awning over several rows of parking spaces, but came back shaking his head in confusion. Eamonn, having just watched Hamill comically slide around those pillars, expertly keeping himself and the massive bottle out of his pursuer's line of sight, struggled to keep a straight face.

Hamill couldn't help himself. He once faked a heart attack in a shop and maintained the distraction long enough for Eamonn to sprint out the door laughing with bin bags rammed full of clothes. Sometimes Ham & Eggs simply grabbed an armful himself and ran, as happened when he burst through the doors of a bar where Magee was sipping a pint one afternoon, closely followed by a couple of breathless and irate cops. On another occasion, one sunny summer's day, Hamill suddenly emerged furtively from a shop, stuffed an unseen item into a nearby bush and joined Eamonn on a wooden park bench. Seconds later a security guard was over for a word.

'Well Eamonn,' he began, obviously recognising the most famous boxer in the country. 'Are you with this man here?'

'I am indeed, mate,' Eamonn said, gently placing a brotherly arm around Hamill's shoulders. 'I've only got him out for a couple of hours and I thought I'd let him get a bit of sun and fresh air.'

Nothing had been planned, but Hamill didn't miss a beat, twitching and gazing around with a vacant look in his eyes. The security guard looked down at Hamill suspiciously.

'I've to take him back to the hospital now,' Eamonn continued. 'He's due his medication and can't be out too long anyway.'

With that he rose to his feet, holding Hamill's arm and helping the Ardoyne's answer to Rainman shuffle gingerly away. The security guard smelled a rat but given Hamill's Oscar-winning performance he couldn't be sure. 'All right then, Eamonn,' he shouted after the pair of conmen. 'Just make sure you keep an eye on this man.'

But keeping an eye on Hamill was easier said than done. Standing beside Eamonn at half-time in Solitude – the stadium of north Belfast's Cliftonville Football Club – on the day Cliftonville won the league, he suddenly decided to jump the barrier, run onto the pitch, place an imaginary ball on the penalty spot and blast it into the top corner as the crowd behind the goal went mad. That performance made Hamill a brief Internet sensation. In another role, Eamonn dressed him up in a suit and tie and introduced him to a visiting *Guardian* journalist as his minder and driver. As Eamonn then led the poor scribe on a merry dance around north Belfast, milking him for expenses at every turn, all five foot five of James Gerard was a step behind, alert to any dangers that may befall his defenceless, welterweight champion of the world client.

***

Back at the official day job, Callahan and Breen were keen to get Magee in the ring again as quickly as possible. By now they were making their rebukes of Eamonn's lack of dedication open to the press. Mike talked about walking away if the boxer didn't give it his all, saying there were no second chances now and that he feared conversations when it was all over about just how good Magee could have been with a different mindset. It was all done in the hope that a hint of a public backlash against a man who held the keys to the world but was unwilling to open the lock would force the fighter to knuckle down. But in truth, they knew exactly what they were getting with him from day one and they had both made their peace with who and what Eamonn was, privately acknowledging that it was they who were resigned to do the knuckling down to help the fighter get the most out of his career. Now that Eamonn was circling in on thirty-two years of age, both felt there wasn't much time to lose.

Mike lobbied hard for a rematch with Hatton, but it was never likely to materialise. He revealed that Eamonn had kept secret an emergency trip to the dentist on the morning of the bout and had fought while on antibiotics for an infection, but the information only served to make Team Hatton less keen on a second dance. Magee had given them all they could handle, so why risk it all over again, particularly if there was a chance he wasn't fully fit first time around. Hatton had also set his sights beyond domestic rivalries now, with bona fide world titles and the likes of Kostya Tszyu and Zab Judah firmly on his radar.

Instead, Callahan turned his attention to the European scene in order to secure his charge a route back to big-money fights and world honours. Eamonn was kept ticking over with another routine five-round victory over Alan Bosworth in September while Mike signed the papers for a shot at the Belgian European Union champion, Jürgen Haeck. The fight was added to the first boxing card to be held at the recently built Odyssey Arena in the centre of Belfast. Ten thousand tickets were available for a show that also featured Jim Rock challenging Mehrdud Takaloo for the vacant WBU super welterweight crown and Neil Sinclair defending his British welterweight title against Bradley Pryce.

Three weeks out from the fight, Magee was busy bullying a sparring partner about Breen's Gym when an attempted uppercut only half landed. A bolt of pain shot up his hand, but he fought on and completed the round, praying there was no lasting damage. Unfortunately no one upstairs was listening to his silent pleas: his thumb was broken and he wouldn't be able to glove up for at least two months. He went to the Odyssey anyway that February in 2003, but only to watch his stablemates in action, ultimately celebrating with Sinclair and commiserating with Rock.

Just as the thumb was regaining mobility, Callahan agreed terms with Junior Witter's people for Eamonn to fight for the Englishman's British and Commonwealth belts. Witter, who had lost just once in twenty-eight fights – his one defeat a decision to Zab Judah when challenging for the American's IBF title – was a slick, world-level operator but he also liked to get involved in a fight and Eamonn was confident of picking him off. It would have been an intriguing contest, but within a fortnight Mike received a phone call with an even better offer. The European Boxing Union had installed Magee as the mandatory challenger to their champion, Oktay Urkal, and expected the bout to take place within three months. Witter was dropped – he instead fought and beat Haeck inside four rounds for the EU strap – and Eamonn began plotting a revenge mission.

Eamonn had had a previous encounter with the German-based Turk. In 1993 Urkal had comfortably beaten an undercooked Magee at the European amateur championships in Finland in the most comprehensive defeat of Eamonn's career. Now, exactly a decade on, Urkal was a thirty-three fight professional with just one loss, against the legendary Kostya Tszyu, on his record. He was already a two-time European champion, ranked at four in the world by three governing bodies, and almost always fought in front of a sold-out and influential home crowd. The joke that you need to knock a home fighter out to secure a draw in Germany may be slight hyperbole, but Magee was about right when he declared he would have to administer a terrible beating on Urkal if he was to get the decision in Magdeburg.

There were no isolated farmhouse camps this time around. Perhaps Eamonn was just too old to keep being treated like a tearaway kid who couldn't be trusted. Maybe Callahan and Breen simply accepted that there was nowhere on the planet they could exile him to where he wouldn't find a way to break curfew and track down a drink or a woman. Instead, Breen tortured Magee in the gym every day, working him into a shape in which he could do a job in Germany. They knew he had to fight differently over there to get the result. In an ideal world he'd become the first man to stop Urkal in a boxing ring, but they had to prepare for thirty-six minutes of sustained attack. Eamonn's back-foot, counter-punching style was not going to win enough rounds in front of 8,000 screaming Urkal fans with three compliant judges sitting at ringside.

With three weeks to go, everything was running smoothly. John was one of the best trainers in the business at judging a boxer's condition and he had Eamonn bang on schedule to reach his physical peak come fight week. Then the Germans called Mike: Urkal had picked up an undisclosed injury and the bout would have to be delayed by six weeks. It may have been genuine, but it was neither the first nor last time a European-based champion would employ the tactic to unsettle a challenger. The 3 May fight was rearranged for 14 June and Magee and Breen were forced to reset and renew their preparation.

When the first bell did finally toll, Eamonn fought with spite in his heart. Words were exchanged in the opening engagement and the vitriol barely relented throughout the fight. Magee began quickly and positively, however, for once the aggressor as he frequently landed on Urkal's solid chin. The Turk was rattled and responded with an entirely deliberate, and wholly unpunished, head-butt in the second round. Magee's leathery skin was famously tough but, for the first time in his career, it split open at the centre of an ugly, swollen, purple welt under his right eye. The wound became Urkal's target for the remainder of the contest.

Enraged, Magee fired in a low one and, as the champion was given an eight count, grinned over to Ian Darke and Glenn McCrory who were commentating at ringside. This was a title fight not a tickling contest, and Eamonn was happy to fight fire with fire. Urkal then won most of the middle rounds as he got the better of the majority of exchanges, before Eamonn roared back in the ninth and tenth when he bloodied his rival's nose.

'You need a big finish now, son,' Breen shouted in the corner before the eleventh began.

'What do you mean?' Eamonn cried back. 'I'm a mile in front.'

'You're not,' John said plainly. 'And what's more, we're in fucking Germany here. Go out there and win it.'

Magee shook his head in frustration. He scored his own fights as he fought them and tended to give himself the benefit of the doubt in any close rounds. There was little margin for error in his style as he attempted to parry the punches that came his way while keeping his powder dry in anticipation of throwing singular, killer blows in response. He was a quality over quantity man, but ringside judges were often disciples of a reverse philosophy. Eamonn didn't like fighting to any instructions that were not his own, but he did go out and push himself towards a grandstand finale. Unfortunately, Urkal was cute and experienced enough to stay out of trouble, safe in the knowledge that he was unlikely to be on the wrong side of any scorecards in Sachsen-Anhalt.

It was a feeling of déjà vu at the final bell. Just as in Manchester the previous June, Eamonn was sure he had won and sure he wouldn't get it. As the rules dictate, he loitered about the ring as the points were tallied and announced, but he was already eager to get out of sight. The verdict was unanimous and predictable and eerily similar to the Hatton result. Eamonn looked to his travelling support and stuck a fat tongue out in resignation, the third Magee brother to fall just short in a European title bid. It certainly wasn't anything that could be described as a Burke-esque robbery; it was just a bog-standard home decision in a keenly contested fight. Both men were convinced they had won and, such is the subjective nature of professional prizefighting, neither were necessarily incorrect.

It is just a part of the game, but it is a part of the game that killed Eamonn. The inevitability of dropping a decision in a close fight away from home depressed him more than anything else this bloody show business put him through. It put dark thoughts in his head, thoughts that none of this was worth it, that it was time to pack it all in. This was another big opportunity lost. It was believed that Tszyu was planning to move up a weight to challenge Cory Spinks and the reigning European champion would then challenge for at least one of the three belts the unified light welterweight king left behind. Those dreams were gone now.

Something else was weighing heavily on Eamonn's mind at this time, something he had kept bottled up inside throughout the build-up to the Urkal fight. His father had been diagnosed with cancer that spring and was struggling badly. Specialists believed there was one operable tumour doing the damage but when they opened Doc up they found another cancerous growth eating him from within. The surgery was a success, but the disease had ravaged a fifteen-stone mountain of a man and left him lying weak in bed, with barely nine stone of meat on his bones. The sight of his dad so frail and in so much distress cut Eamonn deeper than a thousand illegal head-butts in the ring.

Mike did his best to lift the sense of gloom. It was another defeat on the record, but the performance had done little damage to Magee's standing in the division. The BBBofC immediately made him Junior Witter's mandatory but, although dates were pencilled in, few believed the champion would accept such a dangerous challenge for relatively limited reward when he could simply vacate and chase a more lucrative name. In the end the decision was taken out of Witter's hands.

Climbing the stairs to Breen's Gym one afternoon, Magee heard John on the phone saying that Neil Sinclair wouldn't be fit enough. Eamonn's curiosity was roused and, hovering close, he started whispering in his trainer's ear.

'Fit enough for what, John?'

With one hand over the receiver's mouthpiece, John replied. 'WBU title fight. Sinky's out.'

'Against who?'

'Jimmy Vincent,' Breen hissed back, losing his temper at Magee pestering him while he was mid-conversation.

Eamonn had worked Jim Rock's corner when the Dubliner beat Vincent over ten rounds back in 1999. He had also sparred hundreds of rounds with Jim and rarely come off second best. A light bulb flashed to life in his head.

'Fuck sake, John. I'll take it!'

Mid-sentence on the phone, John simply scrunched his face and waved his molester away dismissively. But a couple of minutes later he wandered over to Eamonn, who was wrapping his hands, and announced rather matter-of-factly, 'Okay son, that's on.'

Just like that, Magee was stepping up in weight and fighting for the vacant WBU world welterweight title.

***

Despite *Boxing News* actually tipping Vincent to win, he was not a fighter in Magee's lofty class. The English Traveller known as 'Bad Boy' had been earning a wage as a journeyman until the decision to join trainer Pat Cowdell in 2001 sparked a late career bloom. He captured the British Masters light middleweight title and then got in shape, dropping down to welterweight and reeling off three more victories. That run earned him a fight with the unbeaten David Barnes for the British title and most felt he was robbed to lose by a point over twelve rounds. It was a bitter pill to swallow but the pain was eased when the WBU came calling and offered him the chance to fight for a world title in his forty-first outing.

The game fighter was never really in it against Eamonn that December 2003 night in Cardiff, however. Indeed, after the opening couple of stanzas, the only risk to an Irish victory was complacency setting in. Magee respected Vincent for what he had achieved, but having recently gone twenty-four rounds with fighters of Hatton and Urkal's calibre, he knew that Jimmy shouldn't really trouble him.

The pattern was set early, Vincent trudging forward in straight lines with a high guard and minimal head movement, while Magee fired in two or three hurtful shots as he backed off and then spun away to safety. Whenever Eamonn did pause long enough for Jimmy to wander into range and get off a few of his own, it was the Irishman who had the faster hands and higher boxing IQ. He seemed to land a clean counter for every two or three blows he deflected with his gloves, a tucked elbow or a raised shoulder and it wasn't long before Vincent's efforts took on an almost forlorn and futile hue.

The Englishman was cut at the corner of his eye towards the end of the fourth and his building frustration showed as he began leading with his head and allowing body punches to creep south in the next round. He was repeatedly warned, particularly for his use of the head, but Magee never complained and the South African referee took it no further. Both men probably knew a deducted point here or there would have no impact on the outcome of this one. Eamonn strutted and swaggered about the ring throughout, throwing in Ray Leonard-type feints and sleight of hand when he wanted to show off. Vincent needed to adapt but he didn't have it in him and spent most of the night chasing Magee's shadow after it had cuffed him a couple of times on the side of the head.

Both fighters raised their gloves in celebration at the end, but only one truly believed. Such was his confidence, Eamonn tempted fate by donning a yellow T-shirt with an Irish tricolour on the front and 'The New WBU World Champion' on the back before the scores were announced.

Thankfully there was to be no controversy this time as a unanimous decision in favour of Magee was called. 119–109 was possibly a little harsh on the brave Vincent, but the other two judges certainly overcompensated in the other direction by somehow seeing it as close as 116–112.

Either way, Eamonn Magee was a world champion.

The indefinite article in the previous sentence is a constant source of angst amongst boxing purists to this day. Magee was *a* world champion, meaning one of several. Since mob influence in boxing was busted wide open in the early 1960s and the WBA and WBC emerged from the chaos to govern the sport, precious few fighters have been able to call themselves *the* world champion with any great conviction. In the 1980s the IBF and

WBO joined the party, and in the mid-1990s an Englishman by the name of Jon W. Robinson decided there was room for another seat at the table and launched the WBU.

America's 'great white' promoter, Bob Arum, was a big supporter of the new governing body and three of his boxers, George Foreman, James Toney and Kevin Kelley were among the early champions. Other notable WBU belt-holders included Johnny Nelson, Micky Ward, Thomas Hearns and Ricky Hatton. Still in its infancy, a WBU crown was no fighter's ultimate goal, but Robinson hoped his belts would soon be on a par with all the other baubles bobbing around in the alphabet soup world of professional prizefighting. After all, the Puerto Rican-based WBO was also dismissed as an irrelevance at the outset but is today just as respected as any of the others. And in those early days, the likes of Chris Eubank, Nigel Benn and Steve Collins treasured their WBO belts and were in time regarded as elite and bona fide world champions because of them. Robinson envisioned following a similar path with his WBU and were it not for his untimely death in 2004, perhaps his dreams would have been realised.

Eamonn viewed his title as the ideal springboard to launch himself into a massive 2004. So confident was Frank Warren that Magee would beat Vincent, he had the Irishman signed up to a lucrative six-fight contract with Queensberry Promotions before the opening bell. Vincent was fight number one and if Eamonn kept winning he would never have to worry about money again for as long as he lived.

He enjoyed a break over Christmas before returning to the gym with renewed vigour. The big-name American and IBF interim title holder, Sharmba Mitchell, verbally agreed to not only fight Magee, but to travel to Belfast to do so. The Odyssey Arena would sell out and even Solitude football ground was mentioned as a possible venue, if the infamously inclement Northern Irish weather would allow a first open-air title fight in the country for decades. Irish boxing was buzzing again and Eamonn Magee was the reason.

And then the snow fell.

***

When Joseph Clarke was nineteen years old, British paratroopers forcibly removed him from his parents' west Belfast home. It was just before dawn on 9 August 1971. It was Operation Demetrius. 'If you try to escape, you'll be shot dead,' he was told as he sat alone, barefoot and wrist-bound in the back of an army lorry. Within days, Clarke would wish he had tried to escape.

The teenager was driven to Girdwood Barracks in north Belfast where he was beaten and interrogated. At one point a black, heavy hood was placed over his head and shoulders and he was bundled into a whirring helicopter. He felt it rise before an English voice asked him if he had ever seen the footage of US marines pushing Vietnamese prisoners out of choppers flying over the South China Sea. Suddenly he was shoved in the back and began to fall. Seconds later, laughing soldiers were hauling him back into the helicopter, which was hovering a couple of metres off the ground. They flew to the Shackleton military base in Ballykelly, Co. Derry, where Clarke was stripped, numbered, dressed in a boiler suit, re-hooded and pushed into a room dominated by a relentless, high-pitched, piercing noise. There he was forced into excruciating stress positions for hours and savagely beaten when his body betrayed him.

At intervals, the hood was removed and he was tied to a chair to be interrogated by unseen men hiding behind blinding lights that stung his now hypersensitive eyeballs. When he gave them nothing he was re-hooded and returned to the euphemistically named music room. The torture continued for over a week in which he survived on dry bread, water and one bowl of cold, watery stew. Sleep was denied unless he had been beaten unconscious and this added deprivation led to hallucinations in which Clarke believed he was the bodyguard of the British politician James Callaghan. When not hallucinating he both wished and expected death to soon befall him and end the suffering. He couldn't believe that the British state would risk the world finding out what they had done by releasing him.

One morning he was dragged back to the helicopter and flown to the Crumlin Road Gaol in north Belfast. From there he was taken to the Long Kesh internment camp in Lisburn and thrown in with hundreds of other suspected IRA men being held without charge. In the couple of years he was interned there he probably came across Terrence 'Doc' Magee, but being from the other side of town he wouldn't have known or spoken to him. One man he did meet and befriend was a young Gerry Adams. A physically large man, Clarke would later act as Adams' minder, as he remained close to the republican movement upon release from the Kesh. A feud saw him shot in the side by the Official IRA in 1975 and his brother was murdered by loyalist paramilitaries in 1992.

Clarke and thirteen other men who suffered a similar fate at the hands of British forces in the early 1970s have been fighting for justice for forty-five long years. Initial government denials and inquiry whitewashes gave way to hushed compensation packages, but financial reparation was never the goal of the fourteen 'Hooded Men'. What they wanted was a declaration from the British government that their predecessors had used torture in their interrogation methods in Northern Ireland and a promise that they would never, ever do so again.

The Irish government took up the case and in 1976 the European Commission of Human Rights concluded that the interrogation techniques used were indeed 'a modern system of torture'. This ruling was undermined somewhat two years later when the European Court of Human Rights downgraded the men's ordeals to 'inhuman and degrading treatment' that did not necessarily amount to torture. It was an unfortunate ruling that the Bush administration would later exploit to defend their own savage interrogation techniques in Guantanamo Bay and Abu Ghraib.

The 'Fourteen Hooded Men' have never given up. Today, boosted by fresh evidence that emerged in 2013 and with famed human rights lawyer Amal Clooney agreeing to handle the case, the ten survivors have renewed hope that they will live to hear the British government tell the truth.

2013 was a special year for Joe Clarke for another, totally unrelated reason. At the end of 2012 he bought a EuroMillions lottery ticket in a west-Belfast filling station near his car mechanics garage on the Springfield Road. When he returned to check his numbers the following week, he was told he had won a share of the jackpot. Just like that, Joe Clarke was over ten million pounds better off. Well-wishers swiftly clamoured to congratulate him on his deserved good fortune. He was well liked in the community and known for charity work that included adopting several impoverished children from orphanages in Belarus. It could not have happened to a nicer bloke was the general consensus. There was only one dissenting voice in the crowd, that of an ex-neighbour from Lagmore Dale.

'Joe Clarke is nothing but a coward and a scumbag,' spat Eamonn Magee.

***

Lagmore Dale is a small and quiet cul-de-sac, the type of street where parents have no fears about letting their kids play out front unsupervised. There were several families living there back in 2004, all with children around the same age who enjoyed each other's company. Through the kids the adults became friendly and soon there were regular get-togethers in different living rooms or gardens. One summer's day a barbecue was in full swing when a nine-year-old Eamonn Junior appeared in floods of tears. Junior had been scrapping with Joe Clarke's son and when Clarke emerged to break it up he allegedly threatened to take his own hand to the boy. Enraged, Eamonn went in search of his neighbour. He found him, threatened him and then knocked the fifty-year-old to the ground with a single punch. It was always a massive risk to use fists on anyone who had friends in the IRA, but time passed and nothing more transpired between Eamonn and Joe.

Eighteen months later, snow lay on the ground. Eamonn, still buzzing from a party the night before, spoke on the phone to his mother, who had returned to live in Belfast. Isobel marvelled that, due to the shade her house threw over Holmdene Gardens, her front was an icy white while across the street was clear and bathed in sunshine. Meanwhile in Lagmore, the neighbourhood kids were busy making the most of the cold snap to build rival snowmen on the front lawns and hurl snowballs back and forth. A couple of direct hits soon soured the mood and before long there were only piles of slushy remains where fully-formed sculptures had once proudly stood. The Clarke kids felt they were the main victims in the snowy war and apportioned the blame to twelve-year-old Áine Magee.

Áine believes that Joe Clarke and his wife never liked her because they thought she delighted in antagonising their children. When Big Joe's daughters told him about their wrecked snowman, he marched to the Magee door to remonstrate with Mary about her child's behaviour. He expected Áine to be punished and, seeking to appease Clarke and get him off the doorstep, Mary assured him she would be. Eamonn was informed and Áine was sent to her room with a firm but fatherly slap for her troubles.

But the fact that Clarke had come accusing only Áine, and none of the other kids who were just as guilty, ate away at Mary throughout the day. Finally she decided to walk over to Clarke's to have it out with him. Mary tried to make her case but felt she was shouted down and made to feel small.

In the meantime, Eamonn had gone up to Áine's room to check on his admonished daughter. 'It wasn't just me, Daddy,' she pleaded. When Mary then arrived home in tears, sobbing about taunts and insults from Clarke, Eamonn snapped. With Francis in tow, he stormed towards Clarke's.

More than a decade later, memories of the next three minutes are hazy, but Francis recalls Clarke, clearly anticipating a reaction after the words with Mary, standing in his doorway. When Joe's hand appeared to move towards Francis, the expected response duly arrived. Before he had a chance to react, Eamonn delivered a head-butt which left Joe sitting in the snow with blood running from his mouth, tonguing a loose tooth.

Eamonn arrived home, suddenly and terribly sober with a feeling of dread heavy in his stomach. He peered out his front window and saw Clarke standing in the street on his phone. Mary called a friend, also named Joe, from a nearby street and he flew round to collect Eamonn. The plan was to drive him over to the relative safety of Isobel's in the Ardoyne, but as they left Lagmore Dale, a car entered the estate to pick up Clarke.

'Go for fuck sake,' Eamonn screamed at his driver. 'Let's get out of here.'

They left the Lagmore estate and hung a right onto the Stewartstown Road. They then took the first exit onto the Creighton Road and accelerated, hoping to make it safely along that two-mile stretch to join the M1 motorway. But with the Blacks Road motorway junction in sight, the Clarke car caught them. There was a collision and the pursuing vehicle spun to a halt in front of Eamonn's car. At this point, Clarke and his driver emerged with the pickaxe handle and a baseball bat in their hands.

'Go, go, go!' screamed Magee. 'Put it in fucking reverse and go!'

But the car didn't move an inch. His friend was frozen at the wheel in a state of paralysing shock.

The first swing of the wooden club struck the carbon-steel frame between the windscreen and passenger window, shattering both. Clarke's massive hand then reached in and wrestled the passenger door open. Eamonn, convinced that he was a dead man if he let himself be removed from the car, leaned across and held on to the steering wheel with every ounce of his strength. Joe sat back in stunned horror, guarded by Clarke's companion at the driver's door just in case he got any ideas.

Clarke eventually gave up on dragging Magee out of the car and instead set to work on his kicking legs with the heavy wooden club. Each swing was that of a baseball slugger aiming for the fences, and each direct hit splattered blood onto the road and emitted a sickening crunch of bursting muscle and fracturing bone. Eamonn, convinced he was fighting for his life, didn't feel a thing and it was only when he stole a glance back at Clarke that he noticed he could see straight through his flesh to his own splintered tibia.

'Look what you've done to my leg you big bastard,' he shouted between blows.

Clarke must have looked and the gruesome sight must have interrupted his blind fury, for he immediately ceased the attack and walked calmly back to his car.

Still Joe the driver hadn't moved a muscle but Eamonn soon snapped him out of his daze.

'C'mon you silly bastard!' he managed between gritted teeth. 'Close this door and get me to the fucking hospital.'

Five minutes later the battered car pulled up at the Royal Victoria Hospital with Eamonn's mangled left leg hanging limply out the window. He was rushed into theatre where surgeons worked on the compound fractures of his tibia and fibula and a shattered knee. There was heavy bruising all over his body, and they also discovered a punctured lung. The next day he was transferred to the Ulster Hospital in east Belfast where specialists took muscle from his calf and tissue from his thigh and grafted it over the gaping hole in the front of his leg.

Then, the pain began.

He describes it as a searing hot poker being thrust into his leg, only this agony was constant. He hammered the button for more morphine but nothing could dull the intense burn inside his veins that had him involuntarily weeping for mercy. The consultant was called and immediately diagnosed blood clots. With a pair of surgical tweezers he pinched one and began to pull. As Eamonn looked on, the doctor proceeded to draw out, hand over fist, reams of dark, scarlet, clotted blood and allowed them to coil like sinister skipping ropes on a silver tray.

The next day Eamonn asked the surgeon what his chances of fighting again were. The doctor pulled up a chair and looked him straight in the eye.

'Eamonn,' he said, 'I'm sorry, but I guarantee you that you'll never box again.'

As Eamonn's head dropped, the bleak prognosis got even worse.

'And I have to warn you, Eamonn. You may not even walk again.'

He struggled desperately with the sudden and shocking reality of his situation. For the first time in his life he wept publicly as he told reporters gathered around his bedside of the consultant's words. When Callahan and Breen visited they found their champion boxer agitated and physically tremoring. All three men had tears in their eyes.

'Joe Clarke's going to fucking kill me,' Eamonn whispered to them after a while, his eyes large and fearful.

'No he's not, Eamonn,' Breen soothed. 'I'll speak to Joe Clarke.'

Breen knew Clarke personally and to this day, much to Eamonn's chagrin, he describes him as a big gentleman. He spoke to Joe and managed to negotiate an uneasy truce: if the two men stayed out of one another's way, then that would be the end of it. John was barely through the door in the hospital the following day when Eamonn asked him if he had spoken to Clarke.

'I have, Eamonn,' he answered. 'It's all taken care of, son. Don't worry about any of that.'

But Eamonn couldn't stop worrying. Thoughts of a vengeful Clarke creeping into the hospital under cover of darkness to finish the job he began on the Blacks Road tormented his sleep. Mary soon noticed strange blister-like lesions appearing on his hands and feet. The doctors investigated and concluded they were symptoms of stress, evidence of a tortured mind, but their priority was reconstructing his shattered limb. After surgery it was caged in an Ilizarov frame with metal pins driven into place above and below the break. Later, from ankle to hip, the leg was cocooned in a plaster cast. The blood clots were a major concern and so

Warfarin and constant observation were prescribed. He was in hospital for three months and warned that the protective casing must stay in place for six months before serious rehabilitation could begin.

When the discharge date arrived, Eamonn hesitated to leave for he was unsure where to go. He didn't trust Joe Clarke, and life in Lagmore had become unbearable for Mary and the kids. Living just a few doors from the Clarkes, they had to pass Joe most days and act as if nothing had happened. Equally intimidating was the approach made by other neighbours when they presented a petition signed by all those in the area who wanted Eamonn and his family to pack up and get out. While Mary looked in estate-agent windows, Eamonn took himself off to supplement his painkillers and blood-thinning tablets with his own brand of illicit medication. One night he returned home in such a state of paranoia that he concealed kitchen knives about his person and gathered his family together to spend the night in a huddle on the living-room floor. The spectre of a follow-up attack from Clarke haunted his sleep and he soon decided he couldn't live another day in Lagmore. He spent time with Hamill, with friends in west Belfast and in London. He also spent time with a woman named Maria Magill.

They first met at a charity boxing event in the Chester Bar in early 2002. At the height of his fame, Eamonn was there to hand out prizes and he easily struck up a conversation with Maria at the bar. He claimed to be already separated from Mary at the time and the pair left the bar together that night. It wasn't long before Maria realised that Mary was still very much in the picture, but by then she was in love and didn't care. They snuck around for a year or so, Eamonn spending as many nights in Maria's Glengormley home as he did in the new house he had bought for Mary and the kids in the west Belfast hills. It was only when Maria fell pregnant that Eamonn sat his original family down and told the truth.

Mary was absolutely devastated, but the revelations somehow failed to extinguish the dying embers of her love for Eamonn. He officially moved in with Maria and her young daughter from a previous relationship, and it was in her home that he took his first painful, shuffling solo steps to dumbfound the specialists who ranked his chances of walking unaided again at fifty–fifty.

There are plenty of happy memories from this time, but the drink and drugs and gambling invariably ensured the good days were outweighed by the bad. He was a good partner when he wanted to be, but the violent outbursts continued, as did the gaps when he'd not show his face for days on end. Maria now knows he was back with Mary then, or with any other woman on the side who would take him. It was a destructive pattern that would repeat itself for more than a decade.

***

Incredulous, John Breen watched the pale, hard figure limp across the gym floor and drop his bag unceremoniously in the corner.

'What do you think you're doing?' he asked.

'What?' Eamonn replied.

'What the hell are you doing in here? Do the doctors know you're here?'

'Don't worry about them, fuck sake John. I need to get back in shape. I need to get back in the ring.'

The pins and plaster that held his bones in place had been removed two months earlier than every specialist in Northern Ireland had predicted. Soon after, a pair of complimentary NHS crutches were tossed to the side and never again picked up. Barely five months on from lying in an intensive-care unit with two of his leg bones cracked and exposed to the world, Eamonn was attempting to glove up and step through the ropes.

What drove him on was a steadfast refusal to be dictated to by anyone. Nobody on the planet was going to make his decision to retire for him, even if they insisted upon the career move after around twenty unanswered blows from a three-foot pickaxe handle. Consultant after consultant shaking their head and advising him just to focus on walking again and forget about boxing was more fuel for the fire that burned inside him. He'd show them all.

John managed to restrict his eager fighter to light cardio and shadow-boxing for the first month or so, but by the end of the summer Magee was forcing his way into the ring with a head-guard on, looking for game sparring partners. One of the specialists who had treated him in the Ulster Hospital was aghast to see a photo of the boxer in his gear and immediately phoned with a dire warning. Eamonn was still on a course of Warfarin to thin his blood and the slightest nick could cause him to quickly bleed to death. For once, he heeded the medic's words and continued with non-contact gym sessions until given the green light just after Christmas to start training for real.

As 2005 dawned he was still the WBU welterweight champion of the world. Jon W. Robinson's death had left a void in the organisation and, despite Magee not having fought for over a year, nobody had bothered to strip him of his title. With itchy fists, he started pushing for a return. The BBBofC gathered several independent medical opinions, studied various X-rays, shook their heads in disbelief and renewed his licence. A new moniker, 'Miracle Man', began doing the rounds and the clamour for his return intensified. Sky Sports committed to screen it, wherever, whenever and against whomever. Warren, Callahan and Breen urged their fighter to take on a ten-round walk in the park to test the water, but he was having none of it. The WBU had awoken from their slumber and announced that their champion must defend his title by the end of March or surrender it, and so Eamonn demanded a ranked opponent to satisfy the championship stipulations. Allan Vester, an ex IBF inter-continental champion and world title challenger, was soon nominated.

As this was to be the biggest event in Irish boxing for more than a decade, a suitable venue was required and the famous King's Hall in Belfast fit the bill perfectly. Barry McGuigan had residency in the iconic arena throughout the mid-1980s and another of the great Irish pugilists,

Rinty Monaghan, graced its ring many times in the 1930s and 1940s. Joe Calzaghe versus Brian Magee was announced as chief support and tickets sold out in an instant. This was the biggest fight in Ireland since Ray Close's rematch with Chris Eubank in the same venue in 1994. Eamonn was there that night, making a few extra quid as he worked security on the door, but this would be his first time fighting in the atmospheric, century-old building. To complete the circle, the great Eubank flew over and sat ringside to watch Magee's return in person.

The crowd generated a ferocious din to welcome the first bell. Magee had drawn a crowd even back when he was a young amateur, but there were plenty of new and unfamiliar faces peering towards the ring on this night. Comebacks of any kind stir something inside the average sports fan, but when the long walk back to glory commenced with a brutal, near-death experience, there is an almost morbid curiosity to witness how one of their own breed could possibly do it.

Breen had spoken from the heart in an interview with the *Belfast Telegraph* on the eve of the fight. 'I think the whole of Northern Ireland should be behind Eamonn when he steps into that ring,' he said with conviction. 'We live in a troubled place and Eamonn has had his fair share of troubles, but he's back. I truly believe he's an inspiration to anyone who has been intimidated, anyone who has suffered, because he has come back from the brink. I didn't think he would be back but he just refused to give up; he refused to let anyone stop him from defending his world title. There's only one Eamonn Magee.'

Ian Darke and Jim Watt echoed those sentiments as Eamonn appeared from behind a curtain in front of thousands in the King's Hall and hundreds of thousands watching on television. Darke described it as one of the most remarkable comebacks in the history of all sport before handing over to Watt to complete the tribute.

'It's unbelievable,' gushed the traditionally dour Scotsman. 'If they used Eamonn's life for a Hollywood script they'd have to water it down because it is *too* unbelievable. In his lifetime he's been shot, he's been stabbed, he's been crippled, and here he is defending a world championship after fifteen months out. The man is truly amazing.'

After the almighty build-up, it was a quiet opening stanza. Magee, the counter-puncher so accustomed to lying in wait, was forced onto the front foot by his opponent's timorous reluctance to engage. He pursued Vester with a palpable sense of menace, a look in his eye that promised hurt. Vester, by nature of his soft features and the less than imposing jaunt to his gait as he stepped anywhere that wasn't into range, immediately looked like the occasion might be too much for him. But Eamonn demurred to lash out with the bout still in its vulnerable infancy. Like a hibernating bear emerging for the spring, the fighter was aware of his potency but also conscious of the time his punching muscles had lain in stasis. He pawed after Vester but all the while he was allowing his body to re-associate itself with the environs of the prize ring.

In the third, Eamonn stretched his sinews. A glance from the angle of his shaven skull pierced the skin at the corner of Vester's right eye and the Dane desired refuge immediately. He sought it by bowing down until within an inch of kneeling. It was as if he was faking taking a knee in an attempt to trick Magee into arresting his assault, yet not oblige an eight-count from the referee. But with Vann nowhere to be seen, Eamonn continued, scimitar-like arms swinging scything hooks until his man did drop. Vester complained to Vann, but the Englishman was unmoved, completing his mandatory count just as a drop of Danish blood dripped onto the challenger's bare chest. Magee scented the claret and moved in to draw more. By now he knew that Vester couldn't hurt him and he wanted this all over inside nine minutes. Marching in he got caught with a solid right, but while Vester may have grinned his pleasure at the truest blow he would land all night, Eamonn barely flinched. He backed his man into the corner and an uppercut had Vester two-thirds of the way down before he uncharacteristically turned back for more. Another uppercut was duly served, severing the Dane's guard and blurring his senses. A knee was the quickest way to the canvas, but barely had his patella touched the floor when Magee threw in a spiteful dig that chopped down onto his right ear. Vester rose once more but Eamonn was now in a rage. It was no longer an almost defenceless Allan Vester across the ring, it was Joe Clarke and his three-foot pickaxe handle. Mickey Vann couldn't even complete his wave to motion the action to recommence, for Magee was already on top of his quarry and flailing wildly as a visibly startled Vester scurried about the ring in search of a suitable patch of canvas for this third and final knee. With twenty-eight seconds to go he found it, knelt and removed his gum shield. Eamonn had won in the third round.

There was a distinct inflection to the roar that greeted Vann calling the fight off. It was a more heartfelt sound than anything that had welcomed Magee's previous twenty-five wins as a professional. Within it was admiration, adulation, awe and reverence. 'He's not the Terminator,' said Ian Darke, 'he's the Miracle Man.'

And it certainly felt like he had achieved something very remarkable. He reached through the ropes to embrace Mike and then walked laps of the ring, applauding the fans revelling in what they had witnessed. Eamonn could make himself a hard man to love at times, but that night it was impossible not to feel something in the way of affection and respect towards him.

From his sock he pulled a betting slip on which he had wagered £100 on himself to stop Vester in the third round at odds of twelve to one. He spied Eubank at ringside, upright and applauding heartily. Eamonn dived between the ropes and as Eubank warned him to take care with his new, three-piece, tailor-made suit, Magee grabbed the ex-super middleweight king in a bear hug and held on tight until the Saville Row fabric had absorbed at least a pint of his sweat. Eubank later explained his surprise appearance to local reporters.

'I had never seen him box [live] before,' he began. 'But when I heard what he had gone through, I had to get on a plane and come to watch. I don't know him as a man but as a fighter he has the character and the true grit that seems to be missing quite a bit today. He's a proper fighter.'

Eamonn was calm and measured as he sat on the ring apron and answered Ed Robinson's questions. He made a point of dedicating the victory to all of the doctors and nurses who had treated his leg in the Royal Victoria and Ulster hospitals, and then promised he had much more left in the tank before he hung up his gloves for good.

'It's the only thing I know how to do,' he concluded. 'And I just can't walk away from a game I love so much.'

***

Yet that is effectively what he did for the remainder of 2005. Big fights with Junior Witter, David Barnes and Joshua Okine were all touted and all failed to materialise. In October a deal was agreed to fight the ex-WBU super welterweight champion Mehrdud Takaloo in London, but a month later Eamonn suddenly demanded more money from Frank Warren and the bout was unceremoniously scrapped.

Outside the ring, Magee continued to live the hard life, seemingly intent on confirming people's worst expectations of him. During a long weekend in the Costa del Sol, he and his mates were tossed out of four hotels in as many nights. In one a departing group of English lads gifted them a bundle of fake €50 notes that soon led to the local *policía* ransacking their rooms and dragging a couple of the party to the station for questioning. On their final night Eamonn found time to reacquaint himself with the Spanish taxi drivers with whom he has always enjoyed a hate-hate relationship. When one mistook Magee for a harmless drunken fool and attempted to overcharge him by about €30, and then pulled a telescopic baton from his glove compartment in anticipation of battle, Eamonn had his first fight since Vester and this one certainly didn't go three rounds. The cobblestones were still splattered with dark bloodstains when he passed the spot the next day on the way to the airport.

He returned home just in time to run the Belfast marathon with his brothers to raise money for the NI Chest Heart and Stroke Association. Now back in the limelight for positive reasons, he was regularly asked to participate or show his face at fundraisers for charitable causes. He was always happy to oblige and, soberness permitting, he always did. When the Sacred Heart Club needed equipment, Eamonn was out rattling buckets. When Tinylife, the premature-and-vulnerable baby charity, needed donations, he donned a T-shirt and completed a sponsored walk. Each small gesture gave him a buzz entirely different to the highs he reached on drink and drugs. He liked that wholesome feeling of giving something back, of not always having to be the bad guy. In his twenties he made conscious decisions to abuse whatever substances crossed his path but now approaching his mid-thirties, he would have walked away from it all if the disease were that easy to beat.

It didn't help that he continued to be surrounded by temptation, now even within the confines of Breen's Gym. Fighters were coming from the British mainland to benefit from John's expertise and, in a move of either epic naivety or inexcusable ignorance, boxers battling their own demons with alcoholism and drug use made it up the stairs and through the door. The Glaswegian featherweight world champion, Scott Harrison, was one such man. Harrison was already notorious when he moved to Belfast and insisted that his myriad problems were in the past and he was in Northern Ireland to get his head down, stay clean and out of prison and concentrate on defending his WBO belt. Some genius actually asked Eamonn to give Harrison a room in his home for the duration of the supposed training camp and on the first night the Scotsman slumped onto Magee's sofa and demanded two bottles of Buckfast and a cup of charlie. The best Eamonn could muster was a bottle of Irish whiskey and, when he saw Harrison gulp it down as one might a glass of highland spring water, he took the precaution of surreptitiously spiking the visitor's dinner with sleeping tablets to at least ensure the session ended relatively early. An English boxer who trained with Eamonn back then wasn't much better. At a party one night he was so far gone that he spent an hour cowering in a cloakroom screaming for someone to get the dog out of the house while Eamonn sporadically walked past, barking and howling and scratching at the door with his own human paws. There was no canine other than whatever beast the fighter's paranoid, cocaine-addled mind had conjured up.

In June, Magee flew to Manchester to support his friend Ricky Hatton in the biggest fight of his life against the undisputed light welterweight champion, Kostya Tszyu. After visiting the Hitman's dressing room, he was walking to his seat when out of the corner of his eye he spied a stocky figure bounding from the backrest of one chair to the next, shunting people out of the way as he descended, shouting Eamonn's name at the top of his voice. By the time Eamonn turned and attempted to focus his beery vision on the incoming man, he was held close and squeezed tight by a pair of muscular, tattooed arms. Finally he broke free to see who the happy accoster was. Magee was at the height of his fame then and, this being a boxing show featuring his old pal and rival in a venue Eamonn had graced many times before, it could have been anyone. He expected to face a fan, or a Hatton fan, or just some general, rowdy boxing aficionado. He did not expect to be nose to nose with a beaming Johnny Adair.

Johnny 'Mad Dog' Adair is a loyalist paramilitary, once in command of a Shankill Road Battalion of the UDA believed to be responsible for the murder of at least forty innocent Catholics in the early 1990s. By 2005 he was living in Bolton, exiled from the streets of Belfast under threat of death in the fallout of a violent internal loyalist feud. Yet here he was, embracing Eamonn Magee like a brother. They shot the breeze for several minutes until the lights dimmed in anticipation of the ring walks and Eamonn made his excuses to go find his seat.

A few days later he was crossing the Shankill Road with Hamill on their way back from visiting a friend who was in the Royal Hospital slowly recovering from a punishment shooting.

'Eamonn! Eamonn!' an unfamiliar voice suddenly rang out.

Eamonn and Hamill kept their heads down and quickened their pace.

'Oi Magee!' the voice boomed, now closer and louder.

Eamonn turned to see a large man in a Glasgow Rangers top, his bare forearms plastered in loyalist paramilitary tattoos, jogging towards him.

'Eamonn,' the man continued, slightly out of breath. 'Eamonn, I was talking to Johnny this morning and he was saying he saw you at the fight, so I just wanted to say hello. How are you keeping, mate? Are you fighting again soon?'

'Not too bad, buddy. Yeah, hopefully back in the ring very shortly,' Eamonn replied, the forced and entirely counterfeit nonchalance evident in his tone. 'Just dandering home here from the hospital.'

'Good man, Eamonn. Take it easy, mate.'

'And yourself, mate, good luck,' Eamonn managed before he and Hamill hurried onto Agnes Street in the direction of the Crumlin Road.

'What the fuck …' little Hamilton muttered under his breath as he struggled to keep up.

Eamonn's cross-community support is a phenomenon that has never been championed in the way it was for the likes of McGuigan in the 1980s, McCullough in the 1990s or Carl Frampton in the relative peace of the twenty-first century. Perhaps a Protestant, loyalist paramilitary from the Shankill cheering on an ex-Fianna petrol-bomber from a Catholic, republican Ardoyne family was just too incongruous to be believed.

But I've seen it myself, sitting alongside Eamonn in a fast-food restaurant on the Shankill. A man entered wearing a Linfield replica shirt, Red Hand of Ulster and UDA tattoos immediately evident on his skin. I was facing the door and saw him spy Eamonn and turn ninety degrees to march up to our table. His face was animated as his wife wondered where he was going, but I couldn't gauge whether this was going to be a positive or negative scene. Eamonn didn't seem bothered by the approach, however. Looking back I see he was sure it would be the former.

The man put his hands on Eamonn's shoulders. Up close now I could see the excitement in his eyes. 'You are a legend,' he said, introducing himself. Then louder, looking around as if in amazement that other people were simply eating their lunch without acknowledging the ex-fighter's presence, 'This man is a legend. One of the hardest men in Belfast.'

He called over his wife and posed for photographs with his arm around Eamonn. He couldn't stop touching him, like he was checking this was real. When he went to order his food he left his keys lying on our table and when Eamonn got up to return them the man hugged him and they spoke for another five minutes. I later found his Twitter account, complete with a profile picture of a British soldier walking through a field of poppies. He had already posted several of his photos with Eamonn. 'I met a hero today,' he wrote under one of them.

The Northern Irish Troubles are often described as a religious conflict but, as is the case with most of the so-called holy wars across the globe, territory and nationality are at the heart of the strife. The Troubles were an extension of the centuries-old battle between those who identified as British and others who identified as Irish for a relatively tiny plot of land in the northeast of the island. That it lasted as long as it did is due to the extreme socio-economic poverty of certain pockets of north, east and west Belfast from which the vast majority of the war's foot soldiers emerged embittered and desperate. At their core, these people from districts such as the Ardoyne and the Shankill are the same. A Shankill loyalist has more in common with an Ardoyne republican than he does with a God-fearing, Protestant Ulster Unionist from south Belfast. Likewise, a hard IRA man from the Falls can identify more closely with a UVF member from Tiger's Bay than with a dyed-in-the-wool republican from rural south Armagh.

They say McGuigan, lauded by both sides, united the country during a very dark period. But Barry wasn't from the ghettoes. He never lived there. He never genuinely walked amongst those people. He wasn't one of them, but an abstract figure who came from a village in the south and lived in the newspapers and on the television screen. Johnny Adair, or his 1980s equivalent, would never have warmly embraced Barry McGuigan on the street. Barry had the support of the majority, but why wouldn't he? Most people in Northern Ireland were always totally repulsed by the Troubles and violence and discrimination of any description, so of course they roared the Clones Cyclone on. The vast majority of folk living on the Shankill and Falls are just regular, decent, working-class people, delighted to see anyone connected to the province excel and represent the country well.

But that violent minority, the men who pulled balaclavas over their faces and planted bombs and brutally ended lives – they were the Eamonn Magee fans. They believed he was one of them and, regardless of religion, they could instinctively relate to him. Eamonn lived their lives and that was more important than whether he wore neutral colours or plastered himself in green, white and orange. The fact that his father was a Provo and he was an IRA youth wing soldier was probably part of the attraction. As was the fact that he was as fiercely Irish as a UDA man on the Shankill was fiercely British.

Many believe that to bridge a gap, two sides must move towards the centre. That both must concede ground and appease the other in search of a happy compromise. In the context of Northern Ireland, that means suppressing feelings of nationality and abandoning symbols of representation. No colours, no flags. But that is a quick and short-sighted fix, for it keeps those issues volatile, relevant and inflated far beyond their actual importance. Genuine, long-lasting peace will be the day when a guy draped in a Union Jack flag can stand beside someone decked out in green, white and orange, and both men can drunkenly cheer on the same fighter.

Identity has always been at the very heart of the problems within Northern Ireland and it must be prominent in the solutions. Eamonn always intuitively understood this. He wore his colours with pride and nailed his Irishness to the mast and, ultimately, the men who fought so bitterly against that nationalism respected him for it. In many ways, the success his brazenness had in winning the support of hard-line elements from both communities is much more remarkable than what McGuigan achieved with a neutral approach. His not-my-fault-where-my-da-put-his-cock line may be crude, but it reveals the total lack of prejudice within Eamonn. He will defend his right to be Irish to the death, but he genuinely couldn't care less how anyone around him chooses to privately or publicly self-identify.

***

2006 began with more promise. Eamonn's public persona had never leant itself to inclusion in shortlists for mainstream accolades, but at the prestigious *Belfast Telegraph* awards ceremony in January his recent achievements could not be ignored. David Healy, the Northern Ireland football team's record scorer, fresh from bagging the goal that defeated England 1–0 in September, pipped Eamonn to the Sports Star of the Year prize, but the boxer didn't leave the gala event empty-handed. Such was the Magee story, the *Telegraph* was moved to create a new honour and they called Eamonn on stage to present him with a special achievement award in recognition of the heart and mental fortitude he displayed to come back from life-threatening injuries and retain his world title. As the great and good of Northern Irish life rose to applaud him, he self-consciously lifted his trophy and felt as proud as he ever had when a new belt was placed around his waist in the ring.

Eamonn behaved himself that night but it sparked a month of partying from which he rarely sobered. His fourth child, and first with Maria, arrived during this period and Eamonn stumbled into the hospital and attempted to pour a tin of cider over the newborn to wet his head. Maria blocked his path and then didn't see him again for a week until he came home and picked up one of the congratulatory cards adorning the mantelpiece.

'So you called him Ethan then, I see,' he said.

'Yeah. Well you weren't here and I had to put something down for the birth certificate,' Maria replied.

'I told you I wanted to call him Marvin. After Hagler.'

A little later Maria did go back and amend the records so that her only son's full official name is Ethan Peter Marvin Magill.

In March a criminal-assault trial born from the snowman attack finally reached a conclusion. Throughout his own case, Joe Clarke's defence counsel had focused on the fact that Eamonn had thrown the first physical blow in the confrontation. Their goal was to turn the tables and present Clarke as the victim and Magee as the attacker. Clarke had already pleaded guilty to inflicting grievous bodily harm, possessing a weapon and criminal damage to a car, and received a suspended three-year sentence for his sins. Now Eamonn had to answer before the court on charges of his own. The uncertainty provoked sleepless nights in which Eamonn was tormented by visions of jail time and the end of his career, so it was a huge relief when he was cleared of all the charges against him and declared free to continue the rebuilding process. The next day, he signed the contract to fight Takaloo in the King's Hall in May.

It was a decent run of positives by Magee's standards and Breen hoped Eamonn would enter the gym in a frame of mind conducive to working to squeeze every last drop of potential out of the twilight of his career. The Iranian-born Takaloo was a decent operator: he had beaten Jim Rock, dropped a decision to Daniel Santos for the WBO super welterweight crown, and twice won the WBU title. But he lost that WBU crown when Wayne Alexander knocked him out inside five minutes and Magee had subsequently sparred enough rounds with Alexander in Breen's Gym to slip into the false sense of security that is the scourge of all professional athletes.

That doomed mindset was compounded by the fact that Eamonn's heart just wasn't in it any more. He made the right noises in public, but deep down he knew that the comeback had taken everything he had, both physically and emotionally. Magee was now pushing thirty-five and having fought just three rounds of boxing in two and half years, his tank was all but empty. There were some fumes to run on, but he thought it best to save them for the bright lights rather than the hard yards behind the scenes. Fitness, sharpness, conditioning, weight: everything suffered as a consequence. After an open training session he was asked to pose in the ring for a photographer. With sweat dripping off him he stared into the long lens and waited for the flash. The next thing he remembers was rolling out under the bottom rope and wavering dizzily across the gym floor. Panicking, the photographer made to grab his arm.

'Eamonn, are you okay?'

'Of course I am, what do you mean?'

'You just collapsed. You fell down when I took the photo.'

Eamonn had no memory of that but he felt close enough to Queer Street to sense the snapper wasn't lying.

'Away jump a cat!' he fired back with a smile. 'I've never felt better.'

It is his own creation, that feline-leaping idiom, and it's a turn of phrase he employs daily. It basically translates as *aye right!* or *get outta here!* when he believes someone is pulling his leg or not being entirely accurate with their facts or opinions. He knew he wasn't right and he knew the photographer was not making up stories, but he had to keep going.

Magee's preparation was as bad as when he won the Ulster seniors while still drunk and yet, such was his natural ability in a boxing ring, it was still nearly enough to eke out a result against a younger, bigger, fitter, stronger and more determined Takaloo. The King's Hall was jumping at the first bell, a broiling mass of 7,000 bodies, hungry and restless to see a hero into war. But a bemused silence soon descended as the two soldiers refused to fight. After two minutes of circling and pawing the air like timid, inquisitive kittens, referee Dave Parris actually called both men together to remind them of the purpose of their presence on the canvas. When a bell tolled to mercifully end three minutes of nothingness, the crowd erupted once more, only this time in a seething chorus of jeers at the two pacifists strolling to their stools.

It did improve from that inauspicious opening, but everything is relative and, by any standards, it was an insipid, uninspiring contest. The public responded to any bone Magee threw them, sparking up a chant of his name at the appearance of even singular punches being launched. But even the famous Belfast fight fans struggle to keep a fire lit when starved of oxygen.

By the halfway point Magee was already behind and blowing hard, yet he argued with John in the corner that he was four rounds up and cruising. The reality was that he looked an old and weary thirty-four as he tucked his chin behind a raised shoulder on the ropes and gave his opponent the freedom of the ring. Takaloo certainly did more, but such was his reticence to commit to attacks it was clear he was fighting an intimidating memory of Eamonn Magee rather than the version that stood in front of him that night.

Only in the championship rounds did any action worthy of a championship fight break out, but for Magee at least, it was too little too late. The torpid, ignominious display demanded the derision it received when all involved were finally put out of their misery. The first ringside judge scored it a bore draw, while the second had Takaloo the winner by two points. Only the third adjudicator, Eamonn's old pal Mickey Vann, could save him now. But it wasn't to be: Vann gave the fight to Takaloo by a generous four points and with it, Eamonn's WBU welterweight belt.

After, as before, Eamonn talked a good game in the press the next day. He thought he as champion had done enough to keep his title or, more accurately, Takaloo as challenger hadn't done enough to wrench it from him. But even so, he was embarrassed by the performance and determined not to end his career on such a drab and dismal note. Inactivity and a lack of opportunities for Irish boxers was the problem, he claimed. He demanded a rematch and promised he would be champion again.

Even as he spoke, the reporters could smell the drink on his breath and see the remnants of the previous night's cocaine in his bloodshot eyes. And yet the old routine predictably and depressingly worked. Within months the BBBofC had installed him as the mandatory challenger to the British welterweight champion, Kevin Anderson. While he waited for the contracts to be signed for that one, he fought on, a meaningless six rounder against a nondescript opponent in a hotel in the boxing backwater of Letterkenny. Few were there to see it, and even fewer cheered when he left the ring a points victor over Janos Petrovics. As an indication of the standard of test the Hungarian provided, Petrovics would go on to lose eighty-five times, twenty-one by knockout, in his journeyman career. Even so, that was apparently enough preparation to propel Eamonn into a clash with Anderson, a fresh champion almost twelve years his junior.

He walked to the ring in Motherwell that night on 11 May 2007 to the tune of 'The Irish Rover'. Somehow, it was fitting that he chose an Irish ballad about an old vessel that finally spun and sank to the depths at the end of a wondrous, slightly fantastical journey. His corner had been sheered down to two, just his old friend Jim Rock and the ever-present John Breen, and as he made his way to the ring through a lively melody of boos, he gave the veteran commentator Ian Darke at ringside a friendly clip on the back of the head. It smacked of *one last time then, mate.*

The fight was what it was, a decent domestic scrap. It was Anderson's peak, but just a rather ordinary footnote for Eamonn. Regardless of what the scorecards at the end read, the contest was competitive throughout. In the first half, the Scotsman's youth, and the more vigorous spring which that fluke of birth bestowed upon his step, allowed him to nick all the close stanzas. His work was a little more biting, a little crisper and cleaner, a little more deserving of the benefit of the doubt. That the raucous crowd yelled in delight at his every endeavour, and pointedly ignored whatever came back in return, was enough to sway any judge who hadn't already made up his mind.

But as the young champion's early vigour waned, the wizened challenger's greater ring prowess began to reap some reward for its longevity. An argument could be made for Eamonn winning any or all of rounds seven through ten, with the ninth in particular standing out as one final shining beacon of the extravagant gifts God had seen fit to bless him with thirty-five and three-quarter years before. Yet even as he seized that upper hand, there was a distinct lack of conviction in both his demeanour and gait. Magee was always a relaxed warrior, but as he sat slumped on his stool between rounds there was an indifference in his expression that betrayed the futility he now saw in this savage show in which he was playing a leading role.

He bickered with John when told to get on the front foot and win it.

'Sure he hasn't laid a fucking glove on me for about five rounds,' Eamonn spat at his trainer. It was to be one final tangle with authority as a professional prizefighter.

Fuck it, he then thought, and went recklessly toe-to-toe in the eleventh. It was neither how he boxed, nor how he believed one should box, but he bowed to the accepted wisdom behind the supposed glory of going out on one's shield. With forty-five seconds left of the penultimate session, he set himself to throw a heavy right hook but was thumped, mid-execution, by that same punch coming in the opposite direction. In his two-hundredth professional round, something other than the soles of Eamonn Magee's boots touched the canvas for the very first time. Embarrassed, he sat there a moment. He then applauded and smiled. It was a genuinely sad smile in which he forced a degree of mirth through gritted teeth. He looked over to John. 'Fuck me,' he muttered to himself.

That was his career over, but he still had three minutes and forty-five seconds to go. Rocking now in the face of a feverish Scottish attack, he let his gumshield drop to the floor to buy a few second's repose. As Breen rinsed it for him, he rested his gloves on the top rope and shook his head ruefully. Ten seconds later, that hard, glabrous pate shook again as Magee walked slowly to his corner, this time in pure resignation. Nothing passed between fighter and trainer in the final minute they would share between rounds in that dynamic. Pride then kept Eamonn defiant through to the final bell and, after twelve years and thirty-three fights, that was that.

8

JUNIOR

Many professional athletes struggle to deal with retirement. Having devoted the vast majority of their lives to such an all-consuming vocation, it is very tough to walk away at what tends to be such a relatively young age. In the weeks and months and years after their final appearance, they miss desperately the discipline and structure of training, the adrenaline and thrill of performing, and the adulation and confirmation of self-worth derived from winning. Some feel they can't do anything else, that they have nothing more to offer the world. They feel unprepared for real life, unqualified to survive beyond the confines of a passion that has been their oxygen supply for the previous three decades.

Retirement often hits elite professional boxers harder than other athletes. Boxing is regularly said to be the toughest of sports, the most testing of the human condition physically, mentally and spiritually. The highs and lows are more extreme in prizefighting. It requires more heart and soul than other disciplines and so it follows that a fighter tends to give more, to lose more of themselves in the ring than others do on the pitch, court, course or track. Boxers start young and from an earlier age than most their calling controls them. Rare are the world-class fighters that successfully finish school, almost unheard of are those that ever see the inside of a college or university. They reach the top because they sacrifice everything else, remove the safety nets and let boxing dominate them. It is all or nothing from the opening round.

Eamonn Magee, however, accepted his fate before his final bell had even tolled. When Kevin Anderson's right hand set him down on the seat of his shorts on a twenty-by-twenty stretch of Scottish canvas in the penultimate round, Eamonn knew that life between the ropes was over for him. And when he finally sobered up after that career-concluding chime in Motherwell, he was already looking forward, not back. He'd been fighting in a ring for over thirty years and that was long enough. He'd won far more than he had lost and had claimed titles right up to and including world level along the way. He was totally bereft of regret or any sense of pining for a youth now far behind him. Fully ready to move on, he walked away with his head held high.

But back in the Ardoyne, a terrible pain awaited him. The cancer that lurked within Terrence Magee Senior had re-emerged, emboldened for the final torturous battle. A hospital bed was brought into the living room of the house in Eskdale Gardens which Eamonn had bought for his father, and Doc lay down and waited for the hellish disease to consume him. Eamonn moved in to help care for his dying old man. He spent the final two months of his dad's life with him, sleeping in the room above, often kept awake by the slow, hollow, racking breathing that escapes from the lungs of a cancer victim in the final agonising days. On 31 July 2007 Doc passed away.

Eamonn was diagnosed with depression around that time but knows he had lived with the disease for most of his adult life. 'It isn't the type of thing that just appears from one day to the next,' he says. 'It's something that just creeps up on you gradually. You don't need a doctor to tell you, you sense it yourself. And anyone that has had the life I've had is going to struggle with things like that.' He has tried a variety of prescription drugs to keep the illness under control over the years but he openly admits that he has never followed his doctor's orders when it comes to medication. At times, he will give a course of anti-depressants a chance, adhering to intake guidelines until the drug can take effect, but at the first sight of an adverse side effect the prescription goes out the window. It appears to be an issue of perceived physical control over his own body. One pill was dismissed when it caused a loss of balance. Another when he woke in the exact same position in which he had fallen asleep, suggesting he was almost comatose throughout the night. He likes to have a supply of diazepam close to hand, but he only takes one when he feels himself getting overly anxious or agitated. Some months he goes through more tablets than others.

A decade has passed since the death of his father, but it is still an open and raw wound and a time Eamonn still finds difficult to say much about. As anyone would, he struggled badly with having to look on helpless as his hero wasted away to sallow, waxen skin and bone. His dad's quietus hit him much harder than the almost simultaneous passing of his own boxing career, and for a brief period Eamonn wandered lost within himself. It took one of the few men in the world he truly trusts to ensure he didn't stray too far.

***

With mere words on a page, it is impossible to articulate the bond that twenty years of ups and downs have forged between Eamonn Magee and John Breen. But from discussing it with both men, it soon becomes clear that what they share goes beyond the reach of the traditional attachment of a long-term fighter–trainer relationship. They are both stoic, strong Irish men, predisposed to suppress and deny the emotions that deep friendship evokes. But occasionally, although never in each other's presence, their masks slip. And in those moments, the depth of feeling between the pair is unmistakable. Eamonn would lie down in traffic if it would somehow protect John, and vice versa. In fact, Eamonn has effectively done so on more than one occasion.

For years, John ran a security business providing bouncers for bars and clubs the length and breadth of Northern Ireland. It dovetailed nicely with his day job as the country's premier boxing trainer and he often offered his up-and-coming fighters a few extra quid to work a door somewhere on a Friday and Saturday night. But it was a business that frequently brought Breen and his staff into contact with society's dark and criminal underbelly. In Northern Ireland that means paramilitaries and drug dealers.

With the latter, his approach was simple and unequivocal: drug dealers caught on Breen's shift were promptly handed over to the police. This led to decades of threats on his life from various shady sources, threats serious enough that the police installed a panic alarm in his house and issued bullet-proof attire to him and his bouncers. Even when he was earning enough in the ring to not need the cash or hassle, Magee would regularly strap on a protective vest and stand alongside his trainer.

With the former, the situation was more complicated. John's standing in the community as a decent, honest and hard-working man has ensured that he is on good terms with both republican and loyalist paramilitaries. He was never involved himself, but he came into contact with enough of the top men from both sides of the fence to earn their respect and trust. But as the Troubles wound down and peace limped over the horizon, rogue elements within the violent organisations became harder for command to control.

Breen's beat covered the now-closed Arena nightclub in Armagh, the biggest such venue in Northern Ireland. One night, as the thousands in attendance began their chaotic, drunken 3 a.m. exit, a massive brawl erupted and the security staff were soon sucked into the melée. The fight spilled into the car park, where a couple of the main protagonists suffered a decisive beating from several of the bouncers. John broke it up as soon as he suspected his guys were a little over-zealous in their handling of a volatile situation, but the damage was already done. A few days later he received word that the two who were beaten were connected and they'd be back for revenge the following Saturday, this time with paramilitary reinforcements.

John immediately paid off the door staff involved and told them they'd never work for him again. He then started calling round, trying to get in touch with a senior Provo who would have the authority to end this before it got out of hand. But the weekend arrived and he still hadn't been able to get through to that man. Finishing up in the gym that Saturday afternoon, Eamonn, no longer working doors now he was operating at world level, started the conversation.

'Here, John,' he said, 'are you working at the Arena tonight?'

'I am, yeah,' John replied. 'Why do you ask?'

'I've to meet a girl down there. I met her a few weeks ago and I'm taking her out for dinner tonight. Can you give me a lift?'

'Aye, no bother, Eamonn.'

A few hours later, they were both stood outside the front doors of the Arena. Breen was a little surprised to see Magee sporting a smart black trousers and white shirt ensemble, and even more shocked that he wasn't drinking. Eamonn explained that he was taking this woman to a fancy restaurant and didn't want to smell of booze when she arrived, and that was just about plausible enough to be believed. So they just stood there together in silence and waited.

'Where's this date of yours then, Magee?' John asked several times that night.

'I don't know where she's got to,' Eamonn would occasionally mutter just loud enough for John to hear.

'Give her a ring, for fuck sake,' Breen would say.

'I've left her number in the house,' came Magee's lame reply.

Finally around 10.30 p.m. Eamonn shook his head. 'She must have stood me up, the bitch. I may as well just hang around now and get a lift back up the road when you're going home.'

John looked sideways at his fighter. Finally the penny dropped. There was never any date; Magee just wasn't going to let him face whatever was coming alone. A busload of armed Provos could have turned up that night and Eamonn would not have left his side. 'If Magee is with you, he'll die for you,' John once told me and it is hard to improve on the summation of the strength of Eamonn's loyalty to those he believes deserve it.

***

So when Magee the boxer retired, and Magee the son was bereaved of his father, John welcomed Magee the trainer into his gym. From reputation and resumé alone, Eamonn immediately commands the respect of every boxer, past and present, but he was determined to reinforce the regard in which he was held through his actions in this new career. He was still young and fresh enough to keep up with the lads being whipped into shape in the gym or out on the road, but it was between the ropes with pads on his hands that he really distinguished himself. To this day, when Magee takes a boxer on the pads, he sets out to make it as close to a real fight scenario as possible. There is no let-up in the session as combinations are honed and perfected, and lazy fighters will receive a clip round the head if they are not as alert and mobile as their coach believes they should be. The rounds will also progress in silence, the boxers learning what sequence to throw their punches from the position of Eamonn and his pads rather than any numerical instruction or other artificial indication.

The dark arts of prizefighting are addressed as well. A novice professional fresh out of the relatively clean amateur game needs to be taught the tricks of the trade as far as clinches and inside fighting are concerned. Eamonn is always quick to educate on the value of a well-positioned elbow or subtle jolt of the head, of the benefits of leaning on a foe, or what you can get away with at close quarters in that murky space between the bodies that a referee's vision struggles to penetrate. Every action is designed to prepare a fighter to fight.

Magee is eager to assist young fighters with the business side of boxing as well, an area of the game that can prove as tricky as anything that goes on inside the ring. He has a sharp mind when it comes to numbers, and the promoters he worked with throughout his career soon learned that attempts to pull the wool over his eyes were entirely futile. He is quick to encourage his boxers to demand more for their efforts and to ensure they get what they deserve at the very least. At least one promoter who made the mistake of short-changing a Magee fighter has found himself up against a wall with a hand around his throat, mumbling apologies and scrabbling around to make up the shortfall in the promised purse before a fight night has drawn to a close.

Eamonn also assumed the role of cutman in the corner. Despite the potential importance of this responsibility in a fight, there is no formal training before you begin forcing adrenaline-soaked cotton buds into burst blood vessels and clamping split flesh together between your thumb and forefinger. Magee had very rarely bled himself in the ring, but he had inflicted enough wounds upon others inside and outside the square circle that delving into nicks, cuts and gashes came naturally to him. And it wasn't long before his newfound talent for stemming streams of blood was called into action.

One of the first boxers he worked with was an east Belfast bantamweight by the name of Colin Moffett. Moffett had stuck with his amateur coach, Gerry Storey, when he turned pro but after ten years of four- and six-round battles as a game journeyman, he moved to Breen's for one last hurrah. A couple of fights later, in December 2007, Moffett stepped into the ring in the National Stadium in Dublin to face Eugene Heagney for the vacant Irish bantamweight crown. A phone box would have sufficed, however, as the two went toe-to-toe in a flurry of leather from the opening bell. Moffett simply loved to scrap but he was cursed with fair Irish skin that could be breached by even the most innocuous of blows. When he sat on his stool at the end of the fifth, his nose was broken and he had eight separate cuts leaking blood for Magee to hastily plug. Eamonn did his duty, and Colin went above and beyond the call of his own, and three rounds later referee David Irving interrupted a Moffett assault to save Heagney from potentially damaging harm.

There were tears in Moffett's eyes as he lifted that belt above his head a few moments later, and Magee's weren't bone dry either. A title of any description was all Moffett ever wanted from his tough career; that was his world championship. Despite all Eamonn had just achieved as a fighter, and would go on to accomplish as a coach, helping take Moffett to the top of his mountain remains one of his boxing highlights, a memory from which he still derives so much pleasure. Colin had one more bout, losing a twelve-round decision to Ian Napa for the British title, before he retired a happy and contented man.

Four other boxers in the gym around that time were Neil Sinclair, Kevin O'Hara, Stephen Haughian and Jason McKay. Ex-British welterweight champion Sinclair had fought for a world title back in 2000, but his career was now winding down as Eamonn helped get him in shape for an unsuccessful European title fight under a starry sky in Rome's Foro Italico, before Sinky claimed the Irish super welterweight belt in Belfast.

O'Hara was unlucky to fall just short three times between 2008 and 2010 in bids for Irish, British and Commonwealth crowns. He then returned after a three-year break to fight in a charity event in Belfast City Hall in aid of Wee Oscar Knox, the young Northern Irish boy whose battle against an aggressive form of cancer captured hearts across the UK. O'Hara beat Michael Kelly to claim a Celtic belt that night and was finally able to hang up his gloves a satisfied fighter.

Haughian was another who mixed highs with inevitable lows. The Lurgan welterweight had sparred with Magee as a teenage amateur and was delighted to turn pro under Eamonn's wing. He was unbeaten until he lost a controversial points decision to Giammario Grassellini for the IBF inter-continental title in the King's Hall, but bounced back to defeat Billy Walsh for the Irish title. Haughian's career then petered out when he lost to Kevin McIntyre in a Celtic title fight a year later.

Jason McKay was actually the Irish light heavyweight champion before Eamonn's drive whittled the Craigavon man down to a more appropriate fighting weight. McKay's career highlights were probably the gallant losses to future world champions Andy Lee and Darren Barker, for Irish and Commonwealth titles respectively.

Breen's Gym was a busy establishment in those years and Eamonn was afforded ample opportunity to develop talent at various weights and levels. Three of the bigger names he worked with were Andy Murray, Paul McCloskey and Martin Rogan. Murray was an unassuming Cavan native who fought as a lightweight under the John Wayne-inspired moniker 'The Quiet Man'. With a fine amateur career behind him, he was a skilled technician and excellent boxer, perhaps only lacking an ounce of power to push him through to world level. But with Eamonn in his corner, Murray was an Irish and European Union champion inside fifteen professional contests.

Dungiven's McCloskey was another brilliant boxer. On the same night Haughian lost to Grassellini and Murray won his first Irish title, McCloskey stopped Toncho Tonchev inside four one-sided rounds to claim the IBF inter-continental super lightweight crown. And he wasn't long under John and Eamonn's tutelage, before the elusive southpaw added British and European straps to his collection.

Those successes were matched, and perhaps surpassed, by Martin Rogan's glory nights in the ring. The big, bruising taxi driver from west Belfast burst onto the British heavyweight scene when he won three three-rounders in one night to grab the Prizefighter trophy in April 2008. That crown was then leveraged into a lucrative showdown with the Olympic gold medal winner Audley Harrison and Rogan again emerged victorious to set up a crack at Matt Skelton's Commonwealth title.

Eamonn was in relatively good form in early 2009 as big Rogie stopped Skelton in the eleventh and Haughian and Murray won Irish and European belts respectively. He was loving his new coaching role and a BBC documentary hailing the career of John Breen added to the feel-good vibe bouncing off the walls of the gym. But then a single sad event in May seemed to shunt Eamonn off the positive path he was tentatively feeling his way along. Mike Callahan, the man who had effectively come out of retirement to give Magee his chance as a pro and then guided the fighter's career with integrity and honesty until the end, passed away peacefully. Eamonn carried his coffin and a photo of his flowers and message of sympathy were widely used by the press. His note simply read: 'Deepest sympathy to the Boss's family.'

A week later, Martin Rogan lost his Commonwealth title to Sam Sexton in the Odyssey Arena and Magee's life began to unravel. There are several reasons why Rogan relinquished his belt that night. Ultimately, it was the accidental head-butt which caused his left eye to swell shut, provoking the eighth-round stoppage. Rogan's naivety in hesitating when Sexton was there for the kill, Sexton's gamesmanship with his gum-shield shenanigans and referee Dave Parris doing nothing to help the champion's cause throughout also played a major part. But Rogan, seeking an excuse for defeat like boxers so often do, attempted to make Magee his scapegoat. He called Breen and accused Eamonn of being drunk in the corner and doing a line of cocaine in the toilets before the fight. He gave John an ultimatum on who would continue in Breen's Gym: Rogan or Magee. John didn't blink and Rogan went off to find another trainer and lose more fights than he won for the rest of his career.

The accusations stung Eamonn. While the drugs charge was pure nonsense, he has never hidden his alcohol consumption. Magee needs beer in his system to function and has done for decades. He cracks open a tin of lager as soon as he opens his eyes in the morning and maintains a steady intake throughout the day. Twice a week a man driving a white van knocks on his door and drops off two twenty-tin cases of Carling. John Breen and all the boxers who train in his gym know this. While working there every day, Eamonn will leave a plastic bag of supplies outside the door and neck a tin or two every time he steals out on a nominal smoke break. The fighters couldn't give a damn because they know they can rely on Magee. They know he'll be there when they arrive for training and he'll give them 100 per cent. They actually prefer him with a few beers inside him for the natural shyness dissipates and he finds it easier to open up and share his knowledge and experience. The only days of the year on which he curtails his drinking are when he is working the corner of a fighter. Then, he manages to refrain from alcohol until a couple of hours before the first bell when he'll drink two or three pints to settle him down. It may not be ideal, but it beats having an alcoholic with the shakes dealing with your open wounds at the end of every round.

***

Connolly, Eamonn's oldest friend, once told me that Magee was already a fully blown alcoholic at the age of sixteen. Eamonn laughed out loud when I told him that, but he didn't explicitly refute the claim.

'I certainly liked a beer most nights then, aye,' he allowed.

I immediately countered that he already liked a drink most nights well before his mid-teens. He nodded then and, when I referred back to the stolen bottle of cider anecdote, another childhood memory sparked to life in his mind's eye.

'That bottle of Blackthorn when I was nine, that wasn't actually the first time I got drunk, you know? There was another time I forgot about. Christmas Eve, I was only a nipper because Terry was still in the house. My da was drinking Mundy's fortified wine and he gave me a few glasses. I remember I slept in my ma and da's bed that night. The next day, when my ma and Terry, Noel and Patrick all got up and went down the stairs for Christmas, me and my da couldn't even lift our heads off the pillow. We slept right through Christmas lunch and everything. That was the first hangover I ever had.'

The best estimate the medical profession can give is that genetics account for around half of the alcoholic equation. It is hereditary to an extent, in other words, and then personal choices and environmental factors kick in. If alcoholism is viewed as a contest between nature and nurture, the result is a score draw. Eamonn took the traits his dad passed down to him and ran with them. He was his father's son.

One of Doc's old friends once told me about how they gradually drifted apart over the years.

'It was very sad,' the man said with a wavering voice in an Ardoyne café. 'The drink just got him. He stopped working and you'd just see him walking along the street with his head down and a plastic bag of cans in his hand. He'd go into one of the houses where the alcoholics all hang out and you mightn't see him again for a few days.'

Eamonn has similar houses he goes to most days. There is Hamill's, of course, but Doggy's and especially Hugo's have become more regular haunts. The first time I sat with them in Hugo's house I was sporting a beard, grown out through laziness rather than any fashionable pretensions.

'We don't get many hipsters in here,' Hugo teased me. 'Sit down, mate.'

He went on to say that he'd woken up and gone to get the paper across the road as he does every morning when the newsagents opens at 7 a.m. It was winter and cold and dark as he shuffled out of his cramped cul-de-sac off Ardoyne Avenue. The amount of traffic surprised him for the hour, and he thought he was getting stranger looks than normal from the people he passed and the girl who served him. It was only when he got home and switched on the television that he realised it was 7 p.m.

When we emerged from the empty tins and marijuana smoke about an hour later, Eamonn told me a graver tale. The previous week he had caught Hugo slurring his words earlier in his drunken cycle than usual. Eamonn looked at him directly.

'Hugo, what's wrong with you, mate? Are you feeling all right?'

Hugo managed a weak lopsided smile in response.

'Lift that arm for me, mate,' Eamonn continued. 'Ah, for fuck sake, Hugo mate.'

Eamonn called an ambulance, got into the back of it alongside his friend and spent the night in the hospital with him. Hugo had had a stroke.

The story jarred me, but it was all quite matter-of-fact to Eamonn. These are sick men and I wonder if mild strokes pale into insignificance in the grander scheme of life. Doggy and Hamill have serious health problems as well, but none of the group exhibit any signs of tempering their alcohol consumption. Perhaps they are lulled into a false sense of security by what they have survived to date. Maybe they are now simply content to see out their innings within the confines of this close circle that has been constructed around the bottle. Hamill aside, none of the others ever watched Eamonn fight or have any interest in boxing. They bonded and built their friendship over the disease of alcoholism. But the bonds are genuine. The men both support and enable one another in equal measure.

On our way to see Doggy one day we stopped to pick up some beers for him. Back in the car, Eamonn suddenly considered the strangeness of Doggy not having a drop of alcohol in his house. 'It's not like him at all,' he said, thinking out loud. 'You don't think he's trying to get off it, do you? He does that sometimes. I better call him just to make sure.'

Eamonn has occasionally tried to dry himself out too. With Isobel, Mary and Maria all urging, he lasted a day in the Cuan Mhuire rehabilitation clinic in Newry before the absence of television in his room proved too big an obstacle to overcome. Alcoholics Anonymous meetings can help, he concedes, but he refuses to attend any in Belfast where he fears everyone will know and whisper about him. He has travelled as far as Lisburn, Newry, Newcastle and Armagh to find relative anonymity, but a lack of means to get to these places is a ready-made excuse for not going. At the crux of the matter is the fact he has no current desire to beat his addiction. He is a functioning alcoholic and comfortable with that.

'I'm absolutely fine,' he once said to me. 'I go to the doctor for a full medical every year. The first time I did the doc said I'm fit and healthy. I thought the bastard was just telling me what I wanted to hear. I went mad in his surgery. How the fuck can I be healthy, I shouted at him. I'd told him all about the drinking and drugs. Did you not fucking check my liver, I asked. He said it is all in perfect shape.

'And anyway,' he added. 'What am I supposed to do when I come out of the gym? It's always been the same. I don't read books and I only put the TV on in the background to fall asleep at night. So what do you want me to do? There's fuck all to do in this country that doesn't involve drink.'

Doggy did desperately want a beer that day, but it had struck me how one alcoholic seeking a drinking partner would look out for another like that. As Doggy emptied 500ml down his throat in a few thirsty gulps, I mentioned Eamonn's concern to him.

'Eamonn's a good guy,' he said. 'He's always been a good guy around me. I remember we were all having a barbecue one day, drinking outside, and I mentioned my kitchen was looking old. Eamonn got up, fetched some paint, and painted the whole kitchen there and then while the rest of us sat in the sun drinking. He's a good guy, Eamonn.'

***

With Doggy and Hugo he seems to be able to drink himself into oblivion with few dire consequences, but later on back in his house I feel compelled to push Eamonn on the obvious negativities of his problem with the booze. The physical repercussions are axiomatic so I focus on the mental and psychological changes to his character when he's on the drink.

'You can be intimidating,' I tell him. 'You're more abrupt with people, more aggressive, quicker to lose your temper.'

'Your ballix,' he interrupts. 'Listen, I've the patience of a saint. Now that doesn't mean I won't clip you if you're being cheeky and deserve it, but that goes the same if I'm drunk or sober as a judge. But you ask anyone, it's very hard to cross my line. I've the patience of a saint.'

I look at him sitting on the other end of the sofa, struggling to mask my incredulity. 'I don't know,' I begin before he cuts me off again.

'I don't know,' he mimics back and gets to his feet.

'I'm just being honest,' I continue. 'Your character changes a lot from morning to night when there's a day's drinking in-between.'

'Shocking,' he says in response before flippantly adding, 'Who says the drugs don't work, eh?'

'You know what I mean,' I start to say.

'Jellybean,' he finishes for me and walks into the kitchen for another beer. In less than a minute the atmosphere has soured dramatically but I decide to battle on.

'It's the same for everyone—'

'Not to worry then,' he butts in, the look on his face signifying that this discussion is drawing to a close whether I like it or not.

Only the rasp of yet another tin of Carling opening breaks the ensuing silence.

'You're making me laugh,' he says, but his smile is painted on. I leave the conversation there.

***

The Rogan split began a chaotic summer in which Magee's alcoholism did undeniably impact on him and those sucked into its vicinity. In July he discovered that Mary had struck up a romantic relationship with a local Ardoyne man and Eamonn knocked him out in a jealous rage in Kickhams' GAA clubhouse. He was barred from the premises after that incident but the following month he approached the front doors determined to confront Mary over a financial disagreement. He was under the influence and grew increasingly agitated as a crowd gathered to physically prevent his entry. When a club committee member, and cousin of Mary, confronted him, the man ended up on his back with blood streaming from his nose. Police were called and Eamonn was arrested on assault charges.

In September Magee's combustive on-off relationship with Maria Magill suffered an all-time low when the mother of his fourth child accused him of attacking her in Hamill's flat. He was arrested, charged with assault and released on bail to live with his brother in Newcastle. But Eamonn wasn't long in adding to his rap sheet. On a Christmas visit to see Mary and the kids, an argument spiralled dangerously out of control. He woke in his own bed in the Ardoyne early the next morning, surrounded by police who had entered through an open window. This time he was charged with making threats to kill, and the judge, describing Magee as a dangerous threat to the general public, decided a spell on remand was necessary.

The dynamic which exists between Eamonn, Mary and Maria is difficult for someone looking in from the outside to comprehend. Mary was almost suicidal when she first learned of Maria's existence, and yet less than nine months later she was bringing presents to the hospital to welcome Ethan into the world. The two women are close now, united by a shared love for a flawed man and the strong friendships which their children have built and maintained over the years.

Both Mary and Maria speak of Eamonn in strikingly similar terms. Little is said explicitly, but the spectre of domestic violence, both physical and mental, often hangs heavy between the lines of many conversations. There are allusions to children seeing things they should never have seen and admissions of locking doors and hiding fearful in their own home. They pinpoint drink and drugs as the genesis of all Eamonn's problems and describe a stubborn man, one who refuses to apologise or take responsibility for actions that have hurt others immeasurably. They see a man with a selective memory, quick to create his own truth and then stick fast to it in the face of all contrary evidence. They believe Eamonn is bipolar, a dangerous Jekyll and Hyde character. The most lovely, genuine and heartfelt man in the world one day, then a hateful, hurtful bully the next.

But they remain convinced that underneath it all a warm and generous heart still resides, even if the beat has grown more faint over the years. Eamonn often says that you can count the number of true friends you have on one hand, the test being whether they'd answer a 4 a.m. call with, 'Sure, whatever you need.' Mary and Maria know that, despite his many failings, Eamonn will be there when he is truly needed. And that is why they continue to be there for him, to help and support him, to want the best for him. They are a pair of love-hate relationships, but neither emotion can dominate the other.

***

Eamonn spent the entirety of 2010 in court, in prison or released on bail. He was initially sentenced to six months inside for the GAA fracas, but the conviction was overturned on appeal in early March. That still left the unsavoury incidents with Mary and Maria to be resolved, and the continued contact the three parties maintained with one another only served to exacerbate Eamonn's troubles. In April charges of breaking a non-molestation order against Maria were added and he returned to his cell in Maghaberry Prison. After months on remand, he was released to live in Hull with Vicky, a woman he had met years before while boxing in England, and only permitted to enter Northern Ireland for his own court cases. In the meantime he rented his Eskdale Gardens house out to a character who swiftly covered every inch of the first floor in marijuana plants and a police raid ended that tenancy. The Maria assault trial took place during Eamonn's first visit home.

Called as a prosecution witness, Hamill took the stand and was pushed to describe his friend as a dangerous bully, someone he was afraid of. Several times Hamill swore on his life that he was not frightened of Magee but the cross-examiner wouldn't let up on this line of questioning. Finally, tired of the repetition, Hamill changed his tune. 'Yes, I am scared of him,' he suddenly admitted as Eamonn shook his head and put his face in his hands. But before the satisfied prosecution lawyer could rest her case, Hamill had a sting in the tail. 'I'm scared he'll leave the chip pan on when he goes to bed.' But Hamill's character reference fell on deaf ears and the judge handed down a twelve-month sentence.

Eamonn immediately appealed the ruling and was released back to East Yorkshire, but when Vicky threw him out over the summer he was forced to sneak back into the province. That unauthorised crossing of the Irish Sea violated the conditions of his bail and, after a couple of months hiding out in Ballyclare, the authorities tracked him down and returned him to Maghaberry for the remainder of 2010.

HMP Maghaberry was recently described by the chief inspector of prisons in England and Wales as one of the worst he has visited and the most dangerous in the UK. An accompanying report by the HM Inspectorate of Prisons and the Criminal Justice Inspection of Northern Ireland was just as scathing in its assessment, detailing a litany of defects that included high levels and risk of violence, inadequate health and educational provisions, excessive time spent in lockdown conditions, and a generally unsafe and unstable environment.

But Eamonn's expectations of prison life had been lowered dramatically by his experiences in Crumlin Road Gaol in the early 1990s and he has no complaints about the time he spent in Maghaberry. There were familiar faces from his district to welcome him inside and within a few days of his arrival, fellow inmates had spoken to the prison guards and arranged for Eamonn to be moved to his own single cell. He had no trouble from either the screws or the other prisoners throughout his time behind bars. Fights in the jail were very rare, he says, and if one did erupt he would be the peacemaker rather than an instigator. Unless you identified as being part of a paramilitary group, Protestants and Catholics shared the space and got on with life together inside with few problems. In a strange way it is a more advanced society than the still-segregated streets of the outside world.

He struck up friendships with some of the guards, who'd enter his cell for a crafty fag or just to shoot the breeze about Eamonn's career or the local boxing scene. Tobacco was fine but when the smell of dope wafted into the corridors the screws were forced to intervene. When Eamonn heard the footsteps approach he'd flick the miniature joint out the barred window with unerring accuracy.

'Fuck me, you were quick there Eamonn,' was all the warden said when a quick scan of the cell confirmed pungent smoke but no sign of an incriminating source.

In general, he got on fine with the prison authorities. Eamonn was very much part of the school of prisoner who keeps his head down and attempts to make the most of a bad situation. Hard time passes slower after all. The screws also appreciated the role he could play in breaking up fights and when they saw him deal effectively with a fitting epileptic inmate until medics arrived on the scene, it was another tick in his favour.

In early 2011 Magee decided to draw a line under the legal battles of the previous year. Having now spent more time inside on remand than he had actually been sentenced to, he was in a position to somewhat control his own destiny. Despite maintaining that it was nothing more than a muttered remark in the heat of the moment, he withdrew his appeal against the conviction for threatening to kill Mary and booting her car as he stormed off. Around the same time, Maria declined to give evidence against him and that assault conviction was also overturned. For the first time in eighteen months, Eamonn left court that February with no charges hanging over his head nor trials looming menacingly on the horizon.

***

There is always more than one truth. Eamonn always points to his exceptionally high win rate in court as if that is all that needs to be said about the myriad allegations of assault and domestic abuse that have been levelled at him over the years. He wonders why he has apparently deserved all the badness done unto him, yet when he is the one suspected of projecting the pain and hurt, the victim is a saint and he remains the devil. He just responds to situations, he says. He just stands his ground. He talks of it being a woman's world now, of women with a power over him, an ability to use and abuse and control him. Two in particular have had their claws in him for many years now, he swears. There is always more than one truth.

***

But while he may have been free from imminent legal strife, there were still plenty of battles raging within his soul. The continued drug and alcohol abuse fed into and intensified the mental-health issues with which he has been struggling for decades. The other major issue Eamonn was forced to face up to around this time was a lack of money. Basically, he was broke. Despite earning hundreds of thousands of pounds with his fists, every last penny was now gone or out of his reach. With the big money earned in and around the Hatton fight he had bought separate houses for his parents in the Ardoyne and a large, seven-bedroom property in the west Belfast hills that was to serve as the Magee family abode until Eamonn's philandering scuppered that dream. An additional lump sum was placed in a bank account under Mary's name and it still sits there today, the subject of a rumbling legal dispute between Eamonn and his ex on who deserves what from it. The rest he simply gambled, drank or snorted.

He was now living with a woman named Donna in Ballyclare, the small town twenty-five minutes north of Belfast in which Eamonn enjoyed boxing as a kid. It is an almost exclusively Protestant area and an experience at a funeral a few years earlier had made him a little wary of his new surroundings. When the father of a local middleweight, Willie Thompson, passed away, Eamonn decided to go and pay his respects. Invited back to a pub in the town for post-funeral drinks, Magee was happy to oblige, even though he was sure to be the only Catholic on the premises. He was enjoying his pints and a few games of pool when a dispute over a shot turned physical and the ex-boxer took two or three attackers out before Willie bundled him out the door and hurried him to the sanctuary of his deceased father's home. It was only a temporary refuge, however, as local UVF men gathered with bats and pickaxe handles to exact their revenge.

Police caught wind of the paramilitary vigilantes' intentions and arrests were made, while Mary arrived to spirit her erstwhile partner away from danger. Word soon came from the Shankill that Magee was not to be touched, but as a compromise he was barred from every pub and club in Ballyclare and advised not to show his face again.

Now, just a few years later, here he was living in the town. When the first summer arrived and the foreboding piles of rubber tyres and wooden pallets sprang up from waste ground in anticipation of the Twelfth of July festivities, Eamonn agreed with Donna that a fortnight in the Ardoyne was the prudent choice. But by his second summer he felt more at ease and decided to stick around to see how Protestants celebrate the highlight of the Orange marching season. On the Eleventh Night he strolled across to the biggest bonfire in town, just as the Catholic effigies and Irish tricolour flags were catching fire on the peaks of the towering infernos. Naturally, he was instantly recognised and, within the charged and largely drunken atmosphere that surrounds such occasions, Eamonn held his breath and waited to see what sort of welcome he would receive. Minutes later he'd been handed his first free burger and beer, and the generosity of spirit didn't let up all night. He stood drinking by the flames until the Glorious Twelfth had dawned, and still recalls the experience with fondness and a wide grin.

Back in Breen's Gym, Paul McCloskey was now the top dog and Eamonn focused on getting the County Derry man into shape for a world title shot. After two successful defences of his European crown, that opportunity presented itself in the shape of the WBA super lightweight king, Amir Khan. It remains the only time a fighter who employs Magee to work his corner has been stopped on cuts, and it was a travesty of a stoppage at that, with Khan's corner instrumental in pushing the referee and ringside doctor into one of the most premature halts to a world title fight in recent memory. McCloskey bounced back with a decent victory over Breidis Prescott, but he undid that good work with a shock loss to an aging DeMarcus Corley in the King's Hall. He won his next one but neither Breen nor Magee were impressed with the performance and told their boxer as much. McCloskey disliked the criticism and left the gym, never to win another professional fight.

Two months after the Khan–McCloskey debacle, Andy Murray climbed between the ropes in Cardiff for the biggest fight of his career against local boy and future world champion, Gavin Rees. The Cavan man lost a unanimous decision over twelve competitive rounds, but the night is remembered as much for an incident in the dressing room beforehand as for the fight itself. Barry McGuigan was there to watch his young charge Carl Frampton on the same televised bill and he took a moment to visit Murray's room and bestow a few words of wisdom. Magee felt McGuigan was playing to the Sky Sports cameras and, as the man who had spent two months drilling a game plan into Murray's head, he took umbrage with the Clones Cyclone now offering his own conflicting advice.

'Come on, Barry, that's enough,' Eamonn said sharply. 'Get out of my fighter's changing room.'

Such contrasting characters as Magee and McGuigan were always un-likely to become the best of friends, but the frosty exchange ensured that even cordiality would be a stretch from now on.

That defeat was effectively the end of Murray's career, and it wasn't long before another Breen's Gym boxer was forced to call it a day, albeit in much more tragic circumstances. The young Mancunian lightweight Kieran Farrell had sought out John and Eamonn himself and flew over each week to train in the Belfast gym and sleep in Eamonn's Ardoyne home. He was rewarded with a run of victories which led to a bout with future world champion Anthony Crolla for the vacant English title. Farrell gave it his all in the fight of the year contender and when Breen hoisted him aloft at the final bell it was in genuine hope that Kieran would be awarded the decision. But within seconds, winning or losing became a total irrelevance as Eamonn cushioned Farrell's limp body as it slumped from John's shoulders onto the ring floor. He screamed for medics and a stretcher, and five minutes later the beaten boxer was fighting for his life in the back of an ambulance, an acute subdural haematoma increasing the pressure on his brain.

Although he made a full and miraculous recovery, Farrell would never box again and his retirement coincided with a brief lull in activity in Breen's. There were two young, hot prospects in Jamie Conlan and Marco McCullough coming through, but they were still a year shy of championship level and the pair on their own were not enough work to keep both John and Eamonn busy. More time on Eamonn's hands led to more drink down his throat and more woes of his own making to contend with.

After his niece's wedding in Newcastle, Co. Down, he arrived back at a rented apartment with Donna, Francis and his mother to find a drunk and belligerent Traveller effing and blinding in the communal hallway.

'Will you keep it down?' Eamonn asked rhetorically. 'And don't be swearing like that in front of my mother.'

Irish Travellers are well known for short tempers and a propensity to settle differences with their fists, so it was no surprise when this one re-acted aggressively to Magee's warning. But despite being a mountain of a man, he was no match for an ex-world champion boxer with his back up. Eamonn didn't stop punching until his rival was slumped on the floor with blood splattered across the walls and ceiling. The Magee party called the police themselves and when the local constabulary arrived their hearts sank.

'Aw Christ, Eamonn. There'll be murder now – he's the bloody Gypsy King around here.'

He had just battered to a pulp the hardest Irish Traveller in town and the authorities were keen for Magee to disappear before all hell broke loose. The fact that no one in the wedding party was in any shape to drive was the least of the cops' concerns as they hurried Eamonn to his car, sat him behind the wheel and arranged his safe but drunken passage back to Belfast. A couple of weeks later, he and Donna returned to Newcastle for a stroll along the beach where the Travellers sell donkey rides to kids and anyone else brave enough to straddle their haggard *burros*. Out of the corner of his eye he saw them nudge each other and look in his direction, fearful and awed at the sight of the man who had annihilated their king inside thirty seconds.

It was neither the first nor the last time Magee would scrap with a Traveller. When his relationship with Donna soured, Mary briefly took him back into the big house overlooking the city. But Eamonn's bad days outnumbered his good and the two were often at each other's throats. When he slammed the front door and marched off, he regularly found himself in a nearby watering hole, his anger still simmering below the surface, primed to explode. A local Traveller clan frequented the pub too and violence became almost inevitable when their path crossed Magee's in this mood.

2014 was the year both McCullough and Conlan cemented their status as two of the rising stars of Irish boxing. Marco built on the success of stopping WBO inter-continental champ Willie Casey for the Irish featherweight title by winning the European crown in a Waterfront Hall brawl with Martin Parlagi. Jamie, meanwhile, beat Benjamin Smoes to the vacant European super flyweight title before claiming the WBO inter-continental strap in a war with Mexico's Jose Estrella on the undercard of Frampton-Martinez II on the Titanic Slipways.

But as was his wont, Eamonn managed to mix these professional highs with much darker personal lows and yet another bust-up with Mary led to more assault charges. During the trial Eamonn told the court that this was the nineteenth such allegation against him and it would be the nineteenth time he'd beat it. The judge disagreed, however, and handed down a four-month suspended sentence. Much more serious accusations were then made by a woman following a drink- and cocaine-fuelled incident in a flat in the Oldpark district next to the Ardoyne.

Eamonn insisted that he had acted in self-defence and merely tried to subdue an unprovoked attacker who was throwing Hagler-esque combinations at him. Had he really repeatedly punched the alleged victim as the prosecution claimed, he would have knocked her out cold with the first blow, he said. Again the presiding judge disagreed, this time sentencing Magee to four months in prison.

Eamonn immediately appealed and was released on bail, but in at least one respect the damage was already done. McCullough was due in the ring on the undercard of a huge Cyclone Promotions bill in the Odyssey Arena a few days later, but McGuigan barred Eamonn from working Marco's corner on the night. Magee sat at home and drank and seethed, cursing McGuigan as a self-appointed judge, jury and executioner, but before long he was faced with a tragedy against which all his other trials and tribulations paled into total insignificance.

**

He may have his own ideas, but through his children's eyes, Eamonn is a heady mixture of intimidating old-school, disciplinarian dad, un- predictable cool and crazy dad, and totally inept absentee dad. Francis, the eldest, believes he saw the worst of the strict-father persona, but next-in-line Áine is adamant she bore the brunt of the harsh punishments meted out for minor transgressions. The fact that Áine is most like her father in nature, and attracted trouble quicker and more often than her two brothers combined, leads me to conclude she is probably right. But as well as being a chip off the old block, Áine is also a self-proclaimed daddy's girl.

'I love the bones of my daddy,' she once told me in Eamonn's house in Eskdale. 'I'd do anything for him.'

By way of example she painted a graphic picture of helping her old man with his morning constitutional in the hospital after the snowman attack. 'You're stinking Daddy!' Áine remembers squealing with laughter as she held his leg, encased in plaster from ankle to hip, out straight and aloft as Eamonn concluded his business on the porcelain.

The aforementioned craziness in Eamonn often emerged in family holidays abroad, although his mood and alcohol intake tended to determine if they were positive or negative experiences for the kids. The America trip, with Hamill's antics and constant rowing with Mary, was a bad one for example. But there were plenty in the Mediterranean sun that are largely fond memories, even if still pockmarked by Dad's dangerously erratic behaviour. On a jet-ski excursion with Francis, Eamonn decided the rules on where you could go and for how long did not apply to their craft. The result was a boatload of tourists howling in delight and videoing a shoal of angry Spanish tour operators chasing Eamonn down and wrestling him off the jet-ski. He nearly lost a finger in the melée, and the over-zealous Spaniard who provoked the injury was lucky he wasn't found when Eamonn went in search of him the next morning, but it was all par for the course as far as the ex-boxer was concerned. Back in Belfast, he'd arrive home after days away with the gift of a quad bike, or rouse the house at 4 a.m. to present a life-size fibreglass donkey he'd requisitioned from Slane music festival. 'Daddy, you're not right in the head,' Áine said as she rubbed her eyes and stumbled back into bed on that occasion.

But there aren't as many memories, good or bad, from those formative years as a child would like because, quite simply, Daddy wasn't around as much as he might have been. Part of the blame for that fact lies with his chosen profession, of course. With fight camps ranging from six to ten weeks, Eamonn only needed to box three times a year to already guarantee he'd be separated from his family for close to half of it. But rather than make up for lost time with Mary and the kids in the weeks between one fight concluding and the next picking up steam, Eamonn invariably chose to spend that time drunk and high with his friends. Then, as his career drew to a close, he gathered Francis, Áine and Eamonn Junior together to abruptly break the news of his affair with Maria and the stepbrother they were soon to have.

If Áine was a daddy's girl, then Eamonn Junior was most certainly his mummy's blue-eyed boy. Of the three, he was the only one who ever pushed his father away. Their relationship changed when the details of Eamonn's philandering were revealed. Trust was broken within the family circle and a devastated Junior instinctively stood by his mum. He promised her he wouldn't let his dad hurt her again, and the only time mother and son genuinely argued was when Mary took Eamonn back. Eamonn Junior was the only one in the family who found it difficult to forgive and forget after one of his dad's implosions had left a trail of destruction in its wake. He was just a different character to his father, a more innocent, caring, happy-go-lucky soul. Apart from blood, there was only really one thing the two men had in common: both Eamonn Senior and Eamonn Junior could fight.

Junior and Francis both took up boxing as kids but it was only the younger brother who found he had the gift for it. Trained by Charlie Brown in the Poleglass Club near Lagmore, he was soon ready for junior fights and his dad was there in Beckett's Bar on the Stewartstown Road to watch his debut. Not long after that, Junior carried his old man's WBU belt into the ring for his famous comeback night against Vester and, thrilled by the atmosphere in the packed King's Hall, he returned to the gym even more determined to follow in his father's boxing footsteps.

By the time he reached senior level, Junior was training in the famous Immaculata Club on the Falls Road under the watchful eye of his dad and Gerry 'Nugget' Nugent, the gym's head trainer and an ex-Long Kesh prisoner at around the same time Doc was interned. He had a good amateur career, matching his old man in claiming multiple Antrim light welterweight titles. He went on to become Irish under-21 champion in 2011, lose the 2012 Ulster final by a point and win the Irish intermediates in 2013. But when he lost at the semi-final stage of the Ulster seniors in 2014 at the age of twenty-one, the time to make a decision on turning over into the professional ranks had arrived.

Eamonn was ecstatic at the prospect of working with Junior. He had dreams of an unstoppable father–son team, ably abetted by John Breen, sweeping all before them in and around 140lbs. John spoke to Matchroom's Eddie Hearn about the young prospect too. He explained that while Junior had his dad's blood and talent and was a ticket seller, he was also a clean liver and dedicated athlete. As Chris Eubank Junior and Conor Benn have recently proved, the offspring of ex-world champions are easy sells in the fight game and Hearn was keen to get involved. With his backing, Junior would be fast-tracked onto the undercards of the biggest UK shows and benefit from the unrivalled exposure the Sky Sports behemoth guarantees.

Eamonn brought Junior into Breen's Gym and began working him hard. He had almost forty years of experience to draw upon and was eager to transfer all of that knowledge before the opening bell of his son's professional career. He was kept awake at night thinking how he could ensure that Junior did not repeat any of the mistakes that hampered his own time between the ropes. He also knew what he had done right as a fighter and instilling those qualities in Junior was just as important. But perhaps he wanted it all to work out too much. Maybe he pushed too hard.

There were striking similarities between father and son in how Junior moved physically about a boxing ring, but outside the gym the younger Magee was plainly a very different man. Junior was a college boy, studying engineering at the University of Ulster. He had a long-term girlfriend and a huge circle of friends with whom he socialised regularly. He loved a night out, a dance and a few drinks, but he knew there was a limited time and a place for excess. He was a qualified personal trainer and basically lived in the gym. He started running long distances to get in even better shape and before long he was completing marathons in quicker times than his more experienced running buddies. He was a handsome kid and loved himself too, his mum once told me laughing. He inked his body with tattoos, lay on sunbeds, wore unnecessary designer glasses and arrived home with bags of new clothes every other week. He loved boxing, but it wasn't his life. He had too much else going on. He was dedicated and determined to succeed, but that meant a British title and early retirement to explore all of his other talents to the full. He'd been raised in a different world from that which his dad had been forced to endure. The Ardoyne in the 1970s had made Eamonn into the fighter he was and now, in every session in Breen's, Eamonn pushed Junior with an intensity he imagined might create a similar beast within his son. But in the end, he simply pushed him away.

Breen tried to get him back, but Junior had made up his mind. His dad was working him too hard and, anyway, he was his own man, determined to succeed on merit rather than off the back of a helping hand due to his illustrious surname. He went to Willie Thompson's Spartans' gym in Ballyclare to train and let the Belfast promoter Alio Wilton handle the business side of things. In June 2014 Junior made his debut, stopping the well-known and durable journeyman Zoltan Horvath midway through the second round. Such was the rift, Eamonn wasn't even at ringside that night in Belfast's Holiday Inn hotel. He just couldn't bear to watch his son embark on a pro career under another man's guidance.

But not long after Junior's impressive opening act, father and son went for a long walk together around the Waterworks Lake in north Belfast and got a few things off their chests. Eamonn also attempted to open his boy's eyes to the reality of the boxing game, a business in which the vast majority experience far more downs than ups. The air was temporarily cleared and Junior returned to Breen's, but discord soon usurped the manufactured harmony. A promised slot on a Cyclone Promotions' undercard failed to materialise and Junior's impatience to keep his career progressing got the better of him. He walked out again and when he next fought in March 2015, his father was once more nowhere to be seen.

The ill-feeling caused the absence, but the quality of the bill did nothing to help the situation. Eamonn knew Junior was better than semipro cards under the auspices of the Malta Boxing Commission in west Belfast pubs. He wanted his boy signed up with Matchroom, fighting live on Sky Sports, learning against seasoned journeymen on the undercards of world title bouts. It pained and embarrassed him that Junior chose to operate several levels below that rather than work with his old man. He still harboured the dream of guiding Junior but he was too stubborn to compromise or accept an alternative way of doing things in the gym. He couldn't resist mocking the tattoos that were gradually enveloping Junior's left arm, nor sly digs about the modern diets and supplements that the younger Magee swore by. Perhaps there would have eventually been some movement towards a middle ground, some swallowing of pride and ego, and the two Magee men could have made it work. But sadly, they ran out of time.

Not long after his second fight, Junior went for a drink with his dad and older brother Francis in the Shamrock. There was still a lot of tension between the two but at least they were sitting at the same table sharing a pint. At one point late on in the night, a local hood fancied making a name for himself and grabbed Junior by the throat. Eamonn intervened and calmed the situation. He made the peace, much as a wise old head who has seen it all before might. At closing time outside on Ardoyne Avenue, a bottle flew in the direction of the three Magees. But as Junior's blood rose, just like his dad's had on countless occasions in the past, Eamonn led his two boys away.

'It's not worth it,' he told them. 'It never is. Come on home.'

They all went home and that was the last drink Eamonn ever shared with his son.

Less than two months later, Junior was enjoying Friday night in a flat in Summerhill Park on the Twinbrook estate in west Belfast. He was with Courtney Ward, a girl from his gym with whom he had struck up a romantic relationship just a couple of weeks before. They sat together on the sofa, listening to music and having a few drinks. When they looked at the time they were surprised to see it was already 2 a.m. on Saturday morning, but neither was tired so they ordered some pizza. At 2.40 a.m. Junior opened the back door to see what was keeping the delivery and was met by Orhan Koca springing from the darkness to plunge a six-inch kitchen blade into thigh, buttocks and then his chest. Koca then withdrew the knife and in a frenzy stabbed a further three times before running into the night. Junior tried to rise but merely stumbled forward into the darkness. His blood was found on a child's slide in the back yard, the gate, a parked car and finally the kerbside, where he was found by horrified passers-by. An ambulance was there in minutes, but it was too late.

Eamonn was high on cocaine when he finally answered his phone, but the scene at the hospital soon brought him crashing down to the dark reality of the situation. On the way there his mum had called him in tears.

'Do you know something I don't?' he asked.

'No Eamonn, I promise. Just get here quick.'

Isobel knew but she just couldn't say the words out loud.

It was Eamonn who formally identified the body, his beautiful blue-eyed boy almost unrecognisable with the tubes and wires and dried, black-red blood matting his hair and caking his skin. He stood beside his dead son for five minutes and then took a taxi home and slept, praying he would never wake up and have to deal with the sadness and pain and helplessness that was sure to greet him when he opened his eyes.

He went to Craigavon Magistrates' Court to watch Koca officially charged with murder. It became known that the Turkish national was the spurned lover of Courtney Ward and had warned her on social media to end her fledgling relationship with Junior. Koca was remanded into custody and friends had to physically restrain Magee as he launched a verbal tirade at his child's killer. The following day there was a vigil at the murder scene where hundreds of friends and family lit candles and said prayers. As red, heart-shaped balloons and white Chinese globes were released into the evening sky, Eamonn placed a boxing glove on a fence post behind the steadily growing shrine. The glove had a set of rosary beads wrapped around it and on the wrist label he wrote a simple message: 'To my beautiful son, Eamonn Magee Junior. Dad.'

At the same time in Maghaberry Prison, Koca left his cell to receive a visitor, and an inmate in the line behind him broke his cheekbone with a right-hand lead. It was an old boxing pal of Junior's who threw the punch, a Traveller who had shared the ring with young Magee and, like just about everyone, immediately took a shine to him.

Junior was buried on Friday 5 June in the cemetery in the shadow of St Joseph's Church, Hannahstown, just a stone's throw from the big house where he had lived with his mother.

***

It has been an incredibly tough few years for Eamonn and the whole family since Junior was so violently torn from their lives. Mary has left her son's room virtually untouched, can still smell her youngest from his clothes, and proudly shows me the boxes of letters and cards sent from all over the world when I pay her a visit. She surrounds herself with photos of the child she called her right-hand man and delights in playing short video clips of Junior, full of life, in happier times. She takes comfort from speaking to her departed son through a medium, with messages that he is happy on the free sunbeds up there and that the thrust of Koca's knife ended his life painlessly providing some miniscule mercies.

Yet even in the depths of her own mourning, Mary finds time to worry about how Eamonn Senior is coping with the tragedy. She still sees him regularly and, despite the difficulty Eamonn has talking about Junior, they have occasionally celebrated their son's time on earth. Together, they ran the Lisburn Fun Run which Junior was due to complete for the Tinylife charity. Later they organised a tribute night in the Devenish which old friend Ricky Hatton flew over to host free of charge – a spirit of generosity which the venue's owner failed to share. But Mary fears for the dark thoughts which she knows race through her ex-partner's head when he sits alone in the Ardoyne each night.

And Eamonn did sink low enough to contemplate suicide. The temptation became so strong that one day he walked into his local health centre and asked to see his GP. Despite his obvious distress, the receptionist told him that that would be impossible, that he'd need to make an appointment and come back in a couple of days. Exasperated and embarrassed, Eamonn erupted.

'I'm telling you I'm going to fucking kill myself, and you're telling me to go away and come back in a few days!' he raged at the woman. *Fuck you,* Eamonn thought as he stormed out. *I'm going to stay alive just to spite you.*

A concern for Eamonn's state of mind is expressed by almost everyone I speak to, but it is also invariably tempered by the happy admission he appears to be dealing with the tragedy of Junior's murder better than was expected. He's lost more weight than anyone likes to see and his drinking has not abated, but the hard drugs have been largely left alone. The woman at the centre of the most recent assault allegations dropped the case, leaving him free from legal worries and able to continue working with John in Breen's Gym. Jamie Conlan and Marco McCullough left the team, but Magee is now bringing through a good prospect in young Feargal Mc-Crory. He still gambles more than he should, but it's now just to test his own knowledge rather than chasing winnings or an adrenaline rush. The stakes are small these days as well; they have to be when you're surviving on £75 per week in benefits. Women come and go in generally fraught circumstances, while Maria and especially Mary continue as constants in his life. He spends each weekend with Ethan and sees Áine and Francis when he can too, but although they all love and idolise their daddy, these are somewhat stunted relationships which need more effort from Eamonn if they are to flourish.

He remains just a couple of streets away from his mother and, after everyone I have spoken to about Eamonn, it is still Isobel who appears to know him best. When I sat in her kitchen that first weekend in the Ardoyne, I asked Isobel how she thought her youngest son was currently dealing with the turmoil in his life. It had been an emotional meeting from the moment I walked through the front door, but with this question the tears rolled once more.

'He's struggling on,' she began after a pause to compose herself. Then she opened up.

'My Eamonn is so deep. You see songs, he really listens to them and tells me, ma, listen to these words. Bob Marley songs and that old one, "Who's that Knockin'?" If he dies before me I'm getting "Listen to the Lyrics" engraved on his headstone. That's what he always says. He's very sensitive. He cries his eyes out, cries his eyes out. But then he has an attitude that he just gets on with his life. No matter what happens he doesn't hide away. I used to phone him every night and he'd ask me, "What do you want Ma?" And I'd sing to him, "I Just Called to Say I Love You". Then he'd say, Mummy, sing this song or that song and, like an eejit, I'd be singing down the phone to him. Just to make him ...'

Isobel stops to catch her breath at this point. She peers at me through glassy eyes and transmits that worst-case scenario with the sorrow of her look.

'Because you don't know what goes through his head at night,' she continues quietly, echoing Mary's words. 'I wouldn't like to be inside his brain. I always say to him, you're a thorn in my side but I love you with a passion. I love all my sons so, so much. I feel sorry for Eamonn and I worry about him. Because of what he's seen and where he is now. Because of the different relationships he's had and broken, and what he's left behind. I feel sorry for him because I think he's a lost soul. I really think he is a lost soul.'

***

It is 30 May 2016, the first anniversary of Junior's murder. I woke this morning conscious of the significance of the date and sent a text to Eamonn. 'Thinking of you today mate,' was all I could muster.

About an hour later, Eamonn called.

'How are we finishing this book?' he asked. 'I mean, what's going to be the final scene so to speak?'

I had just ended it with the above quote from Isobel but it was an early draft and I wasn't convinced. The ending is often the hardest part of telling a story.

'I'm not sure yet,' I replied. 'Why? What are you thinking?'

Suddenly, for the first time ever with me, Eamonn sounded a little self-conscious.

'I don't know,' he started tentatively. 'I was just thinking. Last night I drove over to Twinbrook with a friend, Sam Barclay. I'd asked Sam to make up a plaque for Eamonn Junior. Another mate, Fra Lavery, painted the fence for me. Me and Sam went over there around two in the morning and we sat in his car waiting. Then at 2.40 a.m., the time my son took his last breath, I got out and put the plaque in place. It's a sad thing, I know. But it's a nice thing. At least, it's a nice thing for me. Maybe it's stupid but it made me feel good. I think I'd like that to be the end of the book.'

EPILOGUE

I have seen Eamonn on good days and bad days over the past two years. I've sat beside him in bars as he attempted to mask the silent terror and paranoia eating him from within, fearful that someone would soon enter, lead him away and shoot him dead. I've waited outside a Belfast courthouse for him while inside he argued his case in one of the myriad legal disputes that appeared to be omnipresent in his life. I've stood beside him and Mary at their son's grave on what would have been Junior's twenty-third birthday, Eamonn somehow awkward and out of place in the family scene. I've watched from a couple of feet away as he worked wonders in the corner to stem the flow of blood from above a fighter's eye in the sixty seconds permissible within the frantic heat of a title fight. I then sat in the desolation of the same beaten fighter's dressing room as a doctor stitched him in silence, still gloved up, for Eamonn was already AWOL in the Manchester night with the necessary scissors in his pocket. I've met him animated, fresh-faced and positive throughout a day in which he held it together with little more than a handful of pints for support. I've watched him lose other days in a sullen stupor in a squat thick with marijuana smoke and littered with empty beer cans. I've had him call me, only to hang up after less than a minute of quiet sobbing, unable to get even a mumbled word out. 'Forgive me' were his final words on one of those nights. I've had him refuse to talk to me on the phone, paranoid about who could be listening, listing the names of those who have suffered for divulging information across the wires. I've listened to his words tell me he regrets nothing while his eyes betray the truth. I've watched him break down in tears many, many times. Tears of anger, of pain, of a sort of sad happy nostalgia too. I've seen a very stubborn man, one accustomed to forcing his will onto others, one who makes dangerous assumptions on what is right and what is wrong. I've seen a bitter man, someone who will create, nurture and then embrace and harbour a grudge for eternity. I've seen a fiercely loyal man as well, one who continues to personally deliver a bouquet of flowers to the door of his long-dead manager's wife every Christmas Eve. I've seen a sentimental man, sensitive to the point he feels the need to hide that side of his character for fear of a perceived weakness. I've seen a normal man, just wanting a chat, asking how my family and I are doing. I've seen a man still struggling with every single thing that has gone before.

Earlier this year, I flew home to spend a couple of days with Eamonn. I believed I had the skeleton of his life firmly in place and now just needed to round out a few of the many anecdotes I had heard that were fast providing the meat on the bones.

'Will we go through this dictaphone then?' he said when I sat down on his living-room sofa.

After the torture of deciphering his handwriting on the mess of betting slips he was using to jot down notes, I had sent him a voice recorder to capture anything interesting as and when it popped into his head. But we had been through it all the month before and I couldn't see the value in wading back into the mire.

'No,' he corrected me. 'There's new stuff on it now.'

I took a look and he was right. Folder D was now overflowing. One hundred and ninety-seven separate recordings, each a spoken reminder of an event worth writing about. In total, he must have told me over 500 stories across our meetings. Family and friends then filled in the gaps. And very few concerned boxing.

So we began the process, playing the short mumbled synopses on Eamonn's dictaphone and then recording his elaboration of the tale on mine. Some we had to abandon, the background noise of a busy bar drowning out anything intelligible, or Eamonn's words simply too slurred to understand. Others, like 'don't forget about the rope-a-dope' failed to ring any prescient bells. There were occasional drunken repetitions of the same story too, but the vast majority were absolute gold for a writer and I was already cursing the restrictions of my word limit before we were halfway through. They were the usual eclectic mix of shocking violence, slapstick hilarity, glorious human achievement and desperate sadness. But now, listening back to our three-hour conversation that morning, continually interrupted by the tinny crunch of yet another empty can being crumpled in his hand, there is a particularly telling fifteen-minute burst of memories that I realise didn't even make the book.

He told me about Terry McKenna, his gang's lookout while the rest of the fourteen-year-olds raked about under the British Army watchtowers of Flax Street mill in a stolen, beat-up car. Terry got fed up with his passive role and suddenly started hollering that the cops were coming so the other boys would scarper and he could have his turn behind the wheel. 'Peelers, Peelers!' he roared in warning. But Terry was partly deaf and dumb and his pronunciation of words suffered accordingly. 'Pee-lah, Pee-lah!' was what Eamonn and the other joyriders heard that day and, having returned upon the realisation they'd been duped, 'Pee-lah' stuck as young McKenna's new nickname.

He told me about the bars in the Ardoyne all being caged up, a camera and buzzer at the door to control who entered and left. He remembered sitting in the Highfield bar in his school uniform, playing poker with some of the men of the district. Coco McAuley was at the table, the famed hardest man in Belfast, known to have personally knocked out three separate Brits on the city's streets with his bare fists. The player next to Coco annoyed the big man somehow and, without looking up from his five-card hand, Coco knocked the guy off his seat unconscious with just a stinging back-hander.

He told me about a particular British soldier, a physically small man who delighted in lurking behind postboxes and jumping out in front of the teenage Magee to startle and then antagonise him. Eamonn wanted to be like Coco, wanted to knock the Brit out and become part of Ardoyne legend himself.

From there he jumped to memories of his three sons. Of ordering a tearful Francis back outside to continue his fight with an older bully and then watching with pride from the window as Francis emerged victorious. Of saving a choking Junior from a sweet blocking his airways. Of laying a newborn Ethan on his dying father's frail chest.

'Thank everyone for the response after Eamonn was killed' followed when I pushed play again, a reference to the acts of kindness from friends and strangers from both sides of the community. 'I got some T-shirts printed and he wouldn't take a penny. Same with a suit for the funeral. For weeks people were knocking on the door with food they'd made up for me. It was overwhelming. I'll never forget those gestures.'

Then on to a training camp for a major fight ending early when a call from his manager informed him there was something in the house he was staying in. It was the house of a well-known republican so Eamonn didn't hesitate. His bags were packed and he was on his way back to Belfast within the hour.

Next he is a trainer, staying in a London Bridge hotel the weekend big Rogie fought Audley Harrison, and bumping into his old pal Jane Couch, Britain's first professional female fighter. 'We'd both had a couple and I told her she could never land a punch on me if I let her try with my hands by my side. She gave it a go. She threw three right hands at me and each time I moved and let her fist fly centimetres past my right ear. Finally she was so raging she just launched herself at me and we both fell back into a flowerbed. She's great craic is Jane. And if it wasn't for her there'd be no Katie Taylors or anyone else fighting today. Jane was the first.'

Suddenly, we are almost back in the present, standing outside a Dublin hotel having a smoke alongside the referee who robbed him blind in the first Paul Burke fight. John Keane offered him a cigarette and then after an awkward pause said, 'Eamonn, I'm sorry. I got it wrong. You won that fight.' Eamonn hugged him and started crying. His eyes grew moist again as he told me that one.

The next stuttering prompt from the dictaphone is short but not so sweet. 'Friends being shot and dying' was all it said. From drug-dealing acquaintances of the 1990s, to a fan from Leitrim named Frank O'Brien who travelled everywhere to watch Eamonn fight, via Mousey Goodhall, a pal famous for ordering ten whiskeys at a time and falling down the stairs to his death. And there were plenty more in-between.

Doc is never far from Eamonn's mind: his dad, his role model, his hero. He took a phone call from an RUC officer known only as Jock one day, back when he was a fighter living in Lagmore. 'Jock was a good cunt,' Eamonn assures me now. 'There were good cunts as well as bad in the RUC. Just like every other walk of life. He had my phone number and knew me personally because I spent so much time in the company of the cops in those days. Anyway, he told me I needed to get over to Eskdale immediately. They had surrounded my da's house and the old man was losing it. I flew over and it looked like a siege. Jock told me they needed to take my da away, that he was threatening to kill himself. There was an ambulance waiting but the place was crawling with armed police. Get them and their guns away to fuck, Jock, I told him. I'll go in here and I'll sort this out. He's my da and he'll listen to me. Jock gave the order and those other bastards disappeared. I went in and my da was stood in the doorway between the living room and the kitchen, with his hands up on the door frame. I could see it in his face he was in a bad way. It's me, Da, I said to him. Listen, me and you are walking out of here together. Just us two and don't worry about those bastards out the back with their guns. Me and you are walking out the front door and we're getting into the ambulance and we'll get you sorted out, Da.'

We needed to take a break after that one to allow the eyes to dry.

Out of nowhere, a childhood recollection then appears. Eamonn is ten years old in Plouescat in northern France, his first time outside of Ireland. It was a community initiative to show troubled, working-class kids there

311

was a world beyond the struggles of the district and he'd been chosen from Ardoyne youth club.

'I stayed with a beautiful family,' Eamonn remembers. 'They had two kids about my age. At the weekend we went up to see their grandparents on the coast and we went out fishing for crabs. You just snorkelled down yourself and grabbed as many as you could from the bottom while they nipped your fingers. I'd never felt anything like it, being out there in the ocean on my own. The water was so clear. I loved every minute I was there, and they kept inviting me back. I went over on the Cork to Roscoff boat three times to stay with them.'

A pause then before, 'A different world to the Ardoyne.'

It is impossible not to wonder what life Eamonn Magee would have led had he been born in the tranquillity of a sleepy seaside village in Brittany. But he wasn't; he was born in the Ardoyne, where antagonistic British soldiers prowled the street and bloody violence was the norm. Where the bars were caged for their own protection. Where role models were the hard men who drank too much, settled differences with their fists and invariably died too young. Just a different world, as he says.

And he still lives, and will probably die, there. The Ardoyne has changed along with the rest of society in the north of Ireland in the past couple of decades, but it is a district more soaked in the country's violent past than most. Everywhere you look there are murals and plaques and memorials to ensure the horrors and sacrifices of the Troubles are never forgotten. A man arrived on time for a scheduled punishment shooting not so long ago and was left to bleed to death in the alleyway. Father Donegan, the Holy Cross parish priest, talks of twenty-five other local men living under threat of death from paramilitary figures. It seems like every other month there are reports of another Ardoyne youth taking his own life, another victim of the tragic suicide epidemic currently torturing families in the area. Other parts of the city may still be scarred by the Troubles, but sometimes it feels like the Ardoyne is still attempting to cauterise open, seeping wounds.

You may think the harsh reality of life in the Ardoyne would make it fertile ground for bigots to breed future bigots, and yet you find few on its streets. Eamonn is certainly not one. In a perverse way he may be as far from prejudiced as a man can be. He does have plenty of spite, some hate even, in his heart, but it is an emotion totally oblivious to religion, race or creed. He can hate and hurt you regardless of whether you are Catholic or Protestant, Irish or British, IRA or UVF, man or woman.

The district also breeds fighters and Eamonn was a natural. His achievements in the ring, the silver medal in the junior world championships, the multiple county, province and national wins, the Commonwealth and WBU world titles are extraordinary, regardless of circumstance. Put in the context of the shootings, stabbings and shattered limbs, of the imprisonments and exiles, of the drink, drugs and gambling, of the lack of dedication and general turmoil that has engulfed his entire existence, they are almost unbelievable. Some still say he is the most naturally talented pugilist the island of Ireland has ever produced. It eats away at John Breen and Eamonn's brothers that the world never saw the best of Eamonn Magee, but Eamonn is sticking to his story: he has no regrets and his life has been great craic.

I think of my friend Eamonn at least once every single day and I can't help worrying about him. In a recent phone call he admitted that he wasn't eating. That he was 'drinking himself into oblivion'. He had been desperately hoping that a damning verdict and lengthy sentence for Orhan Koca would provide some crumb of comfort and a degree of closure. The leniency shown to his son's killer shattered that hope, but had Koca been sentenced to a thousand years I'm not sure it would have allowed Eamonn to move on. He'll struggle with that terrible tragedy forever.

I hope he will seek help for the twin deadly diseases of alcoholism and depression which are slowly killing him, but I don't believe he ever will. A third affliction he suffers from is a wilful myopia when it comes to how severely the two diagnosed illnesses hurt him and those he loves. He has forgotten, or not remembered in the first place, a lot of his turbulent life and that is, in many ways, a blessing. At times he creates his own truth, but there are terrible memories in his head that he must somehow reconcile with the character of the man he wants to be. A few apologies might be a good start, although he certainly deserves plenty back in return.

I can't help worrying about Eamonn, but even since I placed the final full-stop in this book, several chinks of light have begun fracturing the darkness he faces. He is engaged now. A quiet, sweet girl named Bronagh Cassidy, the latest to try to tame him. 'She just makes me happy,' he says. 'She makes me want to wake up each morning. Fuck knows what would have happened if she hadn't been around the past few years.' He has a new grandson, Eamonn the third, Áine's second-born, to love and adore. He has a new gym too, recently opened on the Ravenhill Road. Being there with John every day, immersing himself in the blood, sweat and tears of young fighters who idolise him, keeps the self-destructive thoughts from his mind for a few hours at least. His nephew Sean, Patrick's boy, turned pro this year to continue the Magee boxing dynasty. Sacred Heart gym is reopening and around the corner a new mural in honour of north Belfast fighters has been painted, with Eamonn and his brothers taking centre-stage. He is undoubtedly struggling, but he knows there are reasons to fight on.

Isobel is right. Her youngest son is a lost soul. But he is a fighter and a survivor too. Life and all its travails have driven him to the edge many times before, but when all he needed was a gentle nudge to jump, he received a violent shunt that riled him and forced him to fight back. That fuck-you attitude is why he is still alive today. 'He'll see us all into the grave yet,' someone once joked with me. I wouldn't be surprised.

ACKNOWLEDGEMENTS

Books as intimate as this one are not possible without the help and cooperation of the subject's nearest and dearest, and I am eternally grateful that I received such support from Eamonn's family and friends. Time and again they opened up and shared personal, and often painful, memories with me, a stranger, when it would have been much easier to dilute or withhold their recollections. Each and every conversation provided new insight into Eamonn's character and added to my understanding of the man and his environment.

First and foremost, I want to thank Isobel, Eamonn's mother. Without her honesty I could never have painted such a vivid picture of the world and family Eamonn was born into. Just as it was Isobel who revealed Eamonn the son, I must thank Noel and Patrick for describing Eamonn the brother; Áine, Francis and Ethan for Eamonn the father; and Mary and Maria for Eamonn the partner.

In the boxing world there are too many to recognise individually. But special thanks must go to Patsy McKenna for his impassioned retelling of tales from Eamonn's early amateur days. To Nicolás Hernández Cruz who was generous with his time and memories of Eamonn the international. To Mike Callahan's wife, Sheila, and daughter, Laura, for sharing what the Boss thought of his wildest and most talented fighter. And of course, to John Breen, Eamonn's closest ally from his professional debut until today.

Outside of boxing, a motley crew of Eamonn's lifelong friends and drinking buddies helped me enormously. I thank Connolly and Hamill for their contributions on Eamonn and his escapades – I would need a second book to include them all. I am also grateful to Hugo and Doggy for welcoming me into their homes. That small band of alcoholics from the Ardoyne and the Bone, of which Eamonn is a prominent member, showed me sides to the disease I did not know existed. On a similar note, thank you to Doc's old friends for their warm but melancholy memories of their comrade and his battle with the bottle.

Thank you to Paul Carson of the *Belfast Telegraph* archives. He not only opened up that massive resource to me, but also went to the trouble of photocopying every article on Eamonn from the mid-1980s onwards. That kindness permitted a level of detail on Eamonn's early professional career that would have otherwise been impossible.

I flicked through several of my old Irish history and politics texts from university while at the desktop research stage in this project, but a new one, *Ardoyne: The Untold Truth* by the Ardoyne Commemoration Project, proved to be the most valuable.

To my friend, mentor and sportswriting idol, Don McRae, you have no idea how important your example and frequent words of encouragement are to me. I'd also like to thank my agent Richard Pike for his support and continued belief in this book in the face of so many frustrating rejections. And I am forever indebted to everyone at Mercier Press for taking a chance and working so hard to produce what you hold in your hands today.

To María, thank you for supporting me emotionally, financially and every other way I can think of as the decision to write this book quickly descended from viable career move to pure passion project. To Sofía and later Erin, thank you for your innate and enduring ability to lift my spirits in any circumstance.

In truth, however, I owe by far the biggest debt of gratitude to the man himself. I was certainly not the first to approach Eamonn with the idea of telling his story, but for some reason I was the first he trusted to do it. To this day, I am still unsure why he chose me, but the leap of faith he took was reciprocated and we formed a bond and built a friendship which surpassed the standard subject–biographer relationship.

When we were together working on the book, Eamonn would repeatedly tell me that this is his life story and no one else's. And so while I welcomed input from anyone with a story to relay, it is ultimately Eamonn's memories and thoughts and interpretations and opinions that lie at the heart of every page. That, I feel, is how it should be. My only hope is that I have managed to do this incredible life story justice.

INDEX